D0629353

Crisis in Command

CRISIS IN COMMAND

★ ★ ★ ★ ★

Mismanagement in the Army

Richard A. Gabriel
and Paul L. Savage

HILL AND WANG · New York
A division of Farrar, Straus and Giroux

AUG 26 '85

Copyright © 1978 by Richard A. Gabriel and Paul L. Savage
All rights reserved
Published simultaneously in Canada
by McGraw-Hill Ryerson Ltd., Toronto
First edition, 1978
Printed in the United States of America
Designed by Paula Wiener

Library of Congress Cataloging in Publication Data
Gabriel, Richard A.   Crisis in command.
Bibliography: p.   Includes index.
1. United States. Army.   2. United States. Army—Officers.
3. Military ethics.   I. Savage, Paul L., joint author.   II. Title.
UA25.G26   355.3'3'0973   77-18689

To our understanding wives,
JANE and KATHIE

Contents

Preface

This book might never have been written. At least we never planned to write it. In fact, we were strongly warned against doing so on the grounds that to suggest reforming an institution with the influence, power, and authority of the United States Army would, at best, go unheeded and, at worst, prompt the growth of "enemies," more of which, alas, we do not need. The book, however, had its beginnings in a series of lectures, papers, and articles which, as each was presented, seemed to call for more development until, as a result of having to refine our positions to several types of audiences, it seemed only logical to tie the whole thing together.

There are advantages in writing a book in bits and pieces. One gets an opportunity to examine critically each aspect of the subject and to expose each argument to detailed criticism. Additionally, by presenting each major point either in a journal or before potentially hostile audiences, one inevitably provokes considerable criticism, much of it cogent. We have thus been forced continually to reexamine our positions, so that by the time they assumed final form, we had a greater degree of confidence in their validity than we probably would have had had we not offered each argument for outside comment. Finally, these responses have increased our confidence in the case for which we have become unabashed proponents.

The central position of this book is that the United States Army and its officer corps are in need of significant reform. The argument for reform is not drawn on ideological lines. It is based on a study of operational performance derived from a detailed analysis of the Army's performance and behavior during the Vietnam War. Additionally, we make the case for reform both historically and cross-culturally by comparing the performance of the American Army with that of other armies in other times. It is our contention that within the Army today there are still severe behavioral and ethical tendencies that threaten the ability of the organization to withstand even minimal combat stress. Further, we suggest that a critical factor contributing to the condition of the Army is the state of the officer corps.

The historical record of the military's performance in Vietnam, and before and since, suggests that something is terribly wrong with the present military structure. Critical to any assessment of the problem is the role of the officer corps, which, we repeat, must bear a large portion of the blame for what went wrong and what remains so; if the mistakes of the past are not to be allowed to shape the future, the role of the officer corps is a critical variable in any calculus of reform.

Its role is central to whatever cause-and-effect linkages relative to disintegration have been uncovered here. The corollary, if reform is to be effected, is that the officer corps will have to play an important part in the attempt, whether initiated from within or outside the Army.

While we have not drawn our case against the Army and for reform of the officer corps along ideological lines, it would be nonsense for us to maintain that this study is "value free" in that it fails to make normative statements. We take our position not out of ideological pique or a sense of messianism, but rather out of a serious concern for what the military has become and what it will undoubtedly remain unless something is done to change it. The consequences of failing to change are, in our view, potentially devastating to the future performance of the military. Since we are both academicians and former military officers, our views are hardly unbiased; we clearly reject the managerial ethos which we see as dominant within the officer corps. At the same time, we openly support what we define as traditional ethics, historically associated with the "way of the soldier" in most successful armies. These ethics are preferable to those now dominant.

Many people stand behind our work; some have given their overt support, others their silence. We would be remiss if we did not mention those individuals and institutions that contributed to the final product. Special thanks are owed to Professor Morris Janowitz of the University of Chicago, who first took notice of our early work on the behavior of the Army in Vietnam, encouraged us, and first suggested the possibility of publication. Certainly of major value was the Inter-University Seminar on Armed Forces and Society, sponsored by the University of Chicago, which provided us with some financial support. The Seminar also provided an extremely valuable forum in which to test our ideas, as well as an extensive network of fellow academics interested in the problems of the military. Many of the members of the Seminar contributed to our work by reading and offering comment on it. The United States Army War College, the National Security Seminar, the International Studies Association, the United States Military Academy at West Point, and the University of Massachusetts at Amherst also provided forums for the expression of our ideas. West Point allowed us to test our ideas on resistance, ethics, and professionalism directly upon their cadets. Worthy of special thanks is Colonel Mike Malone of the Army War College, who has been a constant stimulus to our thinking and a critic of our work, as has Lieutenant Colonel Donald Vought of the United States Army Command and General Staff College. Edward Feit and Milton Cantor of the University of Massachusetts helped in other ways, as did Charles Moskos, whose research provided valuable background data for our study. In the final analysis, however, although our debt to others is a large one, responsibility for any errors or follies must remain with the authors, who reserve the right to blame any shortcomings on one another.

We are not unaware that this book will displease liberals and conservatives alike. The liberals will see in our suggestions the threat of the military slipping its civilian leash, while conservatives, although supporters of tradition, are likely to have difficulty in accepting change in one of our oldest and most tradition-bound institutions. There is some comfort in the fact that many officers agree with what we have said, if only off the record. In the end, we have made a case which we think is a strong one. The obligation for refuting what we have said must rest with those who find it wanting. Indeed, we have asked the Army at each stage in the development of this book to examine our data and to provide us with any information that would contradict our findings. We have made repeated requests since the completion of the manuscript and have even circulated the manuscript within Army channels. To date there has been no response. We are still waiting.

Amherst, New Hampshire
Winter 1977

Crisis in Command

I

The Perspective
of Reform

Reform is almost never anticipatory; more usually it is a reaction against existing circumstances. Examples can be found in congressional efforts to reform the FBI and CIA. In a free society, deeply penetrated by the ethos of self-interest and characterized by spasmodic efforts at social change, reform will probably remain a reactive process. The implication is that in a free society it is unrealistic to expect the impetus for institutional change to be either self-generating or anticipatory in the sense that institutional defects are identified and corrected before they produce near-disasters.[1] It is a paradox that while the United States ranks among the most innovative nations in history, its tendency toward innovation, experimentation, and change has been largely confined to matters dominated by technology and its attendant mechanisms. When addressing the broader institutions of social, economic, and political control, the United States seems to follow the path traveled by other nations in other times. Being habituated to change and growth, we often dismantle traditional value structures to our great loss, as we have in our military system, without being aware of the social costs. In short, we react to events; we rarely, if ever, anticipate them.

Accordingly, it is unfair for academicians and politicians to ask why the Army of the United States could not foresee the strains and stresses which began to develop during the Vietnam conflict and, further, why it did nothing to forestall the inevitable consequences. The question may be unfair because it flies in the face of our history and the "history" of virtually every other country as well. It suggests an attempt to transfer the American penchant for technological innovation and experimentation into the social arena, which is something we have never been able to do successfully. The American Army is deeply rooted in our social structure, indeed perhaps too deeply rooted, and for this very reason was no more capable of anticipating and forestalling the mistakes it made than is any other social institution. In a very simplistic sense, the Army was unable to correct its defects during the Vietnam era because it was institutionally engrossed in developing them!

Once the war began to wind down, however, there were some within the military who began to question what had happened. There was a small discernible movement, however tentative and timid, to cast a cold empirical eye upon the Army and to assess its operations under combat conditions. To be sure, the majority regarded such an examination as either dangerous or an exercise in self-flagellation, and certainly unnecessary. The majority comprised, and still does, those whose careers were deeply rooted in the policies and practices developed during the Vietnam years, and it was this group that finally prevailed. General William C. Westmoreland, the former Commander of the U.S. Forces in Vietnam and later Chief of Staff of the Army, had ordered an empirical study to be conducted by the Army War College into the state of professionalism and leadership in the officer corps.[2] When the study was completed in 1970, the results were so devastating to the image of the officer corps that Westmoreland initially ordered the study classified and limited its circulation to general officers. Naturally, actions of this sort did not lessen the doubts of a growing number of academicians, politicians, and American military men that something was seriously wrong with the officer corps and that we had to learn what it was.

When our independent research into the problems of the Army

officer corps began in 1972, we found that the military had little sense of its own direction. In general, the older officers were opposed to any "outside" examination of the Army's performance and began to develop and use the code word "self-flagellation" to meet the objections of those who felt that much was to be gained by a review of the military's performance. The "old bulls" argued that the military was in the best position to clean its own house and, in any case, the house was not all that dirty. Some of the younger officers, including a handful of recently promoted brigadier generals, openly opposed this view. These were the officers who led the battalions, companies, and platoons in combat in Vietnam and it was they who had experienced firsthand some of the pathologies that had become deeply embedded in the Army as a whole and in the officer corps in particular. The majority were eager to have an accurate examination and assessment of the Army's performance. Unfortunately, the very factors which made them willing to examine their own shortcomings and those of their superiors also made such an examination virtually impossible to undertake. Although they had youth, zeal, and a degree of honesty and openness that was refreshing, these young officers had access to few of the levers of power within the military establishment and control of none. Accordingly, the case for reform was never made from within the officer corps itself and has yet to be made. The tide was allowed to recede.

It is perhaps instructive to clarify one point here. The events of Vietnam, the psychic debacle of an unseemly withdrawal, the collapse of the ARVN, the Watergate affair, the FBI and CIA investigations, and the first resignation of an American President in the history of the Republic all came together in one cataclysmic riptide within so short a period of time as to overwhelm even the most disciplined observer of history. In particular, the role played in Richard Nixon's resignation by General Haig and then Secretary of Defense James Schlesinger may have raised some questions in the minds of some observers as to the reliability of the Army in future situations of domestic crisis.[3] It should be made clear that there is no evidence from our researches that the military has ever contemplated intervening in the political process in an unconstitutional manner. Indeed, the mere thought of such intervention is so foreign to both our history and our traditions of democracy as to border on the incomprehensible. When we refer to young officers who disagree with their superiors, it must be emphasized that their concern has never been to violate the deeply held principle of civilian control of the military. The concern of these officers is focused on the internal conditions of the Army as a whole and the officer corps in particular. Our purpose, consequently, is to examine the internal conditions of the American military structure. We do not question the tradition of civilian control at any point.

This book had its origins in a limited attempt to comprehend the American military failure in Vietnam, specifically as to how that failure was related to the performance of the Army. It surely had become clear to all but the most avid "hawks" that by 1971 the American Army in Vietnam was in deep trouble. To be sure, it had not been decisively defeated on the battlefield as the French were at Dien Bien Phu, but it was unambiguously clear that despite ten years of often desperate efforts, military victory had eluded us.[4] In the strategic thinking of the guerrilla, such a condition could only mean victory. We would have to win; he had only *not* to lose. More and more enemy units were willing to stand and fight, and the enemy units encountered grew ever larger until division-size battles were not uncommon. Again, guerrilla doctrine preaches that as guerrillas are able to place larger and larger units in the field, victory is closer at hand, for such large units require logistical support and intelligence that only an essentially friendly population can provide. General Westmoreland never seemed to grasp this point (as Mao Tse-tung did) and continued to believe that as the enemy's units grew larger, American firepower could finally be brought to bear to destroy them. Both he and British General Gage of Boston and Bunker Hill fame seemed never truly to have understood the nature of political warfare. Westmoreland's failure to comprehend the nature of political warfare was virtually complete and he never understood, as did Mao, that an increase in the size and losses of insurgent military units signaled the ascendancy of the guerrilla, not his defeat. His book, *A Soldier Reports*, makes clear his misunderstanding of the nature of the Vietnam conflict.

Despite increased American air attacks at both the tactical and the strategic level, infiltration of men and supplies from the North continued almost uninterrupted. The Cambodian invasion had proven to be a failure and turned into a quagmire, while in Laos an intensified civil war wracked the countryside. By 1972, despite Richard Nixon's desperate air attacks on the capital of North Vietnam, military indicators predicted that the war was "lost," or at the very least that the price of achieving a military victory had escalated to the point where it would become morally intolerable.[5]

It was at this point that we began our investigations of the military performance of the American Army. Although our data were often less than complete, we began to uncover a portrait of the Army and its officer corps that was less than flattering and which hinted very strongly that serious pathologies were evident within its structure. As our efforts expanded, it rapidly became evident that the Army in Vietnam had literally destroyed itself under conditions of minimal combat stress. Often this process was camouflaged. Further, it had occurred gradually, so that its true dimensions were not clearly and immediately discernible. To be sure, neither Congress, the American people, nor even the general staff had anything resembling an accurate picture of the state of the U.S. Army at the war's end. In the years since we left Vietnam, more data have come to light which support the suspicions we had when we began our work. It is these data that have led us to our conclusions.

In coming to grips with the problems of reform in the Army, it must be noted that the credibility of the military per se had reached a low point. This lack of credibility had been reinforced not only by the events surrounding the Vietnam conflict but also by a series of events which actually had no direct bearing on its performance on the battlefield. The My Lai cover-up, the Lavelle affair, the West Point scandals, further reduced the faith which the American people are willing to place in the military. Additionally, the end of the draft and the introduction of a Volunteer Army (VOLAR) have considerably reduced political support for the military, most particularly the Army. The lack of public faith is important, for even if the Army were undertaking sincere efforts at self-examination and reform—a proposition for which there is precious little evidence—the fact would remain that whatever the results of such efforts they would be greeted with skepticism. The depth of this skepticism is a measure of just how far the case for reform needs to be pressed if significant change is to be brought about within the military establishment and public confidence in it restored. The road back will be a long one.

The credibility of the Army bears heavily upon this study, for the fact of the matter is that we have had to rely a great deal upon information drawn from official military records. This is especially true in analyzing the combat performance of the Army on the battlefields and in the rice paddies of Vietnam. Further, we admit to a certain cautious skepticism about some of the data but suggest that, in the end, we have had little other material available. Even using official sources—and we have by no means relied entirely upon such sources—the case against the Army appears to be convincing regarding its performance in general and that of its officer corps in particular.[6] To the extent that military records and associated official data are incorrect or biased, they are likely to be biased in such a way as to cast the military in the best possible light. Accordingly, to the extent that such data mislead, they do so in a direction favorable to the Army. They thus err on the side of caution.

The major thrust of our argument is that the performance of the American Army during the Vietnam War indicates a military system which failed to maintain unit cohesion under conditions of combat stress. Our data suggest that the Army in the field exhibited a low degree of unit cohesion at virtually all levels of command and staff, but principally at the crucial squad, platoon, and

company levels.[7] The disintegration of unit cohesion had pro-
ceeded to such an extent that by 1972 accommodation with the
North Vietnamese was the only realistic alternative to risking an
eventual military debacle in the field. Indicators of system and subsystem decay were varied, but in most cases unmistakable. The
data indicate a very high rate of drug use among U.S. field forces
in-country, repeated attempts to assassinate officers and senior non-
commissioned officers, combat refusals that bordered on mutiny,
skyrocketing desertion rates in the Army as a whole, and a wide
range of other conditions that played, at the very least, contributory roles. The officer corps should have been appalled, and yet we
find no evidence that it was. Regardless of the cause or causes of
such conditions, it seems evident that to the extent that unit cohesion is a major factor in maintaining an effective fighting force, the
Army in Vietnam had ceased to be effective. Indeed the Army
began to border on an undisciplined, ineffective, almost anomic
mass of individuals who collectively had no goals and who, individually, sought only to survive the length of their tours.[8]

Among the most important factors responsible for the failure of
the Army to cohere under combat stress in Vietnam was the failure
of its officer corps to provide the kind of leadership necessary in a
combat army. It is difficult to escape the charge that the troops
failed (and later sometimes refused) to follow most often because
their officers abandoned their responsibility to lead. Just what went
wrong with the officer corps is a highly complex question. Suffice
it to say, for the moment, that the officer corps manifested severe
pathologies during its experience in Vietnam and that those pathologies combined to reduce its ability to develop and maintain unit
cohesion.

The decline in the quality of the officer corps during the Vietnam War was reflected in several ways—some direct and some hidden. For example, the Army deployed in Vietnam carried with it
an officer corps that had been increased in numbers to the point
that officers were literally tripping over each other. At one time
(1968), as many as one hundred and ten general officers were actu-

ally deployed "in-country," sixty-four of whom were Army. Comparative research suggests that one of the major indicators of a tendency toward discohesion in a military organization is the ratio of officers to troops deployed in the combat area. In Vietnam the officer corps grew in inverse proportion to its decline in quality defined by its ability to act as a cohesive force around which combat units could cluster. Further, as the number of officers proliferated, an expansion of the rank structure occurred so that second lieutenants often did sergeants' jobs while majors did captains' jobs, and so on. Promotions accelerated so that higher and higher ranking officers came to perform tasks normally assigned to lower ranks. Under the doctrine of "equity," a requirement that all officers must serve at least one tour in Vietnam, the quality of individuals allowed to hold commissioned rank steadily declined from year to year. Eventually, given a contrived "demand," the officer corps could correctly be described as both bloated in number and poorer in quality. One result was My Lai. Even the staunchest defenders of the Army agree that in normal times a man of Lieutenant Calley's low intelligence and predispositions would never have been allowed to hold a commission. Indeed, Calley's own defense attorney argued that Calley would never have been allowed to become an officer if the Army had maintained its normal standards for officer selection and that because the Army did in fact lower its standards it must share in the guilt and culpability for the My Lai affair. The lowering of standards was a wound that the officer corps inflicted upon itself.[9]

The increase in the number of officers would have been a problem in and of itself; but it was accompanied by a decline in the quality of officers which resulted from the necessity to fill the increasing number of staff slots required to run the Army deployed in the field. The number of men needed to sustain a single combat soldier in the field (commonly called the "tooth to tail" ratio) expanded beyond all expectation or predictions. But the increase in the number of officers did not occur evenly across the rank structure. Rather, and this was particularly true of those officers who indicated they would "stay for twenty" or reenlist for another tour in Vietnam, promotion rates were accelerated so that the officer corps grew ever more top-heavy with its own brass. That career orientation should begin to set in at these levels surprised no one. On the other hand, the junior officer corps, officers at the rank of captain or lower, who were expected to carry the burden of localized killing combat, became increasingly comprised of young, inexperienced, low-quality men who only wanted to serve their tour and then leave the Army. The breakpoint appears to have been the rank of major. Those who stayed in the Army long enough to make that rank (during the conflict one could make major in only six years with a tour in Vietnam on one's record) often decided to become career men. Those below this rank normally wanted out as soon as possible. The overall quality of the corps deteriorated as a consequence of its personnel, promotion, and rotation policies. That this development did not escape the attention of the enlisted troops, especially the lowest-ranking "grunts" of the combat arms units, is virtually beyond doubt.

If there were too many officers of low quality, it was even more destabilizing to unit cohesion when it became clear to the troops that their high-ranking superiors often absented themselves from combat by positioning themselves in relatively safe areas to the rear. This condition was made at least technically possible by the employment of sophisticated communication and transportation devices known collectively (and derisively) as "the automated battlefield." In theory, it was possible for a commander to communicate with his units without ever leaving his rear command post, a practice to which many commanders seemed dedicated. Additionally, the war in Vietnam was a "circular" war and not a linear war. By contrast with previous wars, troops were deployed in fire bases or base camps from which they would foray forth in search of the enemy. The problem was that these base camps often came to resemble hives that were swarming with officers, most of whom were engaged in various staff and support functions, and, most importantly, who never even risked, much less bore the burden of,

combat and the danger of being killed by hostile fire. Often the individual infantryman would spend days in the field in search of the
enemy only to witness upon his return large numbers of clean-
shaven and starch-fatigued officers going about their business in
their secure environments. The troops developed a series of terms
for these officers, the most derisive of which was "rear-echelon
motherfucker." In the end it was not only a case of too many officers, too much rank, and too low quality. It was the searing
awareness on the part of the troops that large numbers of officers—
often those occupying the higher ranks—simply did not share the
burden of sacrifice that was expected of them.[10]

While it might be argued that the quality of officers was and
remains a matter for debate, it appears clear that in many cases
their behavior was something less than what is normally expected
of a military leader. Often the behavior of officers was openly destructive of unit cohesion and morale. The resentment that resulted
from the ability of a unit commander to direct his troops from the
relative safety of a helicopter "observation and command platform"
without either showing himself to the fighting force or, more importantly, sharing the risks of combat produced anger among the
troops. At the other extreme, one often encountered the young but
career-minded officer who felt that he had to "make his command
time pay" in terms of personal career advancement. In these instances the troops were often led by an officer who sought to use
them as means to his own advancement rather than to care for their
welfare. Accordingly, the troops were likely to perceive him as an
officer who didn't care about them or their welfare—a man likely to
risk their lives to improve *his* combat record. Obviously this problem was particularly acute when the officer was a young "shave-
tail," and it was not uncommon openly to warn such officers that
they had more than the enemy's fire to fear in an engagement. Our
own interviews with enlisted men suggest that many fraggings
were the culmination of a long, gradual process of disgruntlement;
only the most inattentive of officers could fail to grasp that something was amiss. There were often enough warnings to "hard

chargers" before an actual fragging took place and, even then, some of the fraggings were intended to warn rather than kill. Sometimes the warnings took on ominous forms as when one group of soldiers actually took up a collection to raise a "bounty" and then openly offered it to anyone who was willing to "waste" a particularly disliked officer.

Equally destructive of unit cohesion were the brutally disruptive rotation policies in which officers were required to serve only six months in front-line units while enlisted men, "the grunts," had to serve twelve months or until their DEROS (Date Estimated Return Overseas) was reached. The rationale for this policy was based on the notion that rapid rotation of officers would provide a large number of officers with command experience and would have the added advantage of "blooding" the officer, so that a large proportion of the officer corps which stayed on after the conflict would have combat experience. This rationale notwithstanding, the rotation policies operative in Vietnam virtually foreclosed the possibility of establishing fighting units with a sense of identity, morale, and strong cohesiveness. The assignment of individual as opposed to *unit* DEROS dates, plus the frequent rotation of officers, made it clear that the policy was virtually every man for himself.[11]

Not only did the rotation policy foreclose the possibility of developing a sense of unit integrity and responsibility, but it also ensured a continuing supply of low-quality, inexperienced officers at the point of greatest stress in any army, namely in its combat units. To be sure, some officers tried very hard to identify with their men, but such a course was almost impossible when half of a platoon might be individually scheduled to "rotate out" within, say, a three-week period, when many of the replacements were inexperienced and confused, and when the "old-timers"—those who had been there six months—had already seen officers change more than once and felt, not without justification, that they knew more about staying alive than their officers. This set of circumstances, coupled with the behavior of the officers, can hardly be taken as conducive to developing and maintaining combat units characterized by a high degree of unit integrity, cohesion, morale, and, above all, dependability.

The behavior of the officer corps is open to criticism on the grounds that officers did not lead their men or expose themselves to the same risks as the men; it is also open to equally harsh attack on other grounds. A study of the available data concerning the number and type of medals awarded relative to both combat activity and actual casualties taken suggests that as the frequency and intensity of enemy contact declined, the number of awards, many for bravery, actually increased at an astonishing rate.[12] The degree of inversion between the two variables is so great as to border on the ridiculous. Clearly, enlisted men were often the recipients of these awards; but what was most disturbing is the extent to which officers were willing to accept medals and awards which they clearly did not deserve. In fact, so blatant was the practice of awarding medals for actions that were at best marginal in terms of risk that even officers began to refer to these awards and medals in derisive terms. They called them "gongs." Still, they continued to award them to one another and, more importantly, to accept them. It is a not uncommon experience to meet officers and enlisted men who refuse to wear their Vietnam campaign ribbons, which they consider meaningless; far more common, however, is the be-medaled officer who delights in his "combat record" despite the awareness on virtually everyone's part that such awards were indicative of nothing unless it be the preposterous generosity of the local commander who issued them.

The top leadership of the Army condoned awards that bordered on the inane. The policies on which they were based were so loose, documentation requirements so lacking, that, coupled with the encouragement that commanders often received from their higher-ups to "reward" their troops with "gongs" as a means of building unit pride, practices evolved that greatly debased the medals that were presented with so much pomp. In fact, some unit commanders used the number of awards for bravery that a unit had been given as part of a complex formula to measure the combat effectiveness of the unit![13] The tyranny of statistics became complete. Virtually every soldier who managed to survive his tour was given a Bronze Star; if he had seen any combat whatsoever, the tendency was to award him a "V" device to go with it. The Combat Infantryman's Badge, once the symbol of service and hazard that separated the true combat veteran from the "garret trooper," was debased so as to encounter increased derision from all the troops. However, the ultimate absurdity had to be the presentation of various award "packages" to officers and enlisted men. Under this practice a stipulated number and type of medal was automatically given to individuals depending upon their rank and position. There were three such "packages"—the combat package, the service package, and the support package.[14] It is a rather strange experience to wander through a military post and see that almost everyone is wearing the same medals! The idiocy was compounded when officers were awarded higher-level decorations because of their higher rank. As a result, it was almost impossible to encounter a senior colonel who did not display the Silver Star on his chest or to meet a general who did not sport the Distinguished Service Medal. Even the Purple Heart, that traditional symbol of honor, came to mean little. Horror stories proliferated as to the manner in which rear-echelon officers often received this once precious award for mere cuts and bruises sustained in normal administrative or support duty as well as in "other" activities. Such "other" activities include at least one instance where an officer was wounded when a stray enemy mortar round accidentally hit a *maison du joie* in Tuy Hoa, interrupting the soldier at his "work." He was awarded the Purple Heart for injuries incurred in the "line of duty" due to hostile fire! So common were some awards, the Air Medal for example, that they were often given repeatedly to the same man. The second award of the same medal normally entitles one to wear an Oak Leaf Cluster as an indication of the multiple award. So frequent were the number of such multiple awards that the Army literally went over to a numerical system to replace the Oak Leaf Cluster. Accordingly, it was not unusual to see a soldier with the Air Medal with the number five in the middle of the ribbon. In the end, the award system designed to stimulate the morale of the troops undermined it. It became a standing joke. More important, however, was the fact that the officers usually participated in the system with relish, swelling their personnel files with reports of their own bravery and thus increasing their chances for promotion. The troops were rarely fooled.

The officer corps indicted itself by its own behavior in still another way. If Armies are to hold together under stress, then it must be clear to the troops who comprise the fighting units that their officers are willing to share the ultimate risk of death with them. There is no clearer indication of this willingness than to have officers die in full view of their men. The available evidence suggests very clearly that the number of officers who actually died in combat in Vietnam was smaller proportionately compared to the number of Americans killed in other wars and to officer losses suffered by other Armies.[15] Additionally, the risk of death seemed to be directly related to the rank one held. In almost ten years of warfare the United States Army lost only eight colonels to hostile fire and a mere three generals, and the evidence suggests that at least two of those generals were not killed by hostile fire at all but may have actually flown their helicopters into the ground during bad weather. The relation is clear, however, in that the higher one's rank, the lower was the probability that one would meet one's death on the battlefield. Now no one is suggesting that the pinnacle of a successful military career is, to quote General Patton, "to die with the last bullet of the last great battle." However, it is suggested that unit cohesion is, to a large extent, a function of the degree to which the combat troops perceive that their officers are willing to fight and die *with* them. In Vietnam the record is absolutely clear on this point: the officer corps simply did not die in sufficient numbers or in the presence of their men often enough to provide the kind of "martyrs" that all primary sociological units, especially those under stress, require if cohesion is to be maintained. The troops began to perceive that their officers simply were not prepared to share the risk of ultimate sacrifice—and they came to despise them for it.

Our analysis is not meant to indict the entire Army officer corps. Yet, as we shall attempt to demonstrate later, none of our comments are lacking in supportive evidence. The purpose of our description of the behavior of the officer corps is to make it clear that Vietnam witnessed a series of behavioral and attitudinal deficiencies within the officer corps that became so deeply engrained as to constitute true pathologies, that is, real threats to the ability of the Army subsystem to function. It remains a fair question to ask why these events were allowed to occur and, even more to the point, whether the practices and policies developed during Vietnam as they affected the internal quality of the officer corps still obtain.

The problems which plague the Army as a whole and the officer corps in particular were not created solely by the traumatic experiences which the Army endured during Vietnam. The pathologies so clearly present within the officer corps during the conflict were the logical culmination of a series of forces which had been set in motion almost twenty years before the United States ever became enmeshed in the second Indochina war. The military structure had already been conditioned, albeit subtly, so that the pathologies could erupt dramatically in fertile soil.

By the time increasing numbers of the American officer corps took the field in Vietnam in 1964, the American military structure had already become permeated by a set of values, practices, and policies that forced considerations of career advancement to figure more heavily in the behavior of individual officers than the traditional ethics normally associated with military life. In short, the Army as a whole and the officer corps in particular had already moved away from the traditional models and codes centered on "gladiatorial" ethics.[16] The Army had begun to develop and adopt a new ethical code rooted in the entrepreneurial model of the modern business corporation. The traditional ethics which buttressed the code of duty-honor-country had begun to weaken, and in their place the military officer was expected to operate within a code of ethics drawn largely from the practices of the free-enterprise marketplace. That these new ethics would, ultimately, encourage him to consider *his* career to be of the highest personal and professional importance should have surprised no one.

The subtle transformation of the military structure and, along with it, the officer corps seems to have begun during World War II with the influence of Chief of Staff George C. Marshall. Faced with the necessity of pulling together the multiple and diverse centers of economic and social power needed to fight a conflict on a grand scale, Marshall turned to the only model available to him which had some proven experience in the field of organization and that was consistent with the values of democracy and free enterprise. He chose the modern business corporation. Indeed, it was during World War II that the business corporation began to develop many of the sophisticated practices that we have come to commonly associate with it: systems analysis, personnel management, computer-designed decision models, etc. General Marshall could hardly have foreseen that the results of choosing the business corporation as an organizational model would have been the weakening and eventual destruction of traditional military values.

The curiously symbiotic relationship between the American military structure and the modern business corporation which began during World War II has continued to the present. Certainly the rise of huge defense budgets needed to support a large standing Army had much to do with both how and why this relationship developed. Another factor in the pattern of development was the traditional American penchant for free enterprise which required that a close relationship be developed between the two structures in such critical matters as research and development, weapons design, and purchasing. Throughout the fifties, more and more of the internal control practices of the business corporation were adopted by the Army. With the appointment of Robert S. McNamara as Secretary of Defense in 1961, the identification of the two structures was nearly complete. After all, McNamara's previous career involved the production of automobiles with all the attendant concern for modern business practices, cost-benefit analysis, systems perspectives, and "zero defects."

Secretary McNamara is remembered chiefly for his insistence that "good business practices" be applied to the design and purchase of military weapons systems. Yet the symbolism of McNamara's influence runs even deeper. He was the ideal corporate man, and during his tenure as Secretary of Defense the Army moved ever closer to the modern business corporation in concept, tone, language, and style. Further, the individual military officer became identified with the corporate executive to the point where the functions of command were perceived as identical to the functions of departmental management. More and more of its officers were sent to graduate schools to take advanced degrees, almost all receiving degrees in business management or administration. "Systems analysis" became the new Army "buzz word," and officers suddenly became concerned with something called "career management." The traditional aspects of the "military way" collapsed under the impact of new administrative skills, staff reorganizations, and computer models of decision making. The next war was to be fought by corporate executives in uniform equipped with the tools of scientific administration held vital to "managing" the conflict. Military leadership, in the traditional sense, had become obsolete; indeed, it had become unnecessary. The machines, the doctrines, the manuals, would show the way. The era of the "automated battlefield" had arrived.

Had the propensity to imitate the modern business corporation been limited to a selective adoption of some of its technology, then it is questionable whether serious damage would have been done to the Army's values. Perhaps, on the other hand, it is unrealistic to expect the Army to adopt the technology of business without finally adopting its ethics. Whatever the historical options, this major transformation dealt the military a crippling blow: the Army and its officer corps not only adopted the technology of the business world, but began to absorb its language, its style, and, eventually, its ethics. However gradually and subtly, the Army ceased to be a true military establishment in the traditional sense of possessing both a sense of uniqueness apart from society and a sense of ethics deeply rooted in its own experience and traditions that had once come to define the "way of the soldier." The symptoms of the transformation were everywhere. The Secretary of Defense was the perfect corporate man who used "buzz words" that communicated a sense of business-world "newspeak" which the initiated understood but which merely confused the untrained. The extent of the metamorphosis can be seen in the practice of referring to lower-ranking officers, those expected to carry the burden of leadership with combat units in the field, as "middle-tier managers." The officer corps had actually come to believe that leadership and management were one and the same thing and that a mastery of the techniques of the latter would suffice to meet the challenges of the former. The Army has yet to recover from this transformation. The transformation from military institution to business corporation, at least in form, value, and style, may not have been total. Changes seldom are. But it struck roots so deep that even the searing experiences of Vietnam have been unable to reverse it.

Military systems, especially the small-unit subsystems which are expected to bear the burden of killing, are categorically different in nature and function from the modern business corporation and its subsystems. No one expects anyone to die for IBM or General Motors, but the expectation that one will "do one's duty even unto death" is very real in the military and becomes ever more vivid as one moves closer to combat. Thus, the tasks which each system is required to perform are quite different. Consequently, the forces which compel an officer to fulfill his obligations to himself, his command, and his superiors are categorically different from those which press the corporate official to fulfill his obligations.[17] It was the failure of the American military, especially with respect to its ground Army, to realize that combat leaders are not, in truth, "middle-tier managers." To adopt virtually intact the practices and ethics of the business corporation, leading senior officers to equate the internal efficiency of a military organization with "management," and then to assume that this pattern would provide combat strength defined as unit cohesion and a will to fight, was disastrously wrong. This equation was proven demonstrably false in the rice paddies of Vietnam.

Military organizations successful in withstanding combat stress are truly corporative in that they require high levels of individual identification with institutional goals as the primary mechanism for compelling individual behavior. It is this very sense of belonging, of sharing common values, and of being unique that defines a truly cohesive military unit. It is these factors which, in the end, motivate the individual soldier to stand and fight and to risk death in the service of his comrades. By contrast, the adoption of business ethics in the military environment had to portend disaster. In a free-enterprise economy, business "ethics" are dictated only by cost-effectiveness, which, in turn, is directed solely to the maximization of profit. In a sense, the free-enterprise system as outlined by Adam Smith constitutes the negation of ethics in the sense that the pursuit of self-interest at the individual level is expected to result in the emergence of a community of interests at the organizational level. Accordingly, the individual has no *direct* responsibility for developing and following ethical norms that address community goals. Such goals are held to result automatically and, consequently, there can never truly be any conflict between what is good for the individual and what is good for the community. Thus, the "ethics" of business are really not ethics; what is evident is that there is an *ethos* surrounding business practices and this ethos has served too often as a model for the military.

Since business corporations are different from successful military institutions, it is clear that in the former no effort is made to submerge the individual into the organization; the individual is not expected to forgo his self-interest *even in the short run*. To be sure, the individual is exhorted to become a "team player" or "to get on board," but such exhortations are made in the context of the argument that such actions are truly in his self-interest, usually materially defined. Clearly, when this ethical perspective is adopted by the military, the result is to undermine traditional perspectives of community sacrifice and service to one's comrades. As a result, career management becomes the ultimate means to the ultimate value—promotion. The cumulative impact of this change in ethical perspectives within the military has been to bring about the rise and emulation of the "officer as entrepreneur," the man adept at managing his own career by manipulating the system, mastering its technology, usually defined in terms of administrative or managerial techniques, having his "ticket punched," and achieving the "right" assignments. An officer who can master such avenues of career advancement will be rewarded with the ultimate goal: promotion to the rank of general. The entrepreneurial officer and the ethics which motivate him remain one of the major problems afflicting the Army officer corps.

The primary difficulty encountered with this shift from corporative to entrepreneurial perspectives is that in the end it is simply to no one's self-interest to risk death in pursuit of promotion. Accordingly, the officer corps acted rationally when presented with this contradiction and began to institutionalize and minimize risk. It was no accident therefore that officers generally served in command/combat positions for only six months while enlisted troops served in their exposed posts for twelve months.[18] Additionally, the rotation of officers in and out of combat positions appears to have increased the closer they got to combat positions and the further down the rank structure one went. Thus, full colonels often were not rotated as rapidly as, say, captains. The justification for the rotation policy was that it provided a wide range of officers the opportunity for command time. Here we witness a primary example of the displacement of values. Command positions came to be valued not for the purpose of producing effective fighting units, but as a "ticket" that had to be punched in order to sustain the drive toward career advancement. Apparently the Army gave very little thought to the effect of such rotation policies on unit morale and combat effectiveness. No one seemed to realize that the ultimate result of this particular application of entrepreneurial ethics in a military milieu would maximize the role of the manager and downgrade the traditional role of the combat leader. Unable to separate the two because of the constraints of their own entrepreneurial perspective, the Army attempted to "manage the war." The officer corps learned the hard way that members of combat units could not be managed to their death. Combat effectiveness depends heavily upon the willingness to lead, and this willingness is sustained by the presence of competent, brave officers willing to share risks with their men. Such selfless behavior could no longer be justified or achieved by the new entrepreneurial logic that had taken hold within the military.

The adoption of the ethics of the entrepreneur remains one of the major difficulties confronting the officer corps. It is encouraged and sustained by a hundred different policies and practices, ranging from an officer-evaluation system that almost all agree is inflated and measures nothing, to the practice of rotating each officer through a series of assignments and schools in pursuit of the preposterous doctrine that "every second lieutenant is a potential Chief of Staff." While the Army's experience in Vietnam did not *cause* the Army or its officer corps to adopt such an ethical system, it clearly accelerated the process under which such ethics would be subject to stress and eventually proven bankrupt. Consequently, the Vietnam performance of the officer corps of all ranks cries out for an impartial examination aimed at devising means of reform. Westmoreland's suppression of the study of Army professionalism suggests most forcefully that the officer corps must critically reexamine itself with a view toward abandoning the ethics of the entrepreneur. However, it is unlikely that such ethical perspectives will ever tolerate such a reexamination as long as they remain intact. The circle is as complete as it is vicious.

It is possible that our critique of the military is not really to the point. Perhaps the impact of technology upon the American democratic social order has been such as to leave the military no real alternative but to develop an officer corps that reflects the larger societal values and practices.[19] If so, it would be pointless to talk about "reforming" the officer corps if the problem is defined *a priori* as being that of a corps that can only reflect social values. If this is so, then either the "reform" of the officer corps really depends on changing wider societal values or, more likely, we will simply have to learn to live with the entrepreneurial officer corps, because in a democracy there is logically no other alternative to the garrison state.

The argument is not compelling on several grounds. In the first place, there is nothing in the nature of American social values or in the application of technology which, *ab initio*, precludes the development of both a military structure in general and an officer corps constituted along traditional lines.[20] Further, one has only to examine the British, French, and Israeli systems to see that the doctrines accompanying social democracy need not hinder the development of highly cohesive, traditionally based, disciplined, and effective fighting forces. It must be clear that we are not making the case for placing the military totally outside the mainstream of American values. To do so would make the military a potential threat to the political system which it serves. Rather, we are suggesting that there is no inherent contradiction between the values of the wider American society and the ability to develop values which would return to a sense of "the military way" within a military unit. Additionally, the true measure of the strength of any democracy is the extent to which it can tolerate and encourage a diversity of values among its different institutional subsystems. In the real world, few if any societal subsystems require or demonstrate a one-to-one correlation between their own values and those of the society at large. To the extent that congruence must exist, it must do so only in the broadest sense.[21] Thus, the assumption underlying the case for reform, at least as it addresses the larger issue of connective links between the society at large and its military subsystems, is rooted in a pluralistic view of the American social order.

This perspective sees democratic social orders as finding their basic strength and ultimate justification in their acceptance of diversity. The social order is admittedly fragmented. Its specific sub-systems are defined by the values and rituals which it holds dear and which are utilized to define membership. To be sure, membership in social subsystems is frequently overlapping, but the tension inherent in multiple membership remains largely potential and becomes relevant only when some specific issue galvanizes the attention of the group membership to increased salience. This, in turn, often forces choices to be made, but, in the context of American social and economic practices, such choices are almost always made in terms of "more or less" rather than "all or none." Consequently, unless a subsystem were to develop extreme positions which other groups began to perceive as threatening, the lines between the values and rituals of any given subsystem and the wider social order are, by and large, articulated in only very general terms and in most instances are simply not that relevant to the day-to-day operation of the subsystem.[22]

So it is with the military subsystem and with the officer corps in particular. There is a sense in which members of the officer corps reflect larger societal values, but in the day-to-day operation of the corps such issues are not usually salient and, in most cases, not even particularly relevant. As with any other group within the social order, there is a tendency to develop a set of values and rituals (in-group norms) which ostensibly define oneself and one's relationships to other members of the corps. The extent to which these in-group norms are reflective of larger social values *in any particular case* is, as we shall argue later, a function of many factors. In the main, however, there is nothing in the nature of military subsystems per se which implies or compels that system to adopt the *specific* values and rituals of the larger social order of which it is a part. In sum, a well-disciplined, highly cohesive, tradition-oriented military subsystem and the officer corps which provides its leadership is not incompatible with a larger democratic social, political, and economic order.

It is important to understand this position. Our interviews with several dozen high-ranking officers revealed a startling tendency to lay the blame for the difficulties manifested within the Army and the officer corps at the feet of the society at large. It was argued very frequently that the military could not produce good soldiers out of the raw material furnished by a "drug-ridden" and "openly permissive society." Many of these officers felt that the officer corps could not be expected to forgo the values of the officer as entrepreneur when the military establishment had already been structured to reward these values. Finally, it was suggested throughout these interviews that it is impossible for the Army and its officer corps to sustain the traditional values of selflessness, responsibility, and sacrifice when such values receive no support from the larger social system. We find these arguments unconvincing. If the British Army could socialize the Irish peasantry to its sense of the military way and still retain an army fully congruent with democratic values operating in a society that stressed, above all else, the ethics of laissez-faire, then there seems to be no convincing historical reason why the American military cannot develop a highly integrative subsystem commanded by an officer corps whose standards of honor, duty, and responsibility transcend, but do not threaten, the social values of the larger social order. To suggest that the task is an impossible one is really to ignore the fact that history is replete with examples of its successful accomplishment in other democratic societies. More importantly, to imply that the military can be no more than the values of the larger society of which it is a part is to provide the Army and its officer corps with a built-in excuse for continuing the policies which surfaced during the Vietnam War. Down that road can only lie further disintegration.

Once it is agreed that reform of the American military system, specifically the Army officer corps, is possible, then the case for reform must stand or fall on its own merits. An examination of the officer corps requires some standard against which to measure indicators of performance. We shall rely heavily on historical comparisons drawn from the British, French, and German models. It might be argued that such models do not really lend themselves to valid comparisons with the American Army or that diverse military systems cannot be compared across cultural boundaries simply because they are so deeply rooted within their respective and different cultures. This argument does not strike us as particularly strong in light of the fact that social scientists regularly compare political systems, economic systems, and social systems on a cross-cultural basis. Furthermore, our comparisons are drawn from armies within the same ecumene, that is, essentially from those within cultures rooted in the common heritage of the Judeo-Christian experience. The similarities of culture and history are broad enough within this cultural spectrum to make comparisons of military systems and subsystems valid at least in the main.

These comparative models need not be overemphasized, for, in the final analysis, they merely provide us with baselines from which other more sophisticated measurements of military behavior can be made. History, however, does provide examples buttressing those baselines. Historical perspective does help us to judge the behavior of the American Army and its officer corps.

Additional data are marshaled at various points in support of the case for reform. These data include aggregate data, survey data, case studies, dozens of personal interviews, and even our personal experiences as former military officers. In many instances we have had to rely more heavily than we would have wished on official statistics provided by various sources which had some direct or indirect connection with the military itself. Further, it has not escaped us that in some instances the data are incomplete. Such instances are few, however, and where they exist have the single redeeming value of being the only data available.

There is one point that requires attention and that is the charge that the data are accurate and correctly interpreted as they stand but only for the time period that they address. In an earlier presentation of our findings to a group of senior Army officers at the Army War College, there was almost unanimous agreement that the data employed were accurate and that our conclusion, that the officer corps needed reform, was also accurate. However, it was suggested that the data *no longer* accurately describe present conditions but only those that existed during and immediately following the Vietnam War. It was argued that the Army had "turned the corner" and that our data have been rendered obsolete by events. While this argument will be addressed in more detail later, suffice it to say that every effort has been made to update the data wherever possible, sometimes against the open resistance of the Army itself. To the extent that our data may be out of date, it is the responsibility of those who so argue to produce and make available up-to-date information. We have seen no such efforts nor encountered any data which would lead us to believe that our conclusions are wrong.

II

An Army in Collapse

If political systems can be compared, we can also compare the ways in which the military "manage" and conduct wars. More importantly, the performance of military forces should be comparable in specific terms: degree of unit cohesion, discipline, and the quality of leadership. Such comparisons allow the construction of a general standard against which the performance of the U.S. Army may be measured.

Effective, professional military leadership requires that certain standards of officer behavior be met. Officers' attitudes, actions, and abilities contribute to the formation of unit integrity. At a very minimum, these standards do not permit soldiers to be "used" in pursuit of an officer's career. We have suggested that there is a clear and, perhaps, even a growing trend toward the entrepreneurial disposition among contemporary American Army officers. The entrepreneurial disposition is most clearly contrasted to a corporative disposition. In the latter there is stress on traditional military virtues—self-sacrifice, duty, honor, and institutional dedication—whereas in the former, attitudes more typical of the occupationally concerned corporate executive predominate. The entrepreneur, of course, becomes the occupationally oriented "military manager," while the traditional corporative officer has been referred to as the "gladiator." Charles C. Moskos, following Morris

Janowitz in *The Professional Soldier*, observes that the "occupational model" operant in the military system generates what, in effect, is an industrial ethic for the military with traditional military values confined to a shrinking number of self-selected elite units. Development of this sociopolitical quality within the services brings into question the very notion of military legitimacy.[1] With changes in the social ambience of the U.S. Army since World War II, similar changes in officer behavior appear associated with radical changes in the behavior of military units under conditions of combat stress. Toward the end of the Vietnam War the U.S. Army began to exhibit clear signs of disintegration under what appear to have been conditions of relatively minimal combat stress.

A principal concern of this chapter is to examine the indicators of disintegration reflected in the performance of the American Field Army in Vietnam. Elsewhere we shall examine the behavior of the Army officer corps during the same period. This analysis is set against historical comparisons in the context of definable sociomilitary processes which simultaneously appear to affect military cohesion in the U.S. Army. These processes include the following: the replacement of a traditional "gladiatorial" officer stereotype with the managerial combat nonparticipant to the extent that managerial efficiency instead of "honor" becomes the standard of performance. The managerial disposition undermines, it seems to us, the sense of military honor commonly associated with unit integrity. Inasmuch as the latter is involved with "profitless" personal sacrifice, a managerially oriented commander may come to see his troops as a resource to be used to advance his own career rather than as a moral charge, placed upon his honor and rested ultimately in reciprocal trust and self-sacrifice. Morris Janowitz has addressed the problem in the following terms: "Because the military establishment is managerially oriented, the gap between the heroic leader and the military manager has also narrowed . . . The Technologist is likely to be most concerned with means, the manager with the purpose of military policy . . . Presently the military academies are deeply concerned with whether they can adequately present an image of a 'whole man' who, realistically, is both a modern heroic leader and a military manager."[2]

Another major concern is the radical inflation of officer strengths. The percentage of Army officers to troops during World War II and Korea was 7 and 9 percent respectively; by the end of the Vietnam War officers constituted approximately 15 percent of total strength. There is evidence that the swelling of the officer corps corresponded with a decline in quality. The destruction of primary military groups appears to be a critical factor of disintegration within armies. Military units whose essential task is combat resist disintegration principally because of the integrity of the primary military unit—the squad, platoon, or company. The American Army since World War II has experienced a progressive reduction of primary-group cohesion until the Vietnam War, when, it may be argued, it almost ceased to exist at all. There were, no doubt, several factors contributing to this condition, but the proximate cause of primary-group destruction appears to have been the rotation system. Two interrelated hypotheses may be suggested:

1. The U.S. Army underwent a progressive disintegration and finally an accelerating one in the years 1961–71. To a significant degree, the disintegrative process operated independently of sociopolitical factors in the larger American society.

2. The disintegration of the Army, together with the dissolution of its primary-group cohesion, is directly related to the loss of officer professionalism expressed in the increasingly pervasive phenomenon of "managerial careerism."

It is important to define "cohesion" and "disintegration" since they constitute concepts critical to this analysis. The definition of one impacts heavily upon the definition of the other since they are reciprocals. Disintegration of a military organization can be seen in the prevalence of internal conditions which make effective military operations very difficult if not, in some cases, impossible. These conditions are desertion, mutiny, assassination of leaders, and other factors, such as drug usage, which destroy discipline and combat effectiveness. Unit cohesion is the presence of a set of conditions which create the expectation that a military unit will attempt to perform its assigned orders and mission irrespective of the situation and its inevitable attendant risks. Victory or defeat is *not* a condition of measurement, since, clearly, even defeated armies can maintain high rates of unit cohesion, as a multiplicity of examples from British, French, and German history attest. Cohesion is revealed in levels of performance in battle and, like disintegration, is measurable only in relative terms. Deplorably, much of man's history is one of conflict, warfare, and battle. Armies have cohered under seemingly unendurable conditions while others have disintegrated under conditions of minimal combat stress. Certainly the performance of the German Army in both world wars is an obvious example of high cohesion under great stress largely irrespective of the nature of their government. Other examples can be cited, but most striking is the experience of the British Army in World War I. British losses from attrition in the Ypres Salient in 1916 were some 7,000 men per week—"wastage" in the staff argot of the time. The later offensive of Third Ypres (1917) cost 370,000 men in five months. Forty-five square miles of land were gained—8,222 men per square mile. Officer losses were extremely high, as were noncommissioned officer casualties. Despite staggering levels of combat stress, no evidence of a loss of cohesion in any measurable dimension can be found in the British Army records.[3] Indeed, British unit cohesion under almost impossible conditions is so common in British military history that such behavior is not regarded as unusual by British military men. Rather, cohesion under stress is the norm.

Conventional historians and not a small number of political and social commentators believe that military units maintain cohesion in combat because of external behavioral reinforcers such as patriotism, a tradition of militarism (Sparta, Rome, Prussia), ideological beliefs, and, possibly, aristocratically derived imperialism. Some contemporary military sociologists find other explanations to account for cohesion or disintegration. Accordingly, the strength or weakness of a military structure is, by and large, a function of conditions generated within the military structure itself. It is clear that a decline in officer professionalism and the displacement of the military ethos by the ethics of the entrepreneur are more likely to be responsible for disintegration than factors operant in the society at large. We do not deny, of course, that there are linkages between the larger society and its military subsystem, for clearly such linkages do exist. With regard to Vietnam, for example, such linkages were evident in the adoption of a rotation policy designed to avoid putting the United States on a total-war footing, the isolation of elites in colleges which served to reduce the high-quality pool of potential officers, and the obvious restrictions placed upon military operations as a result of domestic political considerations. Another factor yet to be studied is the effect of mass media on troop morale. Did the rising opposition to the war reflected in the media between 1968 and 1971 affect individual military attachment to norms of battle conduct? The data are not yet in, but certainly the question is pertinent. While we do not wish to imply that military structures are totally independent of wider societal forces, we stress that forces internal to the military structure—such as a developed sense of professionalism and an honored military ethic—are far more crucial in understanding the degree of cohesion that an army will maintain under stress. Accordingly, we do not agree with popular notions that indicators of military disintegration are the direct result of factors generated by the external society.

To illustrate the process of military disintegration, historical comparisons are helpful. We have observed British, French, American, and other experiences. Another most useful comparison is that of the German historical model, which presents us with an army that maintained strong cohesion under enormous pressures even during final defeat in World War II. The German model is appropriate for two reasons. It is a product of Western civilization, exhibiting far more in common with other Western armies than differences. Minimal cultural differences aside, one can point to similarities in organizational and value structures, belief systems rested in patriotism, and mass armies based on conscription.[4] The second reason is that the cohesion of the German Army has been studied in some detail by other analysts through the use of empirical data.[5]

Despite repeated catastrophes, the Wehrmacht remained so cohesive that it fought effectively until eventually overrun; and, indeed, never did surrender as it did in World War I. German speed, discipline, and efficiency in the attack, combined with determined, relentless, and methodical resistance over thousands of miles, have been attributed to a multitude of variables, including nationalism, the impact of National Socialist ideology, and the "inherent militarism" of the German people. Little available evidence reveals these factors as important, or indeed that any special *external* sociopolitical factors were major influences on military cohesion. Indeed, the cohesion of the German Army "was sustained only to a very slight extent by the National Socialist political convictions of German soldiers . . . and that more important in the motivation of the determined resistance of the German soldier was the ready satisfaction of certain primary personality demands afforded by the social organization of the Army."[6] German battlefield cohesion resulted directly from the individual soldier's personal reinforcement due to interactions through which he received esteem and respect from his primary group—squad, platoon, and company—and to his perceptions of his immediate officers and NCO's as men of honor eminently deserving of respect and who cared for their men.[7] German Army officers were very carefully selected, virtually all with education superior to the average German. Moreover, the rigorous standards for selecting German officers were maintained throughout the war.[8] Ultimately these standards resulted in producing a German Army which was greatly underofficered, even by their own austere officer manning levels. The low percentage of officers to men had little effect on cohesion.[9]

When restrictive standards in officer selection are combined with very high casualties, the result inevitably is the severe contraction of an officer corps and especially so in one insisting on rigorous qualifications for its replacements. In 1939 the German Field Army

had 81,314 officers and 2,741,064 enlisted men. Officers constituted 2.96 percent of total fighting strength. For the 1939 German
Army as a whole (officers: 105,394; EM: 3,571,215), officers represented 2.86 percent. The officer-enlisted ratio was 1:34.[10] If this officer-enlisted ratio had been maintained throughout the war—
although it was not, because, as noted, the German Army by 1945
was severely underofficered—then when the German Army
reached its maximum strength of 6,550,000 in 1943, the officer
corps would have totaled approximately 194,535.[11] However,
while officer numbers declined, no substantial effect on military
cohesion became evident. In fact, as military catastrophes multiplied, cohesion seems to have remained constant.

Enormous German officer and enlisted losses occurred on the
Russian front in 1944; under ordinary conditions, the German
Army should have collapsed. It did not, and this example illustrates the German military capacity to maintain cohesion and recover from catastrophic reverses. In July 1944, the German Central
Army Group was virtually destroyed by Soviet assault. Of 38 German divisions committed, 28 were put out of action and total
losses were between 350,000 and 400,000 officers and men. The
battle lasted some three weeks. Of 47 generals commanding at
division and corps levels (up to an equivalent U.S. rank of lieutenant general), 31 were lost: 10 killed in action, 21 became prisoners of war. Even more remarkable, the Germans managed to restore a defensive front under these conditions. Even in the face of
catastrophic defeat the evidence of leadership in battle by the highest ranks is overwhelming; their willingness to incur sacrifice was
well above and beyond what the ordinary soldier was required to
do.[12]

German officers consistently suffered losses in much higher proportion than their share of the force strength. Constituting 2.86
percent of overall Army strength, officers accounted for 3.5 percent
of the total number killed. The German Army lost 1,709,739 men
killed in action, including 59,965 officers. One German soldier in
28 killed in action was an officer, while officers constituted only 1

in 34 of the operating strength. Thus 30.8 percent of the German officer corps was killed in action as against 26.1 percent of the enlisted ranks.

If the average German officer's risk of being killed was far greater than that faced by his men, the risk of field-grade leadership was even greater. Of 675 general officers on the German Army list, 223 were killed in action, or 33 percent.[13]

In the German military, rank and social status overlapped extensively; so too did the indicators of sacrifice. Europeans keep track of their nobility by way of such references as the *Almanach de Gotha*. Germans, being the researchers they are, have counted the losses of their nobility in World War II. One source lists 8,284 German noblemen. Of these, 4,690 were lost in action, or 56.6 percent of those listed.[14] Noblemen tended to enter the officer corps and their losses were 25.8 percent higher than the losses of the officer corps itself. In some measure then, the attitude of deference and respect the German soldier showed his social and military superiors was merited by the unambiguous willingness of his "betters" to assume the burden and costs of status.

Certainly a main factor in the cohesion of the primary group in the German Army, namely the company, was the sense of responsibility, performance of duty, and willingness to take combat risks demonstrated by German officers. The data on the readiness of the officers and upper classes to die in battle support this assertion. The concern of German officers for their soldiers was reciprocated by their men, reinforcing the cohesion of combat units that remained so high in the German Army right to the end.[15] To a great extent then, military cohesion can be seen as a function of the quality of the officer corps, its skill, dedication, and its readiness to sacrifice.

The readiness of German officers to lead and to die was apparent to the German soldier.[16] He was a good soldier expended in a bad cause. The "cause," Nazi ideology or even nationalism, was never the driving force in his capacity to fight or his ability to maintain unit cohesiveness. This point is at the heart of the Shils and Janowitz study. These findings, of course, contravene the conventional wisdom which tends to lay military disintegration at the feet of a society badly fragmented, a point later to be addressed in the discussion of the American Army in Vietnam. In all German field operations officers undertook an inordinate share of risk and regarded any insulation of officers from the risks of battle as dishonorable.

The fighting qualities of the German Army can, in large measure, be attributed to the quality of the leadership of its officer corps, a corps remaining throughout the war at a very low percentage of total strength. Indeed, it even declined to half of authorized strength by war's end. The Germans may have achieved a type of optimum officer leadership quotient relying on high quality and low numbers of officers. Officer visibility to the German soldier was apparently maintained at a level which was sufficient to meet the soldiers' needs to be cared for by their officer leaders but which was not overwhelming through an excessive "visibility of brass." Permitting the small-unit officer to exercise responsible control of the fighting forces, the "linear" war fought by the Germans kept senior officers relatively remote from the body of troops. The senior officers, although not overly visible, were not isolated from an appropriate risk of death. Continuous proximity of company-grade officers of high quality emerged as a major factor in primary-group cohesion, with the belief and expectation on the part of the troops that their officers would remain with them "even unto death." Senior officers, noticeably remote from enlisted ranks and rarely interfering in detail with smaller commands, nonetheless bore a substantial share of sacrifice, as the data show and as the German soldier was aware. German officers were not perceived to be in a position of sanctified insulation from the burden of sacrifice and death. As we will see, the opposite was true of American senior officers in Vietnam.

None of the foregoing is to say that the German Army did not, as do all armies, have its "bombproofs": civilians with assimilated ranks, paper generals whose rank was acquired by politics, Nazi party hacks in ornate uniforms (*"die goldenen Fasanen"*), SS rear-area administrators, concentration camp officials, and others. But those in the German military who were entrepreneurs, careerists, military "managers," and others at variance with the German military value structure did not dominate the experience of the line troops, nor did they obtrude so much as to alter the perceived quality of German officer leadership and professionalism. The behavior of German officers remained unambiguously in accord with what cohesive military units require as essential to performance: they were available to their men; they accepted an inordinate share of the burden of death; they were professionally competent and reliable; and, very importantly, they were present at the front. To be sure, other factors affected German military cohesion. Factors such as the sense of a Germany besieged, the traditional deference of a subject-oriented culture, a belief that military service was an honor, some secondary influence of Hitler as a father image, and a fear of the security police all contributed. But these factors remained far less important than the primary group, in the German Army the company, a unit of from 100 to 150 members, and its respected leadership.

An important additional element contributing to cohesion in the German Army was the policy of rotating divisions out of the line for reconstitution of their primary groups.[17] American policy in World Wars I and II, Korea, and Vietnam has been to maintain units in combat for protracted periods, keeping them filled by a stream of replacements and, in effect, considerably reducing the primary-group ties and hence unit cohesion. The effect of American combat replacement policies has been to produce combat units composed of men who do not know each other. Units of strangers are, of course, greater after protracted combat. Still, the practice of treating the American soldier as a "component" instead of part of cohesive units continued during Vietnam.[18]

The German historical model during World War II is characterized by high military professionalism and cohesion. The cement of the German Army was its soldiers' sense of belonging, deferring to and admiring immediate leaders who could be counted upon to accept levels of sacrifice far beyond that demanded of the ordinary soldier. To the extent that casualty data reveal anything, the respect of the German soldier for his officers was well earned if the level of German officer and elite-group sacrifice indicates anything at all. Using even these minimal measures of cohesiveness and professionalism, the American Army provides an interesting study in contrast.

Lest it be thought that the German model is unique, a brief examination of the performance of other European armies provides additional examples of similar cohesion. Incidences of high cohesion accompanied by staggering casualties can be cited almost without end. At Verdun in 1916, for example, over 600,000 total dead were suffered by both sides in an area only slightly larger than three to four times that of Central Park; the U.S. Army 36th Infantry Division on the Rapido in Italy suffered over 1,500 dead in two hours; the German Submarine Service lost 35,000 of 40,000 in action—all dead; the American 3rd Infantry Division in World War II was replaced three times; and the 1945–59 French Expeditionary Force of 151,000 men took 47,048 casualties in the nine-year Indochina war. By any comparison, there is nothing in the American experience in Vietnam remotely approaching the losses in these historical cases, and very little in terms of comparative battle stress. It seems fair to say that the American Army in Vietnam underwent no catastrophic reverses and suffered few losses compared to the countless incidents experienced by other Western armies. It is this "minimal combat stress."[19] which throws into ever starker relief so many indicators associated with discohesion within the American military force in Vietnam.

The evidence suggests that by 1968–69 the American Army had begun to disintegrate under relatively minimal stress. Many have noted the difficulties experienced by the U.S. Army in later stages of the Vietnam War. Some which emerged were considerably higher desertion rates, high levels of drug addiction, mutinies, and "fragging," or the attempted assassination of officers and NCO's.

These conditions—desertion, drug use, fragging, and combat re-fusals—have often been explained as "understandable" expressions of men engaged in a war both unpopular and without home-front support. The conventional wisdom of the present-day military in particular has attempted to explain the lack of discipline of Ameri-can troops as an unavoidable product of the larger permissive soci-ety. Even the draft, it has been argued, exacerbated the problem of cohesion because it was inclined to be invidiously discriminatory, so that mostly the lower classes were called to serve. Those from the upper societal strata were often able to avoid military service, or at least the more dangerous combat assignments. Privileged groups, insulated in colleges and universities by law and the logic of the selective service system, managed disproportionately to avoid military service. This may have some relevance to the ab-sence of cohesion in the American Army. In World War II, 8.5 percent of servicemen aged 20–24 had completed four or more years of college, but by Korea this percentage had fallen to 3.9 per-cent of all veterans. In 1971, during the Vietnam War the percent-age of those who served and who had completed four years of college had fallen to 2.6 percent. Thus, between 1945 and 1971, the percentage of college graduates exposed to the risks of warfare had fallen drastically.[20] Service in limited wars appears to fall less heavily upon the educationally privileged than upon others. Even so, the level of soldiers' education probably has no more than a marginal relation to military cohesion. What is relevant is the fact that the higher-educational system evolved into a device to avoid ground combat by the socially privileged and reduce their potential as a leadership pool.[21]

Still others have explained the 1969–71 disintegration of the U.S. Army as an awakening by the ordinary soldier to the "immo-rality" of the war or the stirring of "true consciousness." We know, however, that military cohesion exists quite apart from issue poli-tics and ideologies in the civilian political system. Specifically, a sense of active patriotism, nationalism, or other ideologies are not demonstrably central to military discipline and cohesion. Responsible scholarship on the subject of military cohesion heavily discounts the conventional psychosocial elements often assumed to be important to military spirit. It appears that a continued sense of "cause," at whatever level of saliency, is not very important to military cohesion. Contemporary literature further calls into question any sense of mission on the part of soldiers other than the immediate tactical mission. The Stouffer Study of World War II demonstrated that the main factor in combat cohesion was found in the primary group. The same factor proved true in Korea. In World War II the American primary group existed at the squad (8–12 men) or platoon (25–40 men) level. During the Korean War, however, the primary group had collapsed to the dyadic buddy system. The smaller primary groups typical of the American Army (compared to the company-sized primary group of the German Army) in World War II, essentially the squad or platoon level, were largely a result of the replacement system which kept divisions in protracted combat, thus tending to keep primary groups small. In Korea the same protracted division combat policy was exacerbated by an individual replacement system which reduced the primary group to a dyad. Additionally, some regard for the immediate leader is essential to cohesion in any military primary group in combat, as demonstrated by the Germans. However, even small-unit combat leadership was weakened in Korea by the unofficial policy of rotating officer platoon leaders from the immediate combat unit to safer positions in the rear as replacement officers became available, weakening in turn the probabilities that reciprocal officer-enlisted regard and respect would develop. Accordingly, enlisted men in Korea served a full combat tour in the line while officers often did not. Later in Vietnam such a policy was put fully into effect with officers in combat units, as we noted earlier, serving approximately six months in combat while their men served a twelve-month combat tour.[22]

If home-front support, ideologies, and "system alienation" have only a limited effect on military cohesion, why was disintegration in the Vietnam War so obvious toward the end of that conflict?

The signs are unambiguous and include the following: rising desertion rates over a ten-year period with a great acceleration toward the end of the conflict, so much so that by 1971 they far exceeded World War II and Korean rates; mutinous outbreaks in combat units; attempted and actual murders of officers by their troops in ever rising numbers; and a drug-addiction plague of vast proportions, especially in the last four years of the war. An examination of each of these indicators allows us to gauge with some accuracy the degree of disintegration evident within the U.S. Army in Vietnam.

One major evidence of disintegration frequently cited is the desertion rate. A deserter is normally defined as a soldier absent without proper authority; he is administratively classified as a deserter usually after a period of thirty days' absence. Table 1* reveals comparative desertion rates for three wars. It is clear from the data that desertion rates during Vietnam well exceeded comparative rates for World War II and Korea. Indeed, the desertion rate reached dangerous levels in the years 1965–71, when it increased by 468 percent! It is highly revealing that after 1968 the level and intensity of combat incidents actually dropped off. Accordingly, the data present a paradox in that desertion rates for U.S. ground forces seemed to increase as the level of combat decreased if we measure the level of combat by the number of troops actually killed in action. While there was a rising desertion rate in the Army as a whole during the years 1969–71, the strength of ground forces in Vietnam, as well as losses measured by killed in action, declined steadily. Table 2 shows the relation between overall Army strengths, total ground forces in Vietnam, losses as measured by the number killed in action, and desertion. From 1968 through 1971, the number of deaths due to hostile action declined steadily each year for an overall four-year decline of 84.6 percent. In the same period, desertion rates steadily increased each year for an overall four-year increase of 60.5 percent. The data thus suggest

*Tables will be found on pg. 181 ff.

that whatever the reasons for increased desertion rates, increased combat loss and risk of death due to hostile fire were certainly not among them. Vietnam desertion rates exceeded those of World War II by over ten per thousand at their height, and by over forty-one per thousand when measured against the Korean War's maximum desertion rates. Indeed, the annual rates of increase in desertions during Vietnam exceed anything in U.S. combat experience despite the fact that the Vietnam conflict, when seen in historical perspective, demanded comparatively low levels of sacrifice.

As an indicator of disintegration, desertion increased radically in Vietnam despite a simultaneous reduction in both the losses and the number of troops actually deployed. At the same time, a peculiar characteristic of the war began to surface. This was the practice of "fragging," defined as attempts to kill with an "explosive device," ordinarily a hand grenade. Table 3 presents the data concerning the number of "fraggings" which the Defense Department admits to during the Vietnam War. The category of assaults by "explosive device" excludes attempts to kill "leadership elements" by other means, such as a rifle, automatic-weapons fire, ambush by claymore mines, and misdirection to hostile ambush. Moreover, the figures released as being official openly conflict with the "official" testimony of Major General Walter Kerwin (data in parentheses in Table 3) before a House of Representatives subcommittee investigating the subject of military assassination. Since there appear to be no historical analogies for large-scale "fragging," official explanations for its occurrence tend to lack credibility. In World War I, only 370 cases of American violence against superiors were brought to court-martial, this in a war that involved over four million American military personnel. This same low ratio is also found during World War II and Korea. In Vietnam, between 1970 and 1972, 363 cases of assault with explosive devices occurred and another 118 were deemed "possible assaults." During this period, approximately 700,000 Americans were in Vietnam. As for the ratio of attempted killings of officers to the number of offenses actually tried, officers in the Judge Advocate General Corps have es-

timated that only about 10 percent of the actual attempts resulted
in the offender being apprehended and brought to trial.[23] Thus it
would seem that General Kerwin's testimony relied heavily upon
the conventional wisdom in referring to the "permissive" society
and enlisted resentment toward officers and NCO's resulting from
necessary "authoritarian" means "proper in a combat environment." He cited as well the boredom and confinement in fire-
support bases and base camps.[24]

One analysis of the "fragging" phenomenon classified types of violent incidents into two categories. The first category of attempted
assassination was undertaken by an individual pursuing a personal
vendetta. In these cases, the perpetrator was likely to be "unbalanced or psychologically disturbed at the time he resorted to violence." ". . . happenstance often determines the ultimate victim,
and the culprit makes little effort to hide his identity." This form
of assassination appears to have been relatively rare. The second
category, that of a premeditated attempt at murder, seems not to
have been so rare. According to Moskos, there are three variants of
this second category: "(a) racially-inspired fraggings, typically by
Blacks against what is regarded as racist white superiors; (b) dope
hassles, fraggings arising from informal groups of drug users seeking reprisal against enforcers of anti-drug regulations; and (c) fraggings in combat groups against a noncom or officer who is seen as
too gung-ho in risking the lives of his subordinates."[25] The second
category of fragging necessarily involves some degree of premedita-
tion and collusion. In one sense, then, fragging in the latter category is closely linked with mutiny, even though fragging is a comparatively short-lived action while a mutiny requires somewhat
more time to occur and be settled. How the data in Table 3 relate
to the above is not known, nor do we know of any studies that
might have conducted such an analysis. Still, it seems reasonable to
say that drug addiction, fragging, and mutiny are definitely linked
to the disintegration of military units. At no time, apparently, has
the ethical quality of the officer corps as a central factor in assassi-

nation been considered by Congress when it has delved into matters of military discipline which led to "fragging."

Concurrently an equally ominous indicator of military disintegration became public—"combat refusals." In more rigorous armies, such incidents would have been called mutiny—which in fact they were. Our inquiries to the Department of Defense extracted the following comment from Clayton N. Gompf, Acting Deputy for Military Personnel Policy and Programs, with respect to mutinous outbreaks: "As to so-called combat refusals, data on incidents of this nature are not maintained by the Department of the Army. I do not know the source of the statistics cited by Senator Stennis."[26] Given the available data, we are limited to noting what Senator John Stennis of the Senate Armed Forces Committee stated during hearings on the nomination of Robert R. Froehlke as Secretary of the Army in 1971. Stennis said there were 68 refusals to fight in 1968 for seven combat divisions in Vietnam, and in 1970, 35 "individual" refusals occurred in the First Air Cavalry Division alone.[27] Certainly, if this latter number of mutinies took place in a division with an extensive and honored combat record, the suspicion is warranted that the level may have probably been higher, for example, in the Americal Division, which was involved in My Lai. Even if each combat division had only the same number of mutinous events as the First Cavalry, then in 1970 there could have been as many as 245 such "refusals" to fight. Without official data, we can only infer that if the progressive and symptomatic military disintegration evidenced by desertions and assassinations of leaders is also reflected in mutinous outbreaks, the number of mutinies was very probably quite large. Moreover, unlike mutinous outbreaks of the past and in other armies, which were usually sporadic short-lived events, the *progressive* unwillingness of American soldiers to fight to the point of open disobedience took place over a four-year period between 1968 and 1971, thus paralleling the data on fragging and desertion to a remarkably high degree. The mutinies in Vietnam appear to represent a pattern of behavior rather than sporadic events, thus lending a substantial degree of credibility to the argument that combat refusals were part of a larger process of disintegration.

It can, of course, be argued that troops have mutinied and murdered their officers in other times and places. The Sepoy Mutiny of 1857, during which native Indian troops killed their British officers as well as British military dependants; the Russian Revolution of 1917; the French Army mutinies in 1917; the German Naval mutiny of 1918; a series of shipboard mutinies in the British fleet during the Napoleonic Wars, all come to mind. However, none of these historical examples is comparable to the behavior in the U.S. Army in Vietnam. The historic cases cited were either relatively short-lived or exhibited social and political qualities not comparable to the American case. The Sepoy Mutiny was a rebellion of colonials against foreign control for what appear to be religious reasons. During the Russian Revolution, a combination of revolution and civil war, which saw the murder of Czarist officers, was characterized by a situation in which troops lived and fought under severely deprived conditions and a uniquely corrupt and inefficient leadership. Similar conditions did not apply to the Army in Vietnam, especially a succession of catastrophic defeats as undergone by the Czarist armies. In the case of the British Fleet mutinies, these were associated with a long period of warfare, extraordinarily brutal living conditions, violent punishment, and large numbers of impressed sailors. Even under these extreme conditions officers were not murdered. Similarly, the French Army mutinies in World War I took place in a matter of days and followed four years of great slaughter characterized by attacks across open areas and notable for their senselessness. Further, the French troops did not refuse to defend, but only to attack. Yet these mutinies did result in the assassination of a few officers.[28] And finally, the German High Seas Fleet mutiny of 1918 was partially the result of idleness in a long war and partially the effect of infiltration by Marxist elements. One example of a sociopolitical setting which, if the explanations offered by the Pentagon are correct, should have resulted in repeated instances of mutinous behavior is the British Army. With the exception of the Sepoy Mutiny, the British Army in its recruitment of "colonials" has experienced surprisingly little rebellion within its military units.

A classic example of cohesion among England's colonials is that of the Irish—a group justly famous for truculence, intractability, and political intrigue—who served for centuries in Britain's armies and wars. Despite coming from an island notable for "risings" against their masters from the time of the Earl of Pembroke, "Strongbow," in 1170 to the present "troubles," they served in their Catholic thousands and died in windrows in all of England's wars. We find in later centuries little evidence of mutiny among the Irish regiments in any of England's wars; not even during World War I, with the great distraction of the 1916 Easter Rebellion. The extraordinary British success in socializing the Irish (not to mention Pathans, Afridis, Gurkhas, Malays, Bedouins, Scots, Amazulus, Ashanti, etc.) into British military discipline and tradition has never been successfully explained in sociological terms and most certainly is not explainable in terms of the Pentagon's attitude toward American "combat refusals" and other troubles. We suspect that successful military socialization is linked intimately to the conduct and leadership of the British officers and NCO's, who always led their men at the front and very often died leading them.

Historical examples of the socialization of "hostiles" into foreign military orders are numerous. Unfortunately, none helps to explain the behavior of the American Army in the last years of the Vietnam War. As a further contrast to other wars in other places, living conditions for American troops in Vietnam were comparatively luxurious: exemplified by the PX, club and resort facilities, and periods of "rest and recuperation" out of the country. The only explanation seems to be that mutinous behavior was only one part of a larger overall pattern of disintegration. While the explanations may vary, the existence of a pattern of disintegration among American troops seems beyond dispute.

The problem of drug usage among American troops in Vietnam,

particularly hard drugs such as heroin, seems to many analysts to have been *sui generis*. No parallel is evident anywhere in military history. The acquisition, organized distribution, and use of drugs cannot be dissociated from crime and corruption at high and intermediate levels of command and staff. Here we find evidence of disintegration, not only among the troops of the line but among their leaders as well. Extensive drug use seems to us to be an absolutely clear sign that disintegration in an army is already well advanced. Further, when members of an allied officer corps are involved, even peripherally, in drug profiteering, it is not unrealistic to expect the stain of guilt to spread to lower-ranking members of the American officer corps and to find that the troops have come to hold their officers in contempt, if only because American officers appeared to tolerate a drug traffic. That troops in battle, however minimal the battle, would be subjected to the organized pushing of hard narcotics is without historical parallel. More extraordinary, drugs were publicly available in places known to officers and men of all ranks and little was done to stem the trade. The higher officer corps was so committed to expedience that the organized distribution of drugs was accepted as necessary to the support of the South Vietnamese government, which often purveyed the drugs that destroyed the Army that defended it. Even though the French operated in the identical area under similar conditions, there is no evidence that the French Army in the first Indochina war experienced a drug problem, or that the French command would, in any case, have tolerated the widespread drug network accepted by the American command in Vietnam.[29]

The true extent of hard-drug usage by the American troops during the last years of the Vietnam War is unknown. One method used for detecting it in Vietnam was to screen men by urinalysis just prior to their departure. By this method, 5.5 percent of the troops were shown to have used heroin, and these data were "officially" accepted as correct. Few students of the subject accept this rate of use as realistic, since the troops devised numerous ways to avoid detection. In a 1971 survey conducted by the Human Resources Research Organization (Humrro) of over forty thousand service people worldwide, the extent of drug usage in the services in general and in Vietnam in particular was found to be over five times as high as "official" figures. Table 4 sets out the Humrro findings. Despite the fact that mass surveys of this sort are suspect, other data support the findings.[30]

The available data suggest that almost a third of the Army in Vietnam had used a hard narcotic at some time, while one in four U.S. soldiers used narcotic drugs worldwide. No comparative modern Western population shows rates of hard-drug usage remotely resembling those of the United States Army in 1971. Clearly the problem had been growing from some time in the recent past, perhaps with the advent of the Thieu-Ky regime. Further, the introduction, distribution, and sale of heroin in Vietnam were clearly tied to an organized system operated and run by high-ranking members of the Vietnamese government. Judgments about the American "Country Team" in Vietnam, headed by Ambassador Ellsworth Bunker, are remarkable in that some American complicity in the drug traffic was clearly evident. In his work on the heroin traffic in Southeast Asia, Alfred W. McCoy provides evidence that not only were the American diplomats and members of the military high command aware of Vietnamese official involvement in the heroin trade, but by concealing the facts and blocking investigations were guilty of continued complicity.[31] Direct complicity was laid at the door of the CIA, which flew heroin and opium shipments from Laos to Vietnam by way of Air America, a CIA subsidiary.[32] Both the CIA and the American diplomatic corps frustrated and blocked investigations of the heroin traffic by other branches of the federal government.[33] In any case, heroin usage in the Army is another unmistakable sign of internal military decay. It is hardly remarkable that an army cannot function, much less fight, when 28.5 percent of its troops use heroin, or that they fail to defer to a leadership that tolerates drug racketeering.

Our analysis has not considered the problem of alcoholism in the Army, which to many appears as serious as drug usage since alcohol itself is a drug. However, the use of drugs is illegal and that of alcohol is not. Thus, alcohol use in the services is not likely to be linked to organized criminal efforts and, therefore, to official corruption. Further, Western armies have always been socialized to the use of alcohol in its many forms, and have devised means to control its abuse. Many British and French soldiers drink heavily, but this drinking does not appear to affect performance. Typically, injunctions exist against drinking on duty and in battle which seem to be largely obeyed. The same is simply not the case with narcotics. Drugs are a substance for which no, or very few, social defenses exist. Additionally, men using them will do so both on duty and in battle. While several drinks are not addictive, several "hits" of "smack" tend to lead to addiction. Finally, there is no evidence that controlled and institutionalized alcohol affects combat performance, but there is every sign that drugs destroy combat capability.[34]

By every historical measure of military cohesiveness, the American Army in Vietnam was in a state of advancing disintegration at the time of disengagement. We know that the basis of a cohesive army, namely, its primary military groups, had been virtually destroyed. We know too that forces and events external to the military system had only limited influence upon, or linkages to, the low state of military cohesiveness. It seems then that the quality and style of American military leadership must be examined since leadership appears historically to be a crucial variable affecting unit cohesion, discipline, and military effectiveness.

III

The Officer Corps

Millions of soldiers have been annihilated over thousands of years for many reasons: fundamental inferiority in strength, tactics, and weaponry; poor organization and strategy, treachery, adverse weather, and repeatedly dismal and poor leadership. One factor virtually guaranteeing poor military performance is bad leadership and its destructive effect on group cohesion. Military groups have often prevailed under circumstances that almost certainly should have resulted in their destruction. Under such conditions the evident cohesion of military groups under great stress appears linked to the quality of leadership most importantly as it operates at the small-unit level. A "small unit" can mean any military group from a squad (8–12 members) to a regiment (approximately 3,000 men), although in more recent times there may be some sense of the combat division (10,000–18,000 troops) as a "group." Whatever the size of the primary military group, and it most certainly varies, history provides many examples of primary-group cohesion under great battle stress.

During the Second Punic War, Rome experienced enormous losses, including the disaster of Cannae, without attendant disintegration on the part of its military units. Roman discipline remains legendary and, from available studies, appears to have been tied less to individual heroic figures than to the discipline and cohesion of small units. Discipline was based on the centurion system: men served for long periods of time with their units, beginning in the legion organization of hierarchically organized small to larger units.[1] In the catastrophe of the Thirty Years' War, the Swedish Army was notable for its cohesive power; during the Seven Years' War, Prussia with its fine regiments and Frederick the Great prevailed with all of Europe arrayed against her. The British Army for centuries has been recognized as a highly successful socializing institution for recruits drawn from a wide array of social, racial, and ethnic backgrounds. In the British case, this phenomenon appears related to the sense of belonging to the "regiment." Equally impressive is the proven capacity of British military units to resist and not break under unusual pressures, which in turn reinforces regimental identity and group cohesion. Other instances of high levels of cohesion can be noted, such as the spirit of Camerone evident in the French Foreign Legion, the tight sense of group loyalty among pre-Meiji Japanese samurai, and of course the remarkable record of Japanese resistance on the islands of the Pacific, where they suffered thirty killed for every man wounded. In the case of American units, the gallantry of Confederate and Union regiments in the Civil War, the U.S. Army 1st, 2nd, 3rd Infantry Divisions and the 82nd Airborne Division in World War II provide convincing examples. All these historic instances of cohesion appear related to the quality of leadership evident at the time and specifically to the individual relationship of officers to men within primary groups. A further aspect of cohesive military units seems to be that their leaders generally remained with them for long periods of time, certainly years and sometimes decades, as was the case in the Roman legions and British Indian regiments. At the very least, then, stability of leadership elements is a fundamental factor in producing unit cohesion.

It should be clear that none of the examples offered are to be taken as instances of a form of military moral purity. Indeed, when we speak of morality and integrity it is as these terms have meaning within the value of a *military* social ambience. To be sure, soldiery has had its share of knaves, tyrants, louts, ruffians, murderers, psychopathic killers, not to mention thieves, rapists, looters, dissemblers, opportunists, pirates, hypocrites, and other varieties of mankind's long list of pathologies. However, there were and are military men of honor, moral integrity, dedication, firm personal moral and religious convictions, and perhaps even a potential saint or two. In short, the distribution of moral characterological types is probably the same in military systems as in the civil system from which they originate. It may simply be that the opportunity for outrage may be more frequent during war.

It is thus apparent that all armies of whatever quality exhibit varieties of leadership from extremely good, as in the case of Lee and the Confederate Army, to very bad, as personified by Samsonov, his officer corps, and the Imperial Russian Army at Tannenberg. It seems to us, however, that there exists some threshold where military cohesion is a composite function of both the quality and numbers of leaders. More than likely no society, especially a mass society, can ever produce more than a very limited number of military leaders who can be expected to lead men directly and to do well in battle. (We are not concerned with the "invisible" officer— the remote and unseen general staff officer, the supply installation commander, public information officers, personnel managers, *so long as they are not directly involved with combat troops*.) Possibly, as we have already suggested, the German ratios of officers to enlisted men evident during World War II are not far from the critical number of good officers needed to maintain cohesion among the troops. But even within an officer corps of small numbers, say 3 to 8 percent of total strength, officers will be found whose personal *military* ethical quality, as evidenced by their actual military behavior, ranges from bad to the disintegrative: these will be careerists, hypocrites, and officers who betray their obligations. Certainly the Germans had a number of these, but clearly managed to minimize the recruitment of such men and, more importantly, to isolate their potentially devastating effect upon the morale and cohesion of the combat units, thus reducing their salience in the perceptions of the troops and then stabilizing the troop assignment of only *effective* officers. Later we will suggest that in this respect the American Army has clearly failed in its officer recruitment policies and that the troops perceived many of their leaders for what they were—officers whose behavior did not inspire confidence, loyalty, and cohesion. One indicator of a poor officer corps is its radical inflation of rank, together with rapid rotation of officer personnel. Germany in World War II, of course, did not permit radical grade inflation and its Army remained cohesive to the very end. The opposite obtained in the American Army in Vietnam.

Critics will no doubt observe that we have not defined "good" leadership. However, we have given some historical examples of heroic unit behavior and suggested from these examples some of the factors which appear important to the effectiveness of those military units. People, having institutionalized violence through war, place great stress on the regulation of violence as it pertains to groups. Without a long digression into the cultural anthropology of aggression, it is our central proposition that since men conduct war in groups, it is leadership which is critical to the behavior of military primary groups.[2] When this leadership elicits loyalty and group dedication or sacrifice, it can be deemed good leadership; if not, it is bad leadership. Earlier we suggested that the gladiatorial officer had become the manager or the careerist officer seeing his men as means. This shift in recent years has, we believe, contributed to a loss of group loyalty and cohesion in the U.S. Army. One classic example of a leadership system that failed is provided by high-level staff officers at the Pentagon who assumed men could be "managed" to their death by rapidly rotating officers in the context of a permanently turbulent replacement system in Vietnam. Men, of course, cannot be indefinitely "managed" to their death. The history of men in military groups testifies that no such thing as "death management" is possible *if* an effective ground army is required. Apparently this lesson of history was lost on the Pentagon planners who attempted to transfer doctrines of systems management to the leadership of combat units. It failed.

Unavoidably, if a cohesive military unit is the goal, then excellence in small-group leadership is essential. A good officer is defined objectively by two criteria. First, these characteristics are defined by the historical necessities of ground combat. The officer *must* be perceived by his troops as concerned about their welfare. Most importantly, however, he must be perceived as willing to share the risks and sacrifices of battle. Second, the institutionalization of an officer's qualifications is ultimately placed in the hands of those who select officers—that is, the officer corps itself, which must state and enforce rigorous selection standards. Officers of high caliber have always been a scarce resource and will no doubt continue to be so. Whenever the numbers of officers are permitted to swell beyond the capacity of the society to produce good officers, a kind of military Gresham's Law begins to operate; bad officers drive out the good. When poor officers are numerically superior, they simply overwhelm good officers. This phenomenon is quickly recognized by fighting troops. As a result, the numerical inflation of an officer corps is almost always associated with a decline in quality.

Despite all the volumes of military history from Xenophon to S. L. A. Marshall, the definition of a good officer remains inexact. Nothing in the *Officer's Guide*, military manuals on combat leadership, or the qualities of the "good officer" as taught at West Point provides clear guides to the nature of officers who, under conditions of enormous battle stress, will remain "faithful unto death" and whose men will follow him into almost certain darkness. However, one important dimension does suggest itself. This dimension involves how the officer corps perceives itself and its obligations, together with the behavior these obligations entail and actually produce. The officer corps of the U.S. Army has studied itself and located some of the failures of leadership which surfaced during the Vietnam War.[3] This study tacitly admitted severe failures in leadership during the Vietnam War. Curiously, the study group recommended that these findings be widely circulated within the Army. The fact is, however, that the distribution of the study was restricted for a time to general officers—a restriction normally reserved for the most sensitive information. Still, the study, while pointing up a crisis of morale and discipline at all levels in the Field Army, does suggest a code of behavior for officers however unclear and timorous. It is appropriate here to give some consideration to the suggested code before examining the officer corps. The study was made because even the Army knew it wasn't doing too well. Given what has already been said, reasonable men could conclude that serious faults in traditional officer leadership behavior surfaced in Vietnam. In order to judge the range of variance from what has been traditionally expected of a good officer, some standard is necessary. Traditional officer behavior has shown itself to be historically effective and thus should constitute the norm. Deviation from the norm of traditional effectiveness can, thus, be viewed as pathological. We suggest that managerial behavior may therefore be pathological to the military system. Having stated that the standard of behavior resides in a traditional military ethic, attention can be more clearly directed toward the officer himself and the ethical and behaviorial code to which he is expected to conform.

Remembering that the following "code" was drafted by the United States Army War College, an institution whose graduates are trained to be general officers, it is worth quoting since it attempts to define "good" officer behavior and would, we may assume, condition the ethical behavior of all Army officers.[4]

An Officer's Creed

I will give to the selfless performance of my duty and my mission the best that effort, thought, and dedication can provide. To this end, I will not only seek continually to improve knowledge and practice of my profession, but also I will exercise the authority entrusted to me by the President and the Congress with fairness, justice, patience, and restraint, respecting the dignity and human rights of others and devoting myself to the welfare of those placed under my command.

In justifying and fulfilling the trust placed in me, I will conduct my private life as well as my public service so as to be free from impropriety and appearance of impropriety, acting with candor and integrity to earn the unquestioning trust of my fellow soldiers—juniors, seniors and associates—and employing my rank and position not to serve myself but to serve my country and my unit. By practicing physical and moral courage I will endeavor to inspire these qualities in others by my example.

In all my actions I will put loyalty to the highest moral principles and the United States of America above loyalty to organizations, persons, and my personal interest.

Apart from its curious timorousness, certain observations can be made about this "code." First, it is scarcely "managerial" in style or intent. Second, it was created in response to what even the Army recognized in 1970 as a crisis of morale and spirit. Third, until the Army War College study, no in-depth studies of military morale or value systems had been undertaken by the Army despite the continuing disintegration. Fourth, to our knowledge it is not a part of Army regulations. It is unspecific in its standards for battle. The Army War College study notes that "visits to the Office of Research and Development, the Behavioral Science Research Laboratory, and the Officer Personnel Directorate revealed no on-going or programmed research in the area of professional value systems." It escapes understanding why the Army, possessing almost unlimited social science and behavioral research resources failed to address so critical a problem as military disintegration among its combat units. Even more to the point, being aware of an *increasing* rate of unit disintegration, why was this phenomenon not studied? Nonetheless, some sense of urgency can be seen in the Army War College study.

Just why General Westmoreland directed the analysis when he did is not known. However, it has been suggested by some that the military was simply unaware that a problem existed. We find from conversations with senior officers who held positions of great power and prestige in Vietnam a curious detachment from the experiences and realities of troop life. In one case, our interviews discovered a retired general officer and a former Vietnam corps commander who expressed shock and surprise that he should be burdened with the charge of irresponsibility when asked why he and his fellow general officers did nothing about the drug traffic. His reply was to the effect that "we knew nothing about this— nothing in our experience prepared us for such a state of affairs and, therefore, since we knew nothing about drugs, how can we be held responsible?" Needless to say, this defense reflects a basic failing in one of the primary military imperatives that a commander is responsible for "everything his command does or fails to do," not to mention the charge in "An Officer's Creed" to devote oneself to the welfare of one's men.

While "An Officer's Creed" exhorts military and moral excellence, it also recognizes the failure of such ethical behavior to manifest itself in the actions of the officer corps; otherwise, why the need for the code at all? As will be argued later, this creed attempts, perhaps too late, to correct leadership lapses in ethical behavior which may be directly associated with a collapsing Army, and an Army virtually devoid of primary military groups. The substance of the creed is revealing in that it levies demands for selflessness, sacrifice, loyalty to subordinates, truth in reports, bravery without arrogance, and the inspiration of like conduct in brother officers and one's troops by example. All these individual leadership qualities which in themselves define a "good" officer relate directly to the level of cohesion of primary military groups within the Army. Without such qualities there is likely to be little military cohesion, if our reading of history is accurate. Despite the importance of these qualities, our data lead us to suspect that dedication to such a creed was and probably remains ruinous to an officer's career.

The Army War College study is a very important document and the point of departure for several additional arguments presented in this book, and we will return to it later. But first, an examination of the behavior of the officer corps during the Vietnam conflict is necessary because this examination reveals data concerning the degree of deviation from traditional military values. An initial reading of the data suggests at the least that the arena of conflict was one for which the military was unprepared. Perhaps even the nature of the arena itself may have induced some forms of pathological behavior. We tend, however, to see the nature of the arena of conflict as playing no more than the role of a background variable. More to the point, we shall focus on those indicators of pathological military behavior within the Army officer corps.

It is worth repeating that the behavior of armies is, in large measure, a product of their leadership and the actions of that leadership in battle. Good leadership, dedication, integrity, loyalty to subordinates, and perceived competence seem clearly historically associated with high levels of military cohesion, which finally defines the good officer. Poor leadership, on the other hand, seems intimately associated with disintegration. Stated more strongly, bad leadership, especially at the officer level, appears to assure that military units will often not retain unit cohesion under relatively mild battle stress. A high desertion rate might be explainable, perhaps even a mutiny or two. But when desertion, fragging, mutiny, and drug addiction converge toward something of a sociopathological riptide effect in a period as short as four or five years, explanations based on references to permissive societies and national "fragmentation" due to unpopular wars simply are not credible.

The behavior of a leader *in battle* is a distinct form of social behavior which has held a special place in the history of Western civilization and, indeed, in most other cultures as well. The role of Battle Leader possesses a special mystique and attendant value system. Combat officers are not viewed as merely another component of the larger societal technostructure that can be created in cooky-cutter fashion from a training base little different from the Harvard Business School. The values, goals, and modes of action required of the combat officer are qualitatively different from those associated with and expected from the commercial manager. We have already observed that no one is expected to sacrifice his life for General Motors or IBM, but military leaders are often required to do just this for their country. Where production workers can be, and most often are, treated as mere tools to the advancement of commercial executives' careers, combat soldiers cannot be so treated if unit cohesion and fighting élan and effectiveness are to be maintained. If combat troops perceive that they are being used to promote an officer's career, they will likely react in a manner destructive of unit cohesion and, perhaps, act to imperil the entire military system. Where the business executive is socially and economically a creature apart from the ordinary worker, the military officer, who has status, privileges, and great personal power, must be perceived as sharing burdens of risk and death at least equal to and preferably exceeding the risks and burdens of his men. Consequently, the moral burden of the officer is qualitatively different from that of the business manager. The measure of an officer corps's performance is therefore to some degree quantifiable and generally measurable against a set of behavioral expectations rooted historically in the fact that the observance of such expectations is strongly associated with unit cohesion and combat effectiveness.

The failure of the officer corps to come to grips with the problem of drug use in Vietnam represented a clear failure of moral expectations. Knowing that the heroin racket destroying their forces was operated by their high-ranking Vietnamese counterparts in apparent collusion with higher American authorities, not a single senior officer in Vietnam resigned or, to our knowledge, publicly protested the situation. A word or two may be offered here in defense of some senior officer neglect respecting the drug traffic. Having noted a conversation with a former U.S. Army corps commander, it is possible that the higher command was at least to some degree ignorant of the devastation being wreaked on their units by drugs. Although later discussed as a sociomilitary phenomenon, we know that the screening of data, false reporting to include lying and the ever-present syndrome of "you can't tell the old man that," most probably affected the willingness of subordinate commanders to in-form higher commanders of the extent of the drug problem. Certainly one result of the prevalent managerial careerism was to block, dilute, and distort almost *any* data that might affect personal performance ratings. The corollary is that if the data on drug usage could be taken as a reflection of a commander's performance it would have been clear that anywhere from 10 to 30 percent of his command were junkies. The argument that combat commanders, especially at the higher levels, were unaware of the drug problem seems weak at best. More likely, they knew but felt there was little they could do without risking their own careers in the process. Accordingly, they officially ignored the problem. In any event, there appear to have been no "protest" resignations over the drug racket. Indeed, the number of protest resignations for any reason at all while the U.S. Army was coming apart as an effective combat mechanism seems pathetically small. Yet a handful of resignations and retirements did in fact occur. One interesting case was that of Colonel David Hackworth, a highly decorated officer, with twenty decorations for gallantry, including two Distinguished Service Crosses and eight Purple Hearts, who retired and publicly directed severe criticism against General Westmoreland for his "managerial" handling of the war.[5] Why did this occur and particularly in this war? There is little evidence that the play of ideologies at home, the influence of the "permissive society," or other factors external to the military caused the process of disintegration. What then of the officer corps as a whole? How well did it lead as indicated by efforts to build and strengthen primary groups, by its burden of shared sacrifice as measured by comparative death rates in battle, or by prolonged exposure to combat compared with the troops? What effect may its large and very visible numbers have had on the troops? The answers to these questions go a long way toward helping us understand how the officer corps came to be an important factor in the process of disintegration which occurred in the American Army in Vietnam.

Among the first factors related to the performance of the Army officer corps is its large numbers. Until 1918 officers averaged about 5.3 percent of the total strength of the Army. In the thirties, officer percentages varied between 7 and 9 percent. At the end of World War II, officers accounted for 7.7 percent of the strength when the strength of the Army Air Force is not included. Table 5 illustrates the expansion of the officer corps over the years. By the sixties, it had stabilized at about 11 percent, fell to an average of 9 percent from 1965 to 1967, and then rose to almost 15 percent of total Army strength in 1972. This meant one officer for every 5.7 enlisted men. Compared to World War II, the number of officers had increased by almost 100 percent! Even compared to 1965, the year in which the large Vietnam buildup began, officers increased from 9.4 percent of total strength to almost 15 percent, or an increase of 59.9 percent. Considered with the data in Tables 1, 2, 3, and 4, disintegration seems to be clearly associated with the large numerical expansion of the officer corps to levels previously unknown.

During a rapid expansion of officer strength, and particularly when the recruiting base is tightly constricted, it is almost unavoidable that the quality of the average officer will tend to suffer. With the withdrawal of so many colleges and universities from the ROTC system, and with the questionable ethical training provided by the United States Military Academy, officer quality had to decline. More specifically, some of the central and dominating characteristics of the officers recruited during the Vietnam period were associated with the managerial disposition. Such a disposition must have affected their individual behavior and, if our analysis is correct, the behavior of their troops as time passed. Even though functioning at a "primitive" level of "business think," perceiving their commands as a means of advancing their careers, it may be that even company-level officers were in part devoid of traditional military values, or at least those values outlined in the "Officer's Creed." These conditions would serve to weaken residual and traditional military values. In any case, potential leaders recruited from the social base and capable of subscribing to traditional military ethics have always been a scarce resource. That this scarcity affected the performance of the officer corps largely by enticing the military to recruit ever-growing numbers of lower-quality officers seems beyond doubt.

From this perspective, where factors external to the military system cannot be related to military disintegration, internal factors are likely to have the greatest bearing on the disintegrative process. Some of the principal internal but generally widespread military conditions linked to disintegration, in association with other influences discussed earlier, appear below:

1. Relative to their number and particularly the higher ranks, American Army officers did not share the burden of death that they asked of the men they sent to fight. Indeed, the number of enlisted men upon whom the burden of death fell were themselves but a small part of the total forces. In 1968, at the height of the buildup, fewer than 80,000 combat forces could be put into the field against a maximum ground troop strength in Vietnam of 543,000.

2. The tactical nature of the war and its manner of logistical configuration created a system that, in contrast to other wars, was circular instead of linear. That is to say, large numbers of officers and men of diverse specialties—mostly noncombat—were placed in base camp areas. Accordingly, combat troops were exposed to large numbers of high-ranking officers with conspicuously greater privileges and greater immunity from harm than in any other war.

3. High-ranking officers were associated with a career system that was manifestly corrupt. Further, the drug traffic and other forms of self-advantage publicly defined as unethical and corrupt by the officers who enforced the code in the first place, resulted in a loss of respect for the officer corps by troops who faced the greater risks of combat.

These conditions, of course, focus more on the officer corps than on the Army as a whole, and in particular as the burden of too many ill-trained, entrepreneurially oriented officers may have affected the military cohesion of the enlisted men.

The significance of the relative numerical strength of the Army officer corps must be understood in historical perspective and in terms of officer-enlisted strength ratios. Table 6 shows the growth, relative to officer-enlisted strength ratios, in the officer corps by rank over a period of three wars. The data indicate clearly that officer-enlisted ratios have changed radically since World War II. The overall strength of the officer corps increased by 71.53 percent between World War II and Vietnam, while the rest of the Army's strength actually declined. Between World War II and Vietnam, the ratio of generals to enlisted men increased by 152 percent, lieutenant colonels by 257 percent, and majors by 168 percent. With such tremendous increases, it is interesting to observe the distribution of casualties by officer grade in three wars. Table 7 provides casualty distribution ratios by rank in three wars.[6] From the data in Table 7 it is clear that there was a distinct shift in the burden of sacrifice away from colonels and generals despite a huge increase in their relative numbers (see Table 6). With respect to senior officer–enlisted ratio losses, 34 percent more enlisted men died in action in Vietnam than did generals when compared to World War II ratios, and 54 percent more enlisted men died than did colonels in Vietnam when compared to World War II loss ratios for that rank. Clearly, the disparity in the sharing of the burden of death borders on the ominous.

There are arguments supporting the growth in senior officer strength, but none seem compelling. For example, the expansion of technology and its "demand" for officer supervision of complex weapons and communications systems, the number of officers in the pipelines, and the increased number of those backed up in various schools are often put forth as explanations. But Vietnam would seem to have required *fewer* officers, not more, for unlike the practice during the Korean War, the reserves and the National Guard generally remained exempt from service. Paradoxically, it may be that in the unused reserve components, some of the resources remained available for recapturing the traditional military ethos and infusing it into the "managerial" Army. Many of the reserve and Guard officers and NCO's had fought in earlier conflicts and may possibly have retained a stronger sense of the primary group than was evident in the "modern" Army which took the field in Vietnam. But whether the reserves and the National Guard would have demonstrated traditional military virtues remains unknown. It is doubtful, however, that reserve and Guard units would have performed significantly better under the conditions of "people's war" than did the regular military establishment.

Yet another argument sometimes put forth is that since the Vietnam War was the only one available, it represented an excellent opportunity to train and "blood" as many officers as possible in combat, thus creating a large reservoir of experienced combat leaders. However, as we have demonstrated, if professionalism is a goal, then the argument will not stand, since the rapid rotation carried out through such a policy is a virtual guarantee of amateurism at the point of greatest stress, namely, the combat-unit level. Thus, while these arguments may, in part, *explain* the rapid inflation of the officer corps, they are by no means strong *justifications* for inflating officer strength beyond all historical experience. More to the point, however, is that even with the inflation of the strength of the officer corps, the data reflect a reduction in relative officer casualties overall, and particularly in the higher ranks. It is suggested that this condition is a clear measure of the failure of leadership behavior, professionalism, and dedication. The burden of risk attendant on combat was simply not fully shared by the officer corps.

Recapitulating the data on strength ratios and the burden of death, Table 8 summarizes the relation between overall strength ratios, officers and enlisted men, and the relative casualty rates experienced in Vietnam by each group. Whereas overall officer deaths in combat may have climbed in Vietnam in comparision to World War II, they have also remained small relative to the total size of the officer corps. The data in Table 8 reveal that in Vietnam officer losses fell substantially below their total share of the Army strength by at least a third. Senior officer strength, majors through generals, expanded from 16.7 percent in World War II to 29.1 percent in Vietnam, while the casualties of this same group of officers fell from 7 percent to 6.1 percent. The data therefore tend to indicate that in Vietnam the burden of sacrifice fell increasingly on the lower grades, in particular on lower-ranking officers and enlisted men.

It may be rightly pointed out, of course, that the officer percentage of *all* deaths in battle in Vietnam (10.7 percent) when compared to World War II (7.01 percent) is substantially higher. However, the measure of officer losses in Vietnam is somewhat misleading since the figures include a very high number of warrant officer losses (679 of 3,269 or 21 percent of total *officer* losses), a category of losses which was comparatively low during World War II and Korea. If warrant officer losses are deducted from overall officer losses in Vietnam, then the actual officer loss rate becomes 8.4 percent of all deaths due to hostile action and substantially below the very high percentage of available officers. It must be pointed out that the position of warrant officers is an anomalous one. They are not, as a rule, perceived by enlisted ranks as full officers, or by officers as having the status of the commissioned ranks. The Army reporting system often separates warrant officer data from both enlisted and officer data. In addition, to the extent that warrant officers saw combat, they rarely did so in field positions: they served most frequently as helicopter pilots. Indeed, it was in this role that the great majority of warrant officers were lost. Few were lost in combat leadership positions similar, say, to that of a platoon leader or company commander. To this extent, then, factoring out warrant officer losses produces a more accurate estimate of the burden of death shouldered by the officer corps proper.

Still another aspect of officer losses must be examined. We know that the assassination of officers became increasingly frequent as the war dragged on and that probably less than 10 percent of the attempted or successful assassinations were ever reported. Accordingly, it is probable that *some* of the officer deaths attributed to hostile action may, in fact, have been due to "fragging" or other means of killing. In this regard, there are some rather interesting data evident in the *Computer Study of Casualties in Vietnam*. These data indicate that the Army lost 89 lives which were attributed to "intentional homicide," 534 to "accidental homicide," and 1,394 to "other accidents," comprising a total of 2,017 deaths. These data were not included in "death due to hostile action" but neither are they explained. Additionally, the losses due solely to helicopter incidents are inordinately high, with 2,352 deaths attributed to "hostile" action and 1,831 to "non-hostile" causes. Of the total 4,183 deaths due to helicopter incidents, 554 were pilots and thus officers or warrant officers actually lost to hostile action. Since these deaths were reported as "in action" (and the Army tends to give credit for battle death when it can possibly do so), then the data suggest that as much as 17 percent of all officer losses might have been associated with helicopter crashes. Further, if it is recalled that the Army lists a category of deaths involving assassination by "explosive devices," it must also be noted that there are few machines easier to sabotage than a helicopter. Regardless of how they died, helicopter pilots and their crews, like the Air Corps crews of World War II, generally died alone. They do not, as a rule, die at the head of their men and, accordingly, their deaths did not have the same personal impact on the troops of reinforcing the perception of a shared burden of sacrifice as would the death of a platoon leader or company commander.

The available evidence strongly suggests that the slightly higher rate of officer casualties in Vietnam compared to World War II found in official statistics is highly suspect. In any event, one would expect that the rate of officer deaths might be similar to that of World War II, or even slightly higher, since Army tactical doctrine in Vietnam stressed personal leadership in "searching out" the enemy. To be sure, the data are not definitive. Yet the fact is that combat enlisted troops did not, as a rule, perceive their officers as sustaining anywhere near the levels of risk and sacrifice that they themselves were experiencing. The sheer number of officers made officer status appear as unnecessarily privileged and, in many documented instances, the troops reacted against it.

If our conclusion is correct that Vietnam witnessed the emergence of a trend in which the risk of death increasingly rested on lower ranks, then the men sent to die not only may have failed to understand the reasons for large staff elements increasingly isolated from the risks of battle, but may in fact have come to resent the privileged persons exempted from risk. If such a military system continued to assign the risk of death to fewer and fewer of its higher-ranking members, while at the same time allowing the nature of the circular war to expose combat troops positioned in their base camps to ever larger numbers of "bombproofs" who, by the nature of their assignments and the organization of the war, remained exempted from the risks of battle, it would not be surprising to discover that the enlisted man's hostility toward officers would increase. In other wars, combat troops would not have encountered the rear-echelon "immunes" in the numbers that were visible in Vietnam, and this fact alone may have contributed strongly to the feeling on the part of soldiers in America's earlier wars that their officers were worth following. Certainly, we have no evidence that soldiers in earlier wars tried to assassinate their officers as they did in Vietnam. Perhaps the fact that the organization of the war in Vietnam was different had its own impact. No longer a "line" war but a circular one, the Vietnam conflict was one set in base camps and fire bases where those who fought and those who did not intermingled frequently, thus providing the enlisted men with an opportunity to perceive the wide differences in life style between combat and noncombat troops, as well as the respective levels of risk to which they were exposed. The thrust of the data in Table 8 and the foregoing analysis is that the leaders who formulated the rules of the game—duty, honor, country—often did not live up to them, the enforcement of which, ironically, was in their charge. It seems likely that the troops knew it, and, in addition, that the officers came to be perceived as careerists driven by the imperatives of a system which isolated them from the risks of combat to which the troops saw themselves increasingly exposed. It is in this context that the earlier indicators of discohesion which we have addressed become understandable.

Except for the numbers of men and levels of technology, the challenge faced by France in Indochina was not radically different in a military sense from that which confronted the United States. At its peak, the deployed strength of the French Expeditionary Force (FEC) amounted to about 151,000. For the French Army as a whole, officers approximated 4.9 percent of total strength, or some 33,000 of a total of 675,000.[7] French officers lost in action in Indochina totaled 2,221, or 6.73 percent of the entire French Army officer corps. Indeed, one in three graduates of St. Cyr during the war years died in Vietnam.[8] Accordingly, with a peak strength of 151,000 in the FEC, the probable level of officer strength at a norm of 5 percent was 7,550. Thus, the 2,220 French officers lost in action constituted some 29 percent of the French officer corps in Indochina. Of total French Army casualties, 11.3 percent were officers, or 5,347 officers of a total number of French casualties of 47,048. For all services killed, missing, dying of battle-related causes in Indochina, losses of French officers constituted 11.89 percent.[9] By comparison, the strength of the U.S. Army officer corps averaged 163,395 for the years 1968 through 1971, and American Army officer deaths due to hostile action amounted to approximately 2 percent of that strength. Further, we can find no evidence of a loss of cohesion among units of the FEC as measured by either the standards we have applied to the German Army or those of the U.S. Army. Neither excessive desertion, drug use, mutiny, nor fragging can be detected anywhere in the experience of the French in Indochina. French officers maintained their numbers and quality and accepted a burden of death in a ratio which far exceeded that of the men they led. We can find no indicators of either wholesale or partial disintegration among units of the French Regular Army or the Foreign Legion, which, although comprised largely of non-French, was exclusively French officered. Further, like the German Army in World War II, the French suffered successive defeats, one of them catastrophic, at Dien Bien Phu. But none of these factors appear to have affected the high level of French Army cohesion.

In many respects, the French Army in Indochina displayed

those "German" qualities of a small but excellent officer corps reflected in the capacity to retain the respect of the troops and the maintenance of primary groups noted earlier. The French Army was largely comprised of volunteers in Vietnam, but the troops were not substantially different in social origin than troops have been historically, that is, they were drawn from the lower social strata. Still by 1970 in Vietnam, 61 percent of the U.S. Army enlisted strength was volunteer. Now it is true that comparisons can be pressed too far. However, it seems clear that French troops fought under conditions far more difficult than those faced by the Americans, if only because they lacked very strong helicopter capability and the massive air support which became almost a defining characteristic of the American effort. On every count, the French ability to maintain cohesion under conditions certainly similar to those faced by the Americans and, in many cases, considerably worse is starkly contrasted with American desertion, officer assassination, drug addiction, and mutiny. Further the first Indochina war was about as unpopular in France as the later American experience in Vietnam was in the United States.

Under ordinary circumstances, the diminished quality of the American officer corps and their high numbers might only marginally have affected operations and discipline. In Korea and World War II, the direct contact by enlisted men with officers and especially senior officers was generally limited. Basic training involved primarily noncommissioned officers and a few company-grade commissioned officers. Upon leaving for overseas in World War II, disembarking, and moving to the lines, few high-ranking officers were encountered by combat troops. The same condition existed during combat, however protracted. Indeed, the more protracted the battle and the higher the officer losses, the less were officers encountered on the enlisted man's "perception horizon." These circumstances obtained in Korea as well. For any soldier who experienced wars other than Vietnam, the linear quality of warfare, however fluid, represented a singular kind of deployment. Even in Russia, despite frequent large gaps in the enormous *Kesselschlachten und Gewühle* (cauldron battles and melees), the front was usually identifiable. This sense of the "lines" provided the configuration of warfare. Linearity in warfare is, of course, probably a product of mass-production technology and the ability of modern societies to mobilize large numbers of men for protracted battles of attrition. In World War I, for the first time, entire land masses could be cut by a single line of battle extending for hundreds of miles. In World War II such lines in Russia extended for thousands of miles. Quite irrespective of how many "bombproofs" served on staffs, the number of officers in linear warfare to which numbers of troops were exposed was generally low. Certainly, those officers the troops did come in contact with were few in number, and almost always confined to combat units; they died at high rates, and acted as leaders by openly sharing the burdens of combat.

In Vietnam, conditions were radically different. The support and operational bases, roughly circular, swarmed with officers. But those who did the actual fighting on a day-to-day basis constituted a minority of all deployed ground troops. Since infantry did most of the fighting, the portion of actual combat troops in most cases constituted only 20 percent or less of any given operational base. While on an operation they were exposed to the overwhelming share of the casualties, they returned to a base structure saturated with officers and NCO's who were largely insulated from the dangers that the combat troops faced. Moreover, the life style of officers, often senior ones, tended to be extravagant. Officer luxury became at times extreme: there were separate and exceptionally well-stocked generals' and colonels' clubs and messes; dedicated transportation for general and other senior officers; the security of every night under sheets. There were ritual visits to remote bases of high-level officers surrounded by innumerable flurries of aides and, worst of all, the very conspicuous presence of large numbers of officers well fed and cared for in the main support bases to which troops returned after a number of days in battle. The troops naturally came to believe that large numbers of their officers never appeared to suffer any deprivation whatsoever.

Aggravating these conspicuous differences was the combat rotation policy. Officers most often served in their combat commands for approximately six months of their twelve-month tour in-country. Enlisted men normally had to remain in a combat assignment for the entire twelve-month tour. The decision to adopt the one-year rotation policy was not one for which the Army can be held totally responsible. Rather, it was the inevitable result of a political policy which refused to mobilize the country for war. Accordingly, the Army faced the problem of command without being able to utilize its officers on tours extending "for the duration." The solution was a policy of frequent rotation based on "equity," the expectation that all officers would serve at least one tour. In this sense, the rotation policy was imposed upon the military structure by the larger society, which rejected the option of moving to full mobilization.[10] The troops most surely were aware that one purpose of such a policy was career advancement ("ticket punching") and not the pursuit of "duty and honor," much less the traditional responsibility placed upon a commander to care for his men. Together with the general rotation system, even more frequent changes in command could only weaken morale and discipline. Further, the rotation system almost guaranteed the assignment of inexperienced commanders to experienced combat units. Often this resulted in a situation in which the commander attempted to demonstrate his competence and advance his career by changes in policy and tactics which appeared outrageous and dangerous to the more experienced troops. Under such conditions, officers could hardly gain the confidence of their troops, much less their respect. The extent and the circumstances of the command structure openly worked against the development of such loyalties. If troops' regard for their officers is important to cohesion, and we submit the evidence is overwhelmingly clear that it is, then in a situation which does not permit such regard to develop, primary-group cohesion cannot but be affected. In Vietnam the result was a kind of "military anomie"—a situation where troops came to have no sense of belonging and became increasingly hostile to their officers.

Another factor contributing to the low regard in which officers were generally held was the excessive burden of battle that was placed upon draftees. The blatant practice of favoring Regular Army volunteers by insulating them from a just share of combat separated the draftee from the Regular Army establishment. As a result, an increasing hostility between the draftee and "lifer" developed; and this hostility naturally often transferred to an officer corps that minimized its own burden of risk through the six-month combat tour rotation policy. The data in Table 9 clearly show that, in both absolute and relative terms, draftees in Vietnam suffered casualties in far greater proportion to Regular Army volunteers. One of the contributing reasons was the institutional arrangement created by the Army itself. Volunteer career soldiers usually received far more consideration in choice of schooling, which tended to center on those schools developing technical, noncombat-associated skills. More important, in terms of its impact upon morale, it was possible in Vietnam to get out of the "bush" by reenlisting for a longer term or agreeing to an extension of one's tour in-country. The "reward" for reenlistment amounted to an assurance that one would receive a noncombat assignment. In short, by opting for the professional Army or an extended tour of duty, it was possible to avoid most of the risks of combat. That career NCO's turned this practice into a fine art was evident to anyone who served with them.

To be sure, the Army was not without a ready defense for those who raised arguments similar to those we have raised. Indeed, some of the higher-ranking officers may even have recognized disintegration and begun to develop an *apologia pro vitis nostris*. One defense suggests that the rapid changes attendant on modern society, accompanied by the dilution of traditional values, the rejection of home, family, country, and duty, in the nation generally and among the young specifically, constituted the root cause of poor military performance. Thus, the Army was forced to bear the impossible burden of coping with self-indulgent youths who had been poorly socialized by parents and were hostile to legitimate authority and indifferent to the national interest. The Army could not be expected to produce good soldiers from such poor raw material and, thus, the pathologies which surfaced in Vietnam were manifestations of ills evident in American society at large. Such pathologies were not caused by the military but were a direct reflection of civilian society. The argument is open to serious question.

Sociological and historical research reveals that effective military units can persist long after the societies which gave them birth have undergone almost revolutionary changes. The disciplinary ethos of the Roman legion, for example, persisted far beyond the decay of Roman society and extended well into the period of the "barbarization" of the Roman Army. Rome herself suffered periods of great political turbulence, experiencing disastrous civil wars at the end of the Republic. And yet the discipline, élan, and cohesion of the legion remained intact. Nor was this cohesion and discipline maintained by the whip—no truly cohesive military system can be so maintained.

From the time of Alexander Severus (A.D. 222) until Aurelian (270), Rome was "ruled" by thirty-five emperors, a number of whom were assassinated by their own men. Civil wars, Praetorian coups, and rebellious generals aside, as a military and social institution the Roman Army outlived its society. It still serves as an example of one of the world's most cohesive military systems. Obviously, the Roman Army changed from the citizen Army of the Republic to the barbarized and ethnically pluralistic legions of the later Empire. Even during the time of Flavius Stilicho, a German (Vandal) serving Rome as a general, the Roman Army still retained the capacity to absorb and socialize large numbers of barbarians. The point is that the Roman military organization established and retained the capacity to socialize hostile colonial elements into its military value system long after the society which it served had decayed. By comparison, the Pentagon's argument that it could not cope with modern American youth seems weak indeed.

Given the many historical instances of the integration, socialization, and successful incorporation of diverse ethnics into so-called foreign armies even in recent times, the British Army and, above all, its Irish component, and the French Foreign Legion represent other instances of highly pluralistic military units bound together by a sense of esprit de corps, high primary-group identification, and low numbers of high-quality officers. The Foreign Legion, although always French officered, was filled over the years by successive waves of foreigners, the last of which were Germans who were recruited into the Legion after World War II. The potentially "hostile colonial elements" fought with complete loyalty to France and the Legion in Indochina and again in Algeria. Even the Prussian tradition survived in an atmosphere of comparative cultural homogeneity and persevered through a number of wars and regimes until 1945. Indeed, its fate in our judgment is not nearly so final as many might assume, since to a large extent the East German regime may be the ultimate beneficiary of its military values. As we have seen with the Roman, English, French, and German Armies, there appears little historical relationship between the quality of an army and the quality, condition, or stability of its parent social order. Given the inherent pluralism of American society and the failure of its Army to socialize and enforce discipline, the Pentagon's argument is devastating in its implications for the future.

The poor quality of recruits assumed in the official explanation of American military performance also overlooks the fact that the "permissive youths" who reject the notions of duty, discipline, and sacrifice tend to be concentrated largely in the middle and upper strata of society. For a variety of reasons, they were protected from the draft and, indeed, did not serve in any numbers in Vietnam. Where they did, they did so mostly in protected noncombat positions. In a word, privileged classes are not typical of the enlisted combat soldier. Enlisted combat ranks tend, on the contrary, to be filled by lower-middle-class and working-class youths lacking the affluence that permits the luxury of "dropping out" or of finding insulated security from the draft at a university or college. Accordingly, Army combat units in Vietnam were not, as far as we can discover, radically different from the enlisted social types which have populated armies in Western nations for centuries, basically rural yeomen and the urban working classes. The implication is clear that the military subsystem and its leadership, not the quality of recruits, are more likely to be at fault when armies lose coherence and begin to disintegrate.

Small-unit cohesion and discipline within American combat units in Vietnam either were destroyed or were in the process of being destroyed because of the overall weakening of traditional discipline within the military system itself. In the Vietnam War, combat troops became psychologically isolated and socially anomic with respect to traditional military values. In this specific sense, they differed little from a mob. For whatever the weight of the social factor, the result was that the Field Army in Vietnam became comprised of a large number of military isolates which constituted *noyaux* far more than functional groups.[11] Under these circumstances discipline became increasingly difficult to maintain, and the reliability of units under combat stress decreased.

Nothing has been said so far about the racial difficulties during the Vietnam War and their impact upon the extent and process of military disintegration. Combat units especially tended to be comprised of a large proportion of black soldiers. Indeed, they comprised much higher percentages of combat units than their percentage in the society at large. In some combat elements, up to 30 percent of infantry units were black, but their officers were almost always white. Charles C. Moskos observes:

The Vietnam Period was characterized by polarization between the races within the context of formal integration. Engendered by real and perceived discrimination, near mutinous actions of groups of Black servicemen in the early 1970's reached such proportions as to undermine the very fighting capability of America's armed forces. . . . Although close living and common danger mitigated racial conflict in combat units in the fields [*sic*], self-imposed informal segregation in the noncombat environment became almost de rigueur on the part of lower ranking black and white servicemen. And it was largely in such off-duty situations that embroilments between races became a common occurrence in Vietnam.[12]

Unfortunately, little of a quantitative nature has been done to attempt to relate racial factors and conflict to indicators of disintegration in Vietnam. The evidence is confusing, as can be seen in the fact that Moskos seems to imply that the racial problem itself threatened the cohesion of the Army, but suggests as well that combat cohesion was not directly threatened by the impact of the racial variable. Our own data show that institutional mutinies did in fact take place, but we can find only limited evidence that such conditions were directly attributable to race. On the other hand, racial friction seems ever to lurk just below the surface. Perhaps the racial problem is neither more nor less than a particular dimension of the larger problem of socialization. Whatever the problems of race in the military, the available evidence is simply not convincing that race played anything but a minor role in the process of disintegration associated with some field units in Vietnam.

While the impact of race upon levels of cohesion is unclear, the fact of racial friction is not. Had the replacement system used in Vietnam been different, rotating unit replacements instead of individual replacements, cohesion might have been greater, even though the quality of leadership was held constant at the low level of quality which characterized it. Maybe if whole units had been replaced instead of individuals and such units organized and trained together at, say, the maneuver battalion level, then not only might the racial problem have been minimized, but several other problems might have been forestalled. We suspect that the common experience of units training together, shipment overseas, common battle experiences with known and familiar officers and NCO's all might have functioned collectively to prevent, or at least minimize, emergence of those factors which we have associated with disintegration. Whatever might have been, race probably scrvcd only as a background variable against which more important forces played out their role in eroding cohesion among combat units in Vietnam.

The lack of effective and professional officers to act as catalysts in the process of military socialization probably caused disintegration to be accelerated by other factors. The nature of the draft brought into the Army a large proportion of soldiers drawn from the lower socioeconomic strata. Men of this social order have often been characterized by sociologists by their impulse toward immediate gratification, sudden urges to violence, and a higher incidence of inability to adapt to military life. If men of these dispositions, facing a heavy burden of combat, are placed in a situation where their leaders are perceived as not deserving of respect, where enforcing traditional and severe discipline is absent, or where effective leadership in battle against a competent enemy is not in evidence, then the incidence of hostile acts against the military system and its symbols will likely increase. Concurrently, if the military system cannot or will not provide a set of constraining values which serve as guides to behavior, then the loss of discipline will be further reinforced. If the military system had tried, in terms of its own logic, to come to grips with the problem of poor recruit material, it would have had to develop a wide range of techniques and subsystems for socializing the recruit to military life and its values. The mere fact that indicators of disintegration appeared in such obvious ways, as our analysis has shown, seems to indicate that the Army gave little thought and effort to the problem of socializing recruits to the imperatives of an army in combat. Under such conditions, the argument that soldiers performed poorly because they were poor recruits to begin with has a certain perverse logic to it. However, the problem of socialization is one which all armies face. What is at issue is the extent to which the American Army came to grips with it. The evidence drawn from its performance in Vietnam suggests that it did a poor job in accomplishing a task which all armies have had to perform.

In addition, senior officers who directed the war in Vietnam

argue with some credibility that opportunities for frequent partici-
pation in battle, and thus direct leadership, were relatively limited.[13] Controlling the movement of hundreds or thousands of
squad-, platoon-, and company-sized units, the continuous operation of multiple and complex communications, and problems of
supply, transport, and evacuation, may have required the presence
of senior officers at command centers in rear-area base camps rather
than at actual battle sites. The Army leadership argues further that
the nature of most operations in Vietnam did not call for the presence of large numbers of generals and colonels during an engagement. Standard tactical doctrine holds that the immediate and junior commander of the unit on the ground is the best judge of the
situation and therefore requires a high degree of tactical autonomy.
The constant presence of senior officers would tend to inhibit decision making and responsibility at the level of unit engagement and
to delay tactical reactions unacceptably. Senior officers should have
absented themselves from battle sites if the argument has any
merit. As we shall see, the argument is spurious. It is weak because
the war in Vietnam was from the outset tied intimately to politics
and especially to the maintaining of the political culture of the
Vietnamese, whose freedom from Communist influence was one of
the war's goals. Accordingly, the objectives were always quasi-
political right down to the lowest unit of combat. By the terms of
the military *ratio* of the war, *all* operations should have been subject
to intense high command supervision in order to ensure that the violence employed was commensurate with the imperatives of *political*
warfare. Commentators have noted that not only were "free-fire
zones" out of place in counter-insurgency warfare, but so was
much of the apparatus of modern warfare, including pattern bombing by B-52 aircraft, defoliation, and population relocation. The
Army should have relied on the employment of multiple small
units patterned after the French Groupes Mobiles, sophisticated intelligence operations, and troop levels held to some 100,000 volunteers but with comparatively long terms of in-country service. Unquestionably, the men needed to fight a political war would have

had to display a certain level of professional expertise gained over many years. Such, of course, was not the case with the American officers and men deployed in-country. Further, the alternatives, based on the experience of similar wars, require that small-unit commanders be constrained from employing the "formal" doctrines of conventional and fire-intensive warfare which dictate tactical autonomy. Instead, all lower-level combat commanders ideally should have demonstrated high competence in counter-guerrilla tactics, which, of course, American soldiers generally did not. At the same time, all operations should have been closely controlled to fit a strict overall counter-guerrilla policy. To perform properly, highly cohesive units led by professionals of integrity and long service are essential.

Unconventional warfare demanding exquisite control of political warfare, tailored professionally to its objects, was clearly beyond the capacity of young American unit commanders and their troops rapidly rotated in and out of the command structure. Little in their military training prepared Americans for this challenge. We remained essentially an army of amateurs. All levels of the Army in Vietnam were totally inexperienced in "people's war," if for no other reason than the rotation system which limited the vast bulk of the forces to thirteen months in-country with the same being true of officers at most levels. Clearly, in so short a period no great expertise could be developed in guerrilla warfare by either officers or enlisted men, however bravely they might fight. Bravery, at best could only play a minor role in success; political sophistication should have been a major part. In the end, the American Army fought with the men and material available. But even if the U.S. Army could not fight a true counter-insurgency war, there was nonetheless a need for the continual presence of highly sophisticated senior officers in battle itself; rather than merely attempting to lead from helicopters, or visiting base camps from time to time.

The character of the American troops employed reinforced the need for the close presence in battle of sophisticated senior officers. The evidence available is that the war was not, in fact, adequately supervised by senior ranks in such a manner as to conduct the war by the rules initially laid down by the Army itself. The rules at issue are those declaiming "winning the hearts and minds . . . ," "unconventional warfare," "civic action," etc. It can be assumed from numerous interviews that the idea spread not only that the generals and colonels absented themselves from battle, as their minor losses show, but that they actually cared little about what the troops did so long as the "forms" were observed, namely, body counts, status reports, reports of "victories," etc. Why should one then be surprised at a rising incidence of signs of disintegration? Eventually the enlisted men's contempt for officers and the system they symbolized was revealed in a number of officer and NCO assassinations, acts of insubordination, and mutinous actions, all of which are clear symptoms of a loss of military self-respect, unit pride, and unit cohesion. The result was disintegration at the small-unit level.

Evidence of a decline in officer quality is beyond question. In examining the pool of men from which officers were to be recruited to conduct the intricacies of counter-revolutionary war, we find a long-term decline in the number of officers available from ROTC. Table 10 shows this decline. Colleges and universities grew less important as sources of officer recruitment, and so the quality of officers declined. Moreover, the college students generally exempted by privileged status and class resisted even the minor demands made upon them by the draft. To be sure, the question of student resistance and its moral justification, or the question of the morality of the Vietnam War itself, is beyond this study. However, the fact of student resistance to military service and the very real insulation provided most college students by the law has raised the question of serious class and status discrimination. The point has great moral as well as empirical relevance since those discriminated against frequently died because of this invidious difference in the burden of sacrifice. As a source of elite-strata recruitment, the Harvard undergraduate class of 1968 offers an interesting study. The class of 1968 numbered 1,203 members. Of this number, available data indicate that 36 served in the armed forces and only 26 in Vietnam. Not a single graduate of that class died in action. Harvard College alumni records show that the burden of sacrifice from this elite school was slight during both the Korean and Vietnam wars. Only 18 members of all the Harvard classes between 1960 and 1971 died in Vietnam. In Korea and Vietnam, of the Harvard classes of 1941 through 1971 totaling 33,468 members, 30 Harvard classmen (including dropouts) died in these wars. From the data available most graduates of this particular elite university appear unwilling to provide the quality of leadership that effective ground forces require.

Equally revealing is the story provided in an article in the *Boston Globe* which describes those few Harvard students who were called to the induction station and the contrived illnesses and disabilities used by them to avoid induction. At the same time, the groups of black and "Southie" inductees are pictured as either relatively docile or even enthusiastic. They appear caught up in a system they but dimly understood. However, because of their social and political status, they were sent to fight many thousands of miles away in a war for which no explanation they might understand can be given. The account is even more revealing in the remarks of one upper-class Harvard student who offers a clear justification for the disparate levels of sacrifice required of the lower social strata. The contention is that the intellectual potential of Harvard students is so high that if anyone must die in what is at best a misguided war, then let those die whose potential is manifestly as low as their status. Harvard indeed produces the physicians, lawyers, scientists, and intellectuals who operate the system. But it seems to us that while European aristocrats have for centuries paid the military price for their privileged status the American elite are manifestly unwilling to do so. What is also clear is that as officer quality declines and their numbers rise, a close association with military disintegration is found. None of this is to say that masses of college students should have been drafted as combat infantrymen, since this may also lead to a loss of cohesion. But to manipulate the political system in such a way that the officer potential in universities is denied to the combat units is most dangerous. It is dangerous because the transmission belt of social values from higher and creative groups to lower and less creative and less value-sustaining strata is broken. While social privilege seems unavoidable in any society, exemplars are equally needed and no more so than in battle.

The evidence seems strong that this vital social transmission belt was broken during the Vietnam War. Between 1960 and 1970, Army ROTC recruitment fell over 60 percent. Concurrently, the active officer corps between 1960 and 1972 increased by 57 percent. Evidently, the Army had some difficulty not only in replacing losses from discharge but in finding the numbers necessary to fill the felt need for an ever-larger officer corps. Officer quality may have declined as radically as their numbers expanded. It is expecting too much to believe that the complexities of the war in Vietnam could have been dealt with by such men, or even by the elite graduates of West Point, whose failings are even more clear today. The argument advanced by the Army is that such numbers of officers had to be obtained even if quality was sacrificed. History suggests otherwise, as the experience of the well-led German, British, and French military forces shows. A large army well led by a small number of dedicated, competent officers exhibiting a sense of the military ethic is always more cohesive than a vast mass of poor officers and badly socialized troops. Much of the evidence points to the fact that the level and rate of disintegration in the Army are related directly to the character, integrity, and competence of the officer corps. Nothing in the data shows any clear connection between disintegration and such external factors as the "permissive society," fragmentation ideologies, or a "nation being torn apart."

Toward the end of the Vietnam War, a large number of books were written about the condition of the American armed services.[14] Stuart H. Loory's account of a "defeated" American military machine is among the most informed.[15] It describes in subjective but convincing detail the prevailing attitudes and conditions in all of the services, together with a credible account of the atmosphere of careerism, self-seeking, and exploitation of the enlisted ranks. Loory did not set out to indict the Army officer corps, but the data will not allow him to avoid the indictment. However, he lets the military off easily. He sees the officer as "victimized" by a system which "politicized" the military, although to the career advantage of the officer corps itself, and he lays little blame at the feet of the officers themselves. Only by implication does he suggest that the officer corps betrayed the ethic of the professional soldier, an ethic which is the very creation of those who are supposed to live by and enforce its rigorous standards. This ethic, expressed insufficiently in three words—duty, honor, country—came finally to be honored by lip service alone. Paradoxically, any real attempt by an officer to fulfill the stated ideals would most likely destroy his career. Utilizing the Army War College study as the source of the military ethic, Loory finds that the ethics of the profession were often more honored in their breach and that actual dedication to ethical standards became submerged in a sea of careerist imperatives.

The Army War College study initiated by General Westmoreland remains the most definitive work done by the Army on the officer corps. With the corps's imperative, "duty-honor-country," in mind, 415 officers were asked in 1970 by questionnaire and rudimentary "Q" sort methodology to evaluate the ethical behavior of the officer corps of the U.S. Army.[16] The behavioral implications of this study are important, for they are based on data gathered from sources very close to the problem, namely, the officers themselves, and are likely to reflect insights which may have been overlooked by outside analysts. Keeping in mind the "Officer's Creed" cited earlier, some of the more pertinent conclusions of the Army War College study are worth pursuing. In the first place, the Army War College study finds: "The ideal standards of ethical/moral/professional behavior as epitomized by 'Duty-Honor-Country' are accepted by the officer corps as proper, meaningful, and relevant for the Army of today." However, it also notes: "There are widespread and often significant differences between the ideal ethical/moral/professional standards of the Army and the prevailing standards . . ." that are necessary for career advancement. Surprisingly, the study notes: "The variances between the ideal standards and the actual or operative standards are perceived with striking similarity by the cross section of officers queried." In point of fact, it would appear that the officer corps itself recognizes the disparity between the ideal and the requirements of career advancement. Indeed, the study suggests that "the junior officers in particular were concerned about the unethical practices they observed and were eager to do their part in correcting the situation."

In addressing itself to the causes of this disparity, the study found: "There was no significant evidence that contemporary sociological pressures—which are everpresent—were primary causes of the differences between the ideal and the actual professional climate in the Army; the problems are for the most part internally generated; they will not vanish automatically as the war in Vietnam winds down and the size of the Army decreases." The report adds: "The Army rewards system focuses on the accomplishment of short term, measurable, and often trivial tasks, and neglects the development of those ethical standards which are essential to a healthy profession."

Among the most frequently recurring reasons for the causes of the gap between the ideal standards of ethical behavior and actual behavior itself are: "selfish, promotion-oriented behavior; inadequate communication between junior and senior; distorted or dishonest reporting of status, statistics, or officer efficiency; technical or managerial incompetence; disregard for principles but total respect for accomplishing even the most trivial mission with zero defects; disloyalty to subordinates; senior officers setting poor standards of ethical/professional behavior." Further, it would appear correct to suggest that evident disparities are encouraged by self-deceptive Army policies "regarding officer evaluation, selection for promotion, career concepts and assignment policies, and information reporting systems." Such circumstances clearly do not aid in the Army's goal of retaining junior officers. The Army War College study notes that while young officers are motivated by principles, these same young officers often find their seniors incompetent, neglectful, and "often out of touch with reality." It is hardly surprising, therefore, that this state of affairs has forced the young officer to choose between the ideals of the code of military ethics and the goal of a successful career.

One element reinforcing careerism, managerial opportunism, is the need to excel at the most trivial task, to please one's rater, and to move in almost yearly stages from one "desirable" assignment to an even more prestigious assignment, a variation of the "up or out" policy determining promotion and retention in the Army. It is important to understand that promotion and higher schooling is exceedingly important to the career of most officers. Not only do prestige, position, and income depend on excelling *within* the system, but so does the long-term security which comes with retirement at a high rank. To achieve some vested retirement status, a minimum of eighteen years of active duty is required by law, a precondition which allows the officer to be retained for twenty years and hopefully at the rank of lieutenant colonel or colonel. Since competition is sharply exaggerated during peacetime, the social and economic costs of even the slightest so-called "blemish" on an efficiency report, however trivial the comment, can be enormous. Being passed over for promotion, loss of the opportunity for higher schooling, and, in the event of sudden "reduction in force," the failure to qualify for retirement pay, may all come to hinge upon a single poor efficiency report. Besides the fear of losing economic benefits, there are peer pressures, and the normal drive for what the system has come to define as success. It would seem that from both a historical and an experimental point of view, an "up or out" policy is grossly pernicious; it results too often in the development of what Presthus calls an "upward looking posture" that requires that professionalism be subordinated to career imperatives. Thus the "military ethic" is reduced to an empty shell insofar as it is capable of generating the kind of overt behavior associated with long-term unit cohesion. While a business corporation can probably afford a form of "up or out" in the pursuit of profit, it is doubtful that an Army can adopt the same policy without disastrous consequences.

Legendary military units notable for their toughness, such as the XX Valeria Victrix Legion of Rome, the British Guards and Scottish regiments, the French Foreign Legion, the Angevin Regiment of France, and the Grossdeutschland Division, all possessed a cadre of long-term small-unit leaders. In all these military units, it was recognized that an officer might well be a superb company commander for his entire career and so little pressure existed to force him to prove that he was a potential field marshal. Higher command and senior officer status were usually the province of the nobility, but not in all cases. In earlier times it was possible and common for an officer to serve his entire career as a company leader, either dying in battle or passing quietly into retirement as a captain or major after twenty, thirty, or more years of service. In more modern times, we find this type of career specialization in the nineteenth- and twentieth-century British Army, both at the regimental level and, of course, in the intelligence system. One might be a permanent lieutenant colonel posted in the North-West Frontier of India with special knowledge of Afghan tribal systems and politics. Such a man might well spend twenty or more years in this area with immense benefit to British power and colonial stability and never go beyond major or lieutenant colonel. He would not, however, be discarded *merely* for failing to be promoted "on schedule."

It was observed by the late John Paul Vann, a retired lieutenant colonel who was killed in action in Vietnam, that "the United States had not been in Vietnam for ten years, but for one year ten times." A military system which places a premium upon a policy of "up or out" and a highly disruptive rotation system can engender little long-term stability, much less develop a corps of dedicated, experienced specialists in Vietnamese history, language, and sociocultural matters. The lack of such expertise was, it seems to us, one of the crucial factors in our failure, a failure evidenced by our inability to create a cohesive South Vietnamese Army; as it was, the ARVN collapsed with extraordinary and embarrassing speed.

Many of the Army War College study findings should scarcely surprise anyone familiar with career patterns in the Army, patterns which tend to create behavior which would be defined as unprofessional in more traditional armies. When most of the institutional reinforcement for officer behavior tends to support careerism, self-seeking, the use of one's charge and command largely as a means to higher career rewards, it is simply unrealistic to expect the military to restore traditional values when the costs of such efforts to one's career are so high. Today there are few perceptible policies that reinforce traditional officer behavior, despite the experience in Vietnam. Every pressure in the Army officer corps still appears designed to achieve what officially is called career management, which, in the end, is destructive of reliable battle performance. It is not likely that cohesive military units can be created by small-unit leaders who are as pressed by the imperatives of the system itself to "go higher or retire." For the combat troops, some center of reliability, of certainty, must exist, especially at the platoon and company levels. If at these levels officers, and increasingly NCO's, move through with production-line speed, each intent on short-range, "zero defect" performances of almost trivial proportions, the result will inevitably be to contribute to the loss of small-unit cohesion. To expect high levels of cohesion under great stress by units so "led" is to expect too much. Thus, disintegration under stress becomes almost a certainty.

One must ask whether these conditions can be changed from within, for a basic premise of our analysis is that conditions of disintegration have been brought about internally. In addressing itself to corrective measures, the Army War College study concluded: "The present climate is not self-correcting, and because of the nature and extent of the problem, changes must be credibly instituted and enforced by the Army's top leadership. . . . correcting the climate will require more than superficial, transitory measures. The climate cannot be changed by admonitions. Modification of the systems of reward and punishment to support adherence to the time-honored principles of an army officer is required." [17] In short, the Army War College study seems to imply that those who have most benefited by the system can be expected and trusted to change it. We find such an assumption highly questionable.

In another part of the Army War College study, we find the following observation, which surely suggests that the Army probably cannot correct its own condition:

> . . . the present climate does not appear to be self-correcting. The human drives for success and for recognition by seniors, sustained if not inflamed by the systems of rewards and management which cater to immediate personal success at the expense of a long term consolidation of moral and ethical strength would appear to perpetuate if not exacerbate the current environment. Time alone will not cure the disease. The fact alone that the leaders of the future are those who survived and excelled within the rules of the present system militates in part against any self-starting incremental return toward the practical application of ideal values. [18]

Reduced to essentials, the Army study leads us to conclude that the military system cannot reform itself because those who enforce the core ethic of duty-honor-country have by the very measure of their own success violated the ethic *ab initio*. Equally important, for such men to begin seriously to reform the system now would constitute a repudiation of their personal histories. Few men can do that.

The Army War College study makes no special reference to the source of an officer's commission or his attitudes. Of the total sample of 450, it must be noted that 105 officers, or 28 percent, were West Point graduates. Further, no significant difference in attitudes was found with respect to the following question: "Do you feel that, within the officer corps as a whole, there is a discernible difference between the ideal standards and those that actually exist?" There are, however, some interesting tabular data in the Army War College study. Table 11 provides data on officer responses to the foregoing question by rank. Table 12 addresses the *mean* intensity of response by several variables, including time in command, commission source, branch (combat or noncombat), and educational level. The data in Table 11 reveal that 313 of the sample, or 76 percent, find a moderate to great variation between ideals and realities, while Table 12 shows that the mean arithmetic response, 73 percent, is uniform. With respect to the relationships of other variables to the question above, they range from nonsignificant to marginally significant, with the most significant relationships being by Grade ($r = -.21$), Military Education ($r = -.29$), and Level of Staff ($r = -.22$). The data clearly imply that the higher one's military status, the less one's tendency to perceive differences between the ideal military ethic and the way it operates in practice. Clearly, higher ranks perceive *less* of what is "wrong" with the Army than lower ranks! A commission obtained from the Military Academy introduces little significant difference in response. The source of one's commission provides no significant correlation with the response to the question of "ideals." There is no evidence to suggest that West Point officers act more honorably than those commissioned from other sources, despite the intensive exposure to the Academy's famous "honor code." There is a certain *majoritarian* perception that all is not well within the Army. Essentially, however, the formal indoctrination received at West Point appears unrelated to the findings of the Army War College study as a whole, so far as actual behavior is affected, whereas the informal experiences of the officer relate highly to the findings. Most disturbing is the implication that within the higher ranks there is a greater perception that the differences between the real and the ideal are minimal. Such differences are perceived as much greater by officers of lower military rank.

We know from our discussion of the drug traffic and addiction in Vietnam that there is evidence that the higher ranks were out of touch with lower-level realities. In the Army War College study we have seen that senior officers are not well informed about lower-level troop conditions. Certainly a lack of honest and frank communication between higher and lower grades is one explanation. Perhaps, as we have suggested, as one rises in rank the flow of information either diminishes or becomes distorted. Given that the majority of generals were originally commissioned from West Point, how does one account for the fact that the moral perceptions of the West Pointer on active duty are not perceptibly different from those of other commissioned officers, even though as a cadet he allegedly was trained in the ethic of duty-honor-country, and also the fact that in the higher ranks, increasingly dominated by West Pointers, there is an apparent increasing lack of moral perception and moral concern?

The Military Academy, unlike most other institutions, lays great stress on its honor code. The ideal that "a Cadet will not lie, cheat or steal, nor tolerate anyone who does" is central. The code is tied in turn to the motto and injunctions of duty-honor-country. Even so, West Point has had its share of scandals, including the most recent, which involved a large number of the junior class.[19] Since the investigation of the Academy is now apparently complete, little else can be said except that several hundred cadets were involved with charges and countercharges of collusion, favoritism, and "toleration"; 152 cadets were ultimately expelled. Some light might be shed on this problem and that of the Army as a whole by a brief consideration of the system at West Point.

Generally, the curriculum at West Point is highly incremental-ized, tending to stress short-range goals. Tests are very limited in scope, highly compartmentalized, and the frequency of testing borders on the ludicrous. At no time, to our knowledge, does the Military Academy give a four-year comprehensive examination in a major field as is common at other schools. Further, all test scores are curved so that there will always be *some* failures. The results of all these mini-tests are cumulative and affect class standing. And class standing affects not only one's assignment after graduation but even promotion in later years. Tremendous personal investment rests on class standing. Many of the tests are very easy to compromise since the instructors do not trouble to change tests or quizzes in the different sections of the same course. They rely on the honor system to enforce the rule against cheating. West Point faculty maintain that the honor system precludes cheating and, further, that the testing system buttresses the honor system itself. Here then is an institution which maximizes temptation and minimizes risk in a way similar to the system as a whole. It seems to us that when 4,000 young men and women are required to place heavy psychic investment in an honor system which forbids cheating, and which at the same time provides great opportunities and pressures for doing so, its occurrence cannot be regarded as surprising. From our observations drawn from interviews with the cadets, we find that they are not one happy band of 4,000 brothers (and sisters), but form into groups of thirty to forty and even smaller numbers of intimates during their four years at the Academy. If the social structure at the Academy is less cohesive than one is led to believe, then we can expect to find small, self-protective groups that cheat because the risk of detection is small. Here we seem to have the cadet model of the "up or out" pattern characteristic of the larger Army, complete with concern for short-range performance goals. Perhaps it is here that the concept of career as an overriding imperative originates and is continually reinforced. If the "up or out" syndrome has the same effect on the cadets as in the Army as a whole, this then may be one of the underlying causes of discohesion among military units in the field. This is to say that the ethical ideal of cadet integrity and honor appears *not* to carry over into the Army either because it may be too weak or because Army behavior has become influenced by the pressure of career imperatives. The argument is made that the honor system is essential to West Point because it not only conditions the cadet to a sense of integrity and honor, but carries over into the Army during his entire career. Yet all the evidence available tends to show that little of the "code" or the sense of duty-honor-country in fact is transmitted to the Army. Thus, what happens at West Point is apparently mirrored in the entire military system. The parallels are striking.

A stark phrase which appears in the conclusions of the Army War College study is "disloyalty to subordinates." If disloyalty in fact ranges all the way down, small wonder that the ethical failure of the officer corps came to be evident to the ranks. We have seen that one of the central elements of cohesion in more traditional armies was the mutual regard between officers and men, that when the time of testing came the officer corps would not forsake their obligations. Might not the reverse have occurred in Vietnam—that in the time of battle and death the officers were not there—especially senior officers? Moreover, the structure of the war in Vietnam tended possibly to reinforce the impression of enlisted personnel that ultimately there was no more purpose to war than the advancement of officers' careers. If the central concern of the more senior officers was career and promotions, what worse way to destroy one's career expectancies than to insist on rigorous ethical standards and then to accept prolonged exposure to the danger of death with combat troops? Under such circumstances, small cohesive groups can scarcely exist, much less overall military cohesion.

The Army War College study affirms the concept that external sociological pressures are not the primary elements in military performance. We find in the Shils and Janowitz study that the cohesion of the Wehrmacht was a function essentially of internal military factors. The Army War College study makes basically the same observation. Further, the study specifically considers popular attitudes toward the war as irrelevant:

There is no direct evidence that external fiscal, political, sociological, or managerial influences are the primary causative factors of this less than optimum climate. Neither does the public attitude to the Vietnam War, or the rapid expansion of the Army, or the current anti-military syndrome stand out as a significant reason for deviations from the level of professional behavior the Army acknowledges as its attainable ideal.[20]

There is no reason to assume that the signs of disintegration emerging from the ranks were primarily derived from external sociopolitical conditions. Accordingly, the connection between an officer corps perceived as unethical and even incompetent and an army of lesser ranks displaying every sign of disintegration is clear. A follow-on study by the Army War College was conducted a year later and completed in October 1971.[21] What this may in fact represent is an effort to find out if the 1970 study might not have been aberrant or parochial because of the small sample of 450 officers. What the 1971 study found was that the lack of ethical dispositions and nonprofessionalism in the Army were widespread. The same pathologies were reported but this time they were found in all ranks, including the enlisted ranks. The 1971 study surveyed a sample of 1,800 military personnel, including 721 enlisted persons, 920 officers (46 generals), 100 cadets at West Point, and 43 Department of the Army civilians. The survey was conducted entirely in the United States at seventeen military establishments. The study uncovered a recurring pattern of the "ambitious, transitory commander—marginally skilled in the complexities of his duties—engulfed in producing transitory results, fearful of personal failure, too busy to talk with or listen to his subordinates, and determined to submit acceptably optimistic reports which reflect faultless completion of a variety of tasks at the expense of the sweat and frustration of his subordinates"—repeating what was found the year before in a study of *officer* values. "Despite concerted efforts to remedy much of the nonprofessionalism illustrated by the theme, the theme persists." We can only observe that where the first study illustrated a clear loss of the military ethic among the officers, further evidence produced by the Army itself suggests that the troops are not unaware of their officers' lack of concern for them. If enlisted ranks perceive their officers in such unflattering terms, little deference, then, can be expected toward such a leadership and certainly not the willingness to sacrifice in battle or produce the military cohesion essential to survival. A study of the Israeli soldier reveals a different attitude toward his leadership in the Israeli Defense Force (Zahal).[22] The Israeli soldier is imbued with neither a fanatic sense of integral nationalism nor deeply hostile feelings toward the Arabs. He does possess a deep sense of military community and unit identification; one absolute in battle is that wounded are *never* left behind. Of overriding importance are the leaders; ". . . it may be said that most of them fit the heroic image of the military leader rather than the manager."[23] Moreover, in Israel the Western concept of the traditional gentleman officer, and in America possibly the gentleman manager, gives way to values of truthfulness in reporting, seriousness in the acquisition of skills, resistance to any form of show-off, unemotional judgment, concern with the well-being of subordinates, humane treatment of prisoners of war and enemy civilians, disregard of personal safety, and rejection of monetary pursuits."[24] Surveys show that. Israeli soldiers gave overwhelming approval to their officers, notably their immediate commanders. Their responses show that he "knew his job" (82 percent), "gave clear orders" (100 percent), "was resourceful" (98 percent), "often praised his superiors" (11 percent), "was interested in men's personal problems" (85 percent), "stuck to the letter of his superior's orders" (43 percent), "gave impossible orders" (3 percent), "had initiative" (93 percent).[25] Writing after the Six Day War, Lieutenant General Haim Bar-Lev stated: "Here lies the secret of our Army's success in the Six Day War. . . . I do not know of any single factor to which so much of historic achievement can be attributed as the human and moral quality of our commanders; of which the readiness to go in the van, their personal valour, their audacity, their readiness to risk their lives are direct products."[26] The striking quality of the Israeli Army and its commanders at all levels, their presence at the front and their willingness to risk losses among themselves, together with visibility to their troops, comprise possibly the central element in Israeli military unit cohesion.

The Israeli Army thus stresses the *led* primary group together with the moral and military responsibility entailed—and these officers and NCO's meet their responsibilities. The evidence drawn from Vietnam suggests American officers did not . . . and still do not.

The U.S. Army in marked contrast exhibited signs of social entropy in the destruction of its basic primary groups, a destruction traceable to the several factors we have noted. However, given first the state of the officer corps, its career obsession and rapid rotation in and out of combat units for the sake of "ticket punching," and second, the condition and perceptions of American enlisted men, especially of their leadership, it is a wonder that any cohesion existed at all. Moreover, it is very doubtful that even had they tried, the officer corps could have created the necessary primary groups since the growth of mutual regard was precluded by the character and inordinate numbers of the officers themselves. Reinforcing all other elements affecting the moral state of the Army in Vietnam was the extraordinary damage done by the drug traffic, which, in the end, the higher echelons of the Army condoned if only by inaction. The existence of an organized drug traffic tolerated by civilian policy makers and the higher officer corps is sufficient evidence of the moral dilemmas of the entire Army.

In the end, factors associated with military decay focus on the officer corps, a corps unsure of itself and its standards of conduct, unable to enforce basic discipline, overmanaged with superfluous staff, and held in contempt by their troops. The American Army in Vietnam was completely unlike those armies which in history have exhibited high cohesion during periods of retreat or even defeat. Primarily because of the character and the quality of the officer corps, the American Army in Vietnam was an army which bordered upon self-destruction primarily because of internal factors.

IV
Reestablishing Traditional Values

The American Army during ten years in Indochina produced a series of behavioral deficiencies which appear almost endemic to the American military structure. Among the most important of these was a military careerism so exaggerated that protection and advancement of an officer's career at all levels seemed to have become the highest value for a substantial number of officers.[1] This metamorphosis of military values was not without its effects on the operational capabilities of the Army.[2] Moreover, the change resulted in a series of moral and ethical failures represented by officers acquiescing in, initiating, or participating in policies and actions which individually they regarded as unethical, but which were followed nevertheless as the way to career advancement. Examples abound, but surely the deliberate falsification of intelligence reports from the hamlet to the strategic level is a classic example. The use of "body counts" and ordnance doctrines such as "bombing enemy approaches" reflect the same type of tendency to "get on board" even in the face of questionable moral and operational policies. False reporting remains a problem today in the case of unit readiness reports. Further, there is no evidence available to us which would lead us to believe that the reasons for these failures have been eliminated.

Why did the officer corps allow itself to participate in a series of

"Vietnam horrors" contrary to the stated ethic of "duty-honor-country"? It seems clear that the exaggerated emphasis upon careerism to the point of acquiescing in almost every policy without opposition could only have happened in a military structure which has consistently failed to develop an ethical doctrine of resistance. Accordingly, such shorthand injunctions as "it all counts for twenty," "don't rock the boat," "you can't tell the general that," while often destructive, were useful attitudes for individual career advancement. To be sure, advancement is then purchased at the expense of a failure to examine higher orders virtually regardless of operational consequences. The Vietnam era witnessed the development of an officer corps whose members acquiesced in policies, orders, and actions with which many strongly disagreed but supported nevertheless as a means of career advancement.

The extent of the problem is obvious and embarrassing. In ten years of warfare, not a single general officer publicly resigned or retired in protest over the policies conducted in Vietnam. Indeed, we cannot find a single instance where a general officer refused by way of resignation or retirement to execute a single policy, although it now appears that several of them may have had serious reservations about the effectiveness of some of these policies. If we can trust the *postwar* statements of some high-ranking officers, they were opposed to such policies as search and destroy and the bombing of rural populations to force them into the cities, where they could be better controlled. Whether they disagreed at the time remains an unanswered question. Despite evidence that specific policies were failing and had been failing for years, not only were there few resignations, but apparently few senior officers protested. We can locate only an occasional colonel or lieutenant colonel who chose to resign as a matter of purely ethical conviction. In fact, the only examples of resignation, early retirement, or protest seemed to have occurred at the lower levels of the officer corps and, even then, only rarely. There are, of course, examples of officers occasionally refusing to execute specific orders, but such behavior was largely sporadic and in almost all cases confined to junior officers who were not career officers but OCS and ROTC graduates who were in "for two and go." The Hamburger Hill incident as well as young Navy and Air Force pilots, mostly young captains, who refused to fly missions are examples of non-career officers who refused to execute orders they regarded as "stupid." In the end, it is difficult to escape the impression that resistance and protest as moral alternatives to acquiescing in orders with which an officer seriously disagreed were not common during the Vietnam conflict.

The marked failure of officers to retire in protest, resign, or to speak out openly against policies which they felt to be morally repugnant or not in the best interests of their commands or their country, was a symptom of a much deeper malaise. The Vietnam experience did not create the tendency for the officer corps "to go along" or to become "team players" in support of policies with which they may have privately disagreed. Rather, as we have seen, that propensity was well established as a consequence of the shift from traditional, corporative institutional values to entrepreneurial values. Once the Army was perceived to be an "occupation," logic compelled an individual to assess the responsibility to obey or object to policy purely in terms of the requirements of the "marketplace" in which his career would be played out. Had the Army remained an institution in the traditional sense, the responsibility to object to given policies would have been predicated upon the secure grounds of a shared sense of the violation of agreed-upon moral and ethical values.[3] A logical result of the shift within the military from corporative to entrepreneurial values is for an officer to support policies with which he disagrees.

The documented willingness of the officer corps at all levels, but especially at the higher ranks, to acquiesce in policies that they individually felt to be either wrong or detrimental "to the good of the service" is at once a result and a reflection of a lack of moral integrity. At issue is the extent to which modern entrepreneurial practices within the officer corps demonstrate the clear necessity to develop codes of *organizationally based morality*. We do not charge that individual officers are not men of integrity in their personal lives. Indeed, there is no real need to question the proposition that individual officers may even be men of personal integrity who exercise their formal responsibilities within the military structure. What is at question is the extent to which a developed sense of organizational morality can be relied upon to support the decisions of individual officers which are based on *their* concepts of what constitutes personal integrity. In short, is there a tension between the individual's sense of ethics and the ethics espoused by the organization of which he is a member?

Now clearly there are few saints among us; few individuals can be expected to stand alone against an organization if they are sustained only by the comfort, probably small, that what they do represents their own sense of what is right. It seems unrealistic to expect individual officers to question, resist, and, at the extreme, refuse to comply with orders and policies that they find morally objectionable unless there is some expectation that what they are doing is somewhere, somehow rooted in and supported by the formal and informal norms of the institution. The erosion of corporative values appears so complete, and the replacement of these values with ones rooted deeply in the entrepreneurial ethos so thorough, that to all intents and purposes it seems fair to conclude that there is no formal code of moral behavior which defines acceptable behavior for a member of the officer corps. Worse, there is no place where an individual officer can find an effective code. A corporative institution requires a code of ethics and behavior which serves as a moral anchor relevant to behavior in combat, and the American Army and its officer corps have failed to evolve such a code. The Army officer corps has no mechanism for socializing its members, especially newly commissioned officers, to a corporative ethical standard that would establish the "price of belonging" to the corps itself and serve as a guide to judgmental actions both on and off the battlefield.

It might be objected that there is no need for a formal ethical code since informal assents given to informal norms actually come to function as a mechanism for socializing young officers to the corps by providing them with a set of ethical guidelines. Such an argument is devastating to the case for an ethically responsible officer corps, for it implies that the penetration of entrepreneurial values has gone so far as to preclude the need for a formal code. Instead the officer is encouraged to rely upon informal "gists" which are gained through experience and which, in the end, are rooted in the necessity to succeed within the system. Accordingly, the ethos of the marketplace, to succeed within the system, becomes the basis for most informal norms. Norms which required action that is not "systems supportive" would be regarded as "irrational." When these conditions obtain, the values attendant on a corporative system are dead. Careerism as the highest value becomes of necessity an *individual* reward, whereas the true measure of a corporatively oriented officer corps is the extent to which individual actions benefit and serve *communal* goals. While informal norms are important, they cannot act as adequate guides to behavior within an entrepreneurial environment. Precisely because they are informal, one suspects that they are not derived from some higher definition of what constitutes a good officer, namely, his ability to abide by a code of honor congruent with both the individual's sense of integrity and that of the officer corps within which he claims a special membership.

The proposition that there is no formal code of ethical behavior set forth for officers and, further, that there is no mechanism for inculcating such a code might be disputed on the grounds that officer candidate schools, the ROTC, and especially the Military Academy at West Point all do much to instill a sense of personal integrity. Anyone familiar with both ROTC and OCS realizes, however, that whatever ethical discussions occur are purely perfunctory parts of the training program and tend to be rooted in legalistic terms rather than moral ones. Most often they take the form of a course addressing the Uniform Code of Military Justice. West Point, however, may be another matter insofar as it affirms and applies the famous West Point "honor code."

As for the honor code at West Point, the cheating scandals over the years raise some legitimate doubts as to the extent to which the code is succeeding.[4] This aside, however, a close examination of the manner in which the honor code actually operates suggests that the problem of socializing individuals to a higher moral code which defines an officer corps goes far beyond the capabilities of the Military Academy. In the first place, the code is too general to guide an officer in a given situation. The stipulation that no cadet will "lie, cheat or steal, nor tolerate anyone who does" offers no real help to the officer in search of moral guidance. The West Point honor code represents the morality of the college fraternity house in that it addresses trivialities. There is no effort to tie the code to specifically *military* situations to which it may apply beyond campus life. It tends to address problems evident to the individual while at the Academy, not when he leaves it, and, in this sense, bears a strong similarity to codes of behavior found on virtually every college campus.

The objection that the Academy's honor code, especially the nontoleration clause, turns all "brother officers" into potential stool pigeons is a real one. The prerequisite of any successful corporative institution such as an officer corps is to inculcate within the individual officer a sense of what is to be done and what is not to be done. This most certainly does not require that every member of the corps keep watch on the behavior of every other officer, or that an officer's unethical conduct be "betrayed to his superiors." The experience of other service academies in allowing the individual some discretion based upon individual choice in dealing with unethical conduct has been uniformly good. However, when a condition exists in which every comrade is a potential informer, it forces the individual to play it safe. More importantly, it tends to destroy any sense of community based upon mutual trust and community attachment to a set of values. It creates officers who come to depend upon their ability to manipulate the system as a substitute for ethical judgment. When in doubt, it is simply much easier to "follow the rules," to go along, and to become a team player by getting on board. To paraphrase Machiavelli, it becomes important to *appear* religious, not to be religious. Such advice is appropriate for the officer who would be an entrepreneur; it is deadly for those who perceive themselves as members of a corporative institution.

The West Point honor code has very little relevance to conditions in the "real Army," a fact which even the instructors at West Point openly acknowledge, and which tends to reinforce our earlier suggestion that the honor code is really intended to operate primarily as a behavioral force at the Academy and not in the Army. Our own analysis suggests that the degree of transferability of the code to behavior, especially as that behavior is supported by the organizational norms of the Army, is minimal. A common occurrence and one which brings wry smiles to the faces of experienced officers is to see a young West Point graduate report another officer for an honor offense! While there is little doubt that such situations lend humor to daily life at the company level, they clearly imply that officers in the "real Army" simply do not expect the provisions of the West Point honor code to apply in the field. Part of the education of the young officer is to learn that these provisions are simply not in force. Consequently, after having the provisions of the honor code hammered home to him during his four years at the Academy, after being exhorted to act honorably, after some of his classmates may have been dismissed for failure to observe its provisions and, perhaps, after having turned in a comrade for violating the code, the young officer is suddenly confronted with the fact that virtually no one in the Field Army takes the code seriously. It is inevitable that after a period of confusion the search for another ethic begins, and here the young officer finds only the informal, intuitively perceived, and experience-learned rules of the entrepreneur. He can find no equivalent to the codes of honor learned at West Point for the most elementary of reasons—the Army has never developed such a code. Indeed, the use of ethics derived from the entrepreneurial marketplace of values makes such a code superfluous.

The fact that the Army has not found it necessary to develop a

moral code which can be transmitted to the officer corps is reflected in the practices at the Military Academy itself. Paradoxically, while the Academy is preaching duty-honor-country and
exhorting its cadets not to lie, cheat, or steal, it refuses to attempt
to develop a broader sense of ethics which the cadet would find
applicable in his day-to-day life on duty with an Army unit. Accordingly, in the words of several faculty members at West Point,
the Academy does not seek to teach or inculcate what they call
"prescriptive ethics," namely, a code which would apply beyond
the confines of West Point and serve as a moral base on which an
officer could organize his life. To the extent that the term is applicable, there is no attempt to develop a moral *Weltanschauung* related to the behavior of the cadet as a future commissioned officer.
In its place, the faculty is content to teach what they refer to as
"descriptive ethics," which acquaints the cadet with a history of
ethical theories. From this it is felt the student will extract those
ethical precepts with which he "feels most comfortable." The problem is immediately obvious in that descriptive ethics fails to develop and systematize a specific code of behavior required of a commissioned officer. Further, no attempt is made to define a code of
ethics which will come to define the "good officer" on the assumption that the individual's sense of integrity will ultimately provide
him with such a code to live with as a military officer. The further
assumption is that a group of officers each secure in his own sense
of personal integrity will, as if by magic, produce a code that is
applicable for the officer corps defined as a community. To be
sure, this is a curious application of the free-market notion of the
invisible guiding hand to the field of ethics!

The fact of the matter is that the moral failures of the officer
corps have only partially been the result of the failure of individual
officers' sense of ethics. *It has been the failure of the Army as an organization to develop an institutional sense of ethics that is supportive of individual notions of integrity and, further, to ensure that individual officers
are trained in a sense of what the ethics of the military institution are.* It is

simply wrong to assume that a collectivity of individual officers with individually derived codes of ethics will automatically produce an ethical code for a community as a whole. Precisely the reverse is likely to obtain. A community sense of ethics can be used to socialize individual members to the community, and it is this process which results in establishing the "price of belonging" so necessary to the cohesion which is characteristic of a corporative institution.

Equally disturbing is the manner in which the West Point code is used by the faculty and staff of the Academy. Indeed, its practice is such as to virtually encourage its violation. For example, each cadet at West Point is subject to a whole host of regulations in addition to the honor code. The point is that a violation of regulations is not necessarily an offense that should involve the honor code. However, in an effort to enforce the innumerable regulations, West Point's faculty and staff have routinely made violations of regulations into honor offenses. Thus cadets are forbidden by regulation to marry while enrolled at the Academy. The recently abandoned practice of making a cadet sign a statement to the effect that he is not married after each return from furlough unnecessarily invoked the honor code when it should not be invoked. Even offenses against minor rules that restrict cadets from certain areas of the campus after a given hour are frequently turned into honor violations when they are, in fact, nothing more than violations of administrative regulations. The point is that by linking routine regulations to the honor code, the faculty and staff have a much easier time of enforcing such regulations while the onus for observance is placed squarely on the cadet rather than on the staff member whose responsibility it is to see that regulations are observed. Virtually any offense can be considered an honor offense, and so frequent is this the case that it has debased the honor code by making it virtually impossible to observe because the situations in which it is held to apply have multiplied beyond reason. In the end, the cadets appear to be behaving as typical entrepreneurs insofar as they conspire among themselves to protect each other from a code whose application has come to be perceived as increasingly capricious.

West Point simply does not prepare the young officer for the kinds of moral choices and situations he may someday have to confront in the field. The major fault of the honor code is not that it sets an impossible standard or that it is outdated; rather, it is irrelevant, for the lessons it teaches do not transfer very well to an Army that has forgone corporative values for entrepreneurial ones. Consequently, this abandonment has led the Army—and West Point—to expect that a group of officers of high levels of personal moral integrity will somehow come to constitute a moral community, namely, an officer corps which has a well-defined sense of ethics and moral values as well as the courage to act upon them. Such a perspective represents an attempt to transform an entrepreneurial organization into a corporative one by allowing the forces of the "moral marketplace" to run unchecked. The attempt is as absurd as is the economics metaphor; its priorities are reversed.

What is clearly required is a code of honor for the officer corps which could become the basis for socializing young officers to its membership. Moreover, the presence of a group of individually moral officers in a milieu that lacks a sense of community morality must inevitably result in situations in which there is little organizational support for individual moral decisions, thus producing irresistible tensions between the press of conscience and the imperatives of career. This is what happened so often in Vietnam. The lessons of that war suggest that only a very few very strong individuals can be expected to withstand this kind of pressure. Most often, in the absence of overt organizational support for what the individual regards as morally imperative action, the most likely course is to avoid his original impulse to do what is right and, eventually, to abandon responsibility to the norms of the organization.[5] In these circumstances the officer as entrepreneur becomes the dominant role model for the young officer, for that is the surest way to survive in the organizational environment in which he must operate.

The failure to abandon the ethics of the entrepreneur and to develop a code of ethics consonant with the nature of corporative institutions has left the Army with an officer corps without any formal organizational sense of ethical guidelines. Whatever ethics exist within the corps is largely rooted in the experiences of the individual *qua* individual and not as a member of a community. Further, there is no place to learn a code of honor, since none exists for the officer corps. The problem is a major one from the practical as well as the moral perspective. An officer confronted with a moral dilemma has only two alternatives: he may resign, or he may acquiesce in the policy to which he objects. If he acquiesces at a high cost to his integrity it does the Army little benefit, for he shuts off the flow of information which may serve to correct policies that may have gone astray. If he resigns, the military has lost an officer of integrity, a commodity which the experience in Vietnam suggests may be in particularly short supply.

If the Army is ever to recover from the debacle of Vietnam, it must first undergo a "moral renaissance," an essential precondition for further operational rebuilding. Among its first priorities must be to ensure that officers develop the capacity to more responsibly balance moral and career considerations. Such a capacity is required at all ranks, but most certainly at the general officer level, where policy is made. Accordingly, it is imperative that the Army develop a doctrine of moral protest for use by the officer corps. It is beyond question that such a doctrine must be consistent with the values of a democratic society and continued civilian control of the military apparatus. Any doctrine violating these basic precepts would be unacceptable and dangerous, and tend to provide the justification for a possible coup d'état.

What, then, are the morally permissible avenues of protest for the military officer consistent with democratic values and civilian control of the military? Are there courses of action an officer may properly take when ordered to execute or acquiesce in policies which he finds morally unacceptable? Four courses seem open, all consistent with the basic precepts already discussed: (1) resign or retire; (2) request for relief in protest; (3) appeal orders to a higher command; and (4) refuse to execute an order. None of these alternatives conflicts with the democratic persuasion. All of them are congruent with the military tradition of Western civilization. Since none is inherently associated with collective resistance, the menace of a coup d'état cannot be associated with any of these alternatives. It is important to observe that the American Army has never developed, nor has it made an effort to develop, any doctrine of moral resistance to immoral or ethically unacceptable orders.[6] It was precisely in this moral vacuum that the exaggerated value of careerism could flourish in Vietnam.

The most obvious way in which a military officer may demonstrate his disagreement with or moral outrage toward official policy is to resign or retire in protest. Further, resignation can be accompanied by a public declaration of the reasons, thus exposing the policy in question to public scrutiny and debate. Such a course of action is perfectly consistent with democratic values and in no way challenges civilian control of the military. Moreover, in a practical way, resignation presents evidence to the "system" that policies may be in serious error. To that extent, resignation may increase system "rationality."

Resignation is almost always a powerful tool when used by a general officer. Indeed, it is the most effective means of protest that a general officer can employ. Since he is likely to be closer to the policy-making level than his subordinates, his resignation can be expected to have the greater impact on policy.[7] At the same time, he is identified in the public mind as a powerful figure whose resignation would have great impact.

Drawing on the doctrine of *respondeat superior*, it may be argued that the general officer, because of his superior position in the authority structure of the Army, has a greater moral obligation to act than a junior officer, simply because his position carries with it a stronger moral charge to see to the welfare of his subordinates and those he has sworn to serve.[8] In any event, resignation or retirement in protest, while surely appropriate for all officers, cannot reasonably be expected to occur in large numbers among the junior officer corps, except in extreme cases. Indeed such an event would be highly dangerous to the whole system. More importantly, the resignation of junior officers, unless done en masse, is likely to have little or no effect on policy.[9] Accordingly, what is needed are other channels of military protest available to the officer below the rank of general.

Although resignations of officers below the general officer rank are not very common or effective under present conditions, the junior officer is still obligated to take action in the face of policies he considers immoral.[10] Accordingly, when confronted with "local" policies or orders which are morally objectionable, an officer must be provided with an option to make a moral choice. Confronted with immoral local policies or orders—shooting prisoners and civilians, burning civilian dwellings, poisoning wells, etc.—an officer should have the option to request formally that he be relieved of participating in such practices and be transferred. Such a formal request should explain why he feels the policies are immoral or illegal. The request, written as well as oral, immediately engages the Army bureaucracy and has the effect of creating a documentary record as well as bringing the case to the attention of superior command and staff. This creates a set of circumstances in which the junior officer has discharged his obligations to himself and to the Army by making improper practices known to his superiors. At the very least, this action reduces the possibility that his superiors can hide behind the doctrine of "plausible denial," a cover story, by claiming that they did not know what was going on in the field. It might be added that the "plausible denial" doctrine, at least implicitly, was the defense pled by Captain Medina and, ultimately, Major General Koster in the My Lai massacre proceedings. It is precisely the doctrine of "plausible denial" which violates *In Re Yamashita* and the responsibility attached inescapably to all commanders under the historical doctrine of *respondeat superior*. Yamashita was hanged not because he ordered atrocities. Indeed the evidence was that General Yamashita had little knowledge of the conduct of his forces at the time and even less control. He was hanged because of the clear application of the ethical principle that a commander is responsible for *everything* his men do or fail to do. We add that this is a principle long applicable to American military custom and practice.

To be sure, not all requests for transfer will be granted. Yet, if the issue raised is truly one of illegality or immorality, our experience with the military bureaucracy suggests the request will not be blocked at the lower levels. Rather, we suspect that in an effort to avoid making a difficult decision, a tendency toward upward "buck-passing" will cause such requests to be rapidly transmitted along the chain of command at least to the general staff level. In any case, the option to request a transfer on the grounds that local policies are immoral or illegal does provide an officer with a viable and feasible mechanism for exercising his moral obligations within the military hierarchy.

The assumption in any military structure, especially one as dedicated to democratic values as our own, is that illegal or immoral orders will not be deliberately issued as a matter of official policy. To be sure, a local commander may overtly or covertly condone and encourage the torturing of prisoners, but such a "policy" is decidedly local and is not the official policy of the Army. This distinction opens up still another avenue an officer may choose in effectuating a moral position for the purpose of changing a practice or policy which he regards as immoral. An officer confronted with a moral dilemma may legitimately take the step of "going over the head" of his superiors as a formal means of protest. Whereas the purpose is clearly to bring immoral orders to the attention of higher authorities in the hope that they will be changed, the implication is that the commander who issued the illegal orders is exceeding his authority by formulating policies or ordering activities which his superiors would not permit *if* they knew about them.[11]

To a minor extent, the military does provide for this alternative through the office of the Inspector General. However, such protests evoke a feeling of disloyalty and are often dealt with in an officious, bureaucratic, and slow manner. If the concerned officer goes to the relevant superior *within* the chain of command, remedial action may take place relatively rapidly. This can be of great importance if the policy objected to is the torturing of prisoners or the shooting of civilians! Some evidence suggests, however, that these remedies are often not pursued because of the compulsion to "team playing." Even so, a determined officer has avenues of redress if he chooses to pay the career price.

We have suggested possible avenues of moral protest available to the military officer and the practical difficulties involved. Yet the difficulty of a given course of action should not obscure the basic point, namely, a moral obligation not discharged in the face of practical difficulties remains no less a moral obligation.[12] There is likely to come a point when the officer has attempted to effect change in other ways ("don't resign, stay in and change the system") or when the practical costs of implementing his moral imperative may become ruinous to his career. Nonetheless, the moral obligation remains.

The ultimate decision that a military officer can make regarding illegal or immoral orders is to refuse to carry them out. Such action is clearly one of last resort, and is based on the assumption that the individual is willing to accept the consequences of his decision *if* it is later judged to have been wrong.[13]

The refusal to carry out an order issued by a legitimate authority is *prima facie* illegal, although not immoral. While refusal to obey is a way to make a moral choice, any refusal to obey an order immediately engages the military's legal structure, namely, the court-martial, in much the same way that the technical violation of a civil law engages the civilian courts, which then become the mechanism for testing the law which was disobeyed. The engagement of the courts-martial system because of an officer's refusal to execute an order he believes to be immoral or illegal provides two opportunities. First, it provides a forum in which the individual may state his moral case in public in an attempt to justify his action. Second, it provides the military structure with the opportunity to evaluate the case and to take appropriate action against the officer who gave the order, if justified. Thus, the court-martial is a two-way street. Like the American legal structure, a court-martial can only respond to a justiciable issue and, again like the civilian legal system, a justiciable issue can only be considered *after* some law or directive has in fact been violated. Viewed in this light, the act of refusing to carry out an order deemed by the individual to be immoral really constitutes an appeal within the military legal structure to higher authority for a judgment on the original order. Refusal becomes the military equivalent of technical disobedience in the service of a higher moral cause. It is not equivalent to cowardice or disloyalty in any *a priori* sense.

Clearly some avenues of protest are more practical than others. Moreover, certain forms of protest carry greater risks. Even so, all the choices outlined above are legitimate in that they are consistent with the dominant values of the democratic polity that the officer swears to serve. Further, they are equally consistent with the military values of "duty-honor-country" when properly understood. The first moral obligation of any officer is to ensure that his conduct and that of his superiors is basically consonant with the values of the society and the constitution that he has sworn to uphold and with the moral constraints of the military system. From that perspective, none of the courses of action available to effect moral protest may be construed as a moral basis for mass disobedience of civilian authority by the military structure. In short, the question of coups d'état drawn on moral lines is placed beyond the scope of the argument.

The principal Western democratic nation, the United States, has been unsuccessful in developing a doctrine concerning the problem of moral protest while other nations have indeed developed a functional ethos of protest within their own armed services. For example, both the British and French Armies have long recognized the right of the military officer to resign in protest and, indeed, he is expected to resign over questions of honor.[14] With respect to the Germans, the mechanisms of moral protest have been preserved in the operation of the Board of Honor (although this "Board" could function as well to discipline officers failing to meet standards of honor) and in some extreme cases, even in the legitimation of suicide as a permissible course of action.[15] The Japanese code of Bushido, which literally required the suicide of an officer who felt himself in moral disagreement with military policy, is too well known to require further elaboration here.[16] To be sure, some of these measures are extreme, while others, such as the French and English examples, are entirely consistent with democratic values. The point is, however, that military structures in other societies have developed functional doctrines of protest for the military officer caught between the demands of conscience and the orders of his superiors.

The widespread behavioral irregularities in Vietnam may be linked to a failure to evolve a mechanism for moral protest. That this failure had serious consequences for the behavior of the officer corps during the Vietnam conflict is beyond question. However, the failure to develop a *formal* doctrine of moral protest is only part of the difficulty. The fact is that formal rules of any bureaucratic structure will be effective only to the extent that they are supported and reinforced by the informal norms and values of that structure.[17] Thus, the moral failures of the American officer corps in Vietnam were possible not only because the officer corps had developed no formalized doctrine of moral guidance, but also because the informal rules of the military subsociety—"don't rock the boat," "it all counts for twenty," "be loyal to your superiors"—would have effectively worked to undercut the operation of any such doctrine. The lack of a traditional code and the emphasis on personal advancement stand in opposition to doctrines requiring the officer to make moral choices. Violation of traditional codes of honor not only paid off in terms of an officer's career, but were in fact demanded by the system itself.

The tension between informal norms serving individual career advancement and any attempt to develop a formalized doctrine of moral protest within the officer corps can be expected to persist even in the face of the most sincere efforts at reform. Even if a formalized code of moral behavior is developed, *the fact remains that informal norms have to be developed and deeply embedded in the military structure so that the officer who exercises his moral prerogatives is not degraded or discriminated against by his peers or superiors.* Members of the officer corps at all ranks must come to realize that the exercise of moral prerogatives is a loyal and moral manner of acting and the means by which careers are advanced. As things now stand, the officer who goes over his commander's head, resigns from the service in protest, or goes to the Inspector General is commonly viewed as "disloyal" or a "quitter." In a very real sense the military has made individual loyalty an absolute, while almost ignoring or even neutralizing the moral commitment the military system requires if it is to be at all cohesive. At the least, such commitment is regarded as damaging to an individual's career. So long as the principal stress is upon individual loyalty and not a higher one, so long as violations of the latter are allowed to remain functional to career advancement, then it is unlikely that any formalized code of behavior relevant to moral resistance will take root.

A formalized doctrine of moral protest within the military structure is not without its opponents, especially regarding resignation and the refusal to execute orders. Concerning the latter, the argument against developing and implementing such a code is simply that if every commander had to explain every order to every officer or at least demonstrate that it was not immoral in order to gain compliance, then the military structure would be paralyzed. The argument is not convincing. Questions of moral choice do not, as a rule, arise frequently. Few orders would have to be justified to subordinates in advance. Indeed, if conditions are such as to provoke a substantial number of officers to demand such justification, this in itself would be a clear indication that the military structure was already breaking down. In a word, if a large number of officers are forced to conclude that certain policies require questioning, then we would be witnessing the symptoms of a disease which in all probability was already terminal.

Resignation as a course of action to effectuate moral protest is most often criticized on the grounds that it amounts to "quitting." Why not, the argument goes, stay within the system and work to bring about change? To the extent that the argument has any merit, it is clearly more applicable to the general officer, whose mere oral disagreement may provoke policy change. To be sure, we can't predict, but available evidence drawn from the past suggests that remaining within the system and trying to change it simply does not work. Consider that during the ten years of the Vietnam conflict, a multitude of individuals faced the problems of moral choice over one policy or another. Yet, since *no one* resigned at the general officer level, we may assume that some men stayed on in order to continue their efforts to change the system. However, it seems clear that for all their efforts little in the way of major policy change was accomplished and the "Vietnam horrors" continued.[18] The conclusion seems clear that the alternative of "working within the system" really begs the moral question since the evidence we have available points overwhelmingly to the fact that such a strategy simply did not work. It seems more probable that the system changed the dissenters!

In assessing the failure of the American military to develop a doctrine of moral protest legitimated for use by its officer corps, it seems clear that one major effect of this failure was the tendency for career functional norms to take precedence over or act as substitutes for moral guidelines in the face of questionable orders and policies. Accordingly, careerism as a value tends to be greatly in evidence, constituting a danger to truly effective military organization and operations. It tends to provoke the worst type of disloyalty under the guise of loyalty, namely, a marked failure to question policy or practices which either don't work (falsification of intelligence reports, search and destroy, etc.) or else extract too high a moral price for their success (bombing rural populations in order to force them into cities as a way of increasing control). What is clearly needed is the development of a formal Army doctrine which teaches officers the accepted avenues of moral protest and encourages them, through the support of informal organizational values, to travel these avenues when urged to do so by the press of personal courage and morality.

The fact that other cultures and military organizations have developed such doctrines to serve the same ends in their armies is proof enough that the task is not an impossible one. We must, of course, always take care to ensure that the pathways of moral protest for the military remain consistent with the democratic values of the polity as a whole and are never allowed to become an excuse for coordinated military action against properly constituted civilian authority. In the end, we are tempted to conclude that we have far less to fear from a coup d'état than we have from a military organization saturated with careerist values. Such an organization can only become increasingly out of touch with the values of the society which it ostensibly serves.[19] Further, it risks disaster for that society and for itself, not through design, but through incompetence.

V

The Specifics
of Reform

Given its performance in Vietnam, a performance characterized by disintegration and a tendency toward collapse, to deny that the Army is in need of fundamental reform is to risk the possibility of future military failure. The danger is that we will learn nothing from our experience in Vietnam and refuse to come to grips with the evidence. Institutional changes, however, rest upon deeper changes in the ambience of an organization, its élan, and sense of mission. The objective of reshaping the background ambience of the Army along traditional lines is to create a military community based on widely shared corporative values. The contemporary Army is rooted deeply in the ethos and practices of the managerial bureaucracy instead of in the "monastic" corporative institution dominated by traditional military values existing apart from its parent society and its dominant commercial ethos. General William Westmoreland, himself the ideal managerial officer, adequately reflected the state of current military values when he was quoted as saying that "good management is good leadership." We submit to the contrary that good management does not necessarily provide good leadership. Good leadership involves good management, to be sure, for a combat leader cannot mismanage his ammunition supplies or other logistical items. However, more importantly, a leader cannot "manage" his men to their deaths, as the evidence from

Vietnam clearly suggests. Good "management" in no sense affords good leadership. Still, the dominant role model evident in the Army today is that of the manager and his attendant values instead of the leader constituted along more traditional lines. The dominant ethic is that of the business corporation, with, it seems to us, the selection process for high position laying far more stress on preparation to manage a corporation rather than to lead men in battle. The practice of senior officers who upon retirement shift almost immediately to defense contractors, is often justified precisely on the grounds that their principal military skills fit them perfectly for adjustment to the values and practices of the modern business corporation.

If experience in the Army, especially at higher levels, is more fit for the boardroom than the command post, then it is this experience that must be altered before successful institutional change can be advanced. If major institutional change is attempted without first changing the value structure, which constitutes the bedrock reform, the persistent informal managerial norms will, in all likelihood, subvert the attempt at changes. In a general sense, the Army must "move back" to being like a "church" and a combative one at that. The heart of the matter is that a successful army centers itself on the values and experiences associated with combat and it must cohere under life-and-death conditions. Little in the way of military cohesion can be achieved unless the men involved have a well-developed sense of responsibility to their fellow soldiers, with leaders regarding their men as moral charges and not as mere steppingstones for upwardly mobile "military managers," "getting their command time in." In a successful military structure, something of the ethos of the legion must permeate and activate the perceptions of individual soldier and officer. It is the sense of the "military way," not tinsel militarism, which is to be stressed and which comes to be expressed as values related to combat risk. Unquestionably, then, the values of the Army cannot be entirely congruent with the values extant in the larger society.

Major institutional changes are usually fiercely resisted in all organizations since reform means a change in both the status quo and the anticipated status quo, each of which guarantees the personal career investments and expectations of large numbers of people, in this case high-ranking officers. It is a fact of political experience, and all armies are political, that when reform is not publicly resisted it is often bureaucratically and covertly sabotaged, so that the shadow of change is often projected while the substance of organizational vested interest remains intact. Elites do not easily relinquish their power, prestige, and income, nor do individuals readily repudiate personal histories. No one who has examined the proliferation of federal agencies, their redundancy, their ineffectiveness, and often their irrelevancy and sometimes malignancy can escape this conclusion. The history of political and governmental reform is not a happy one.[1] Even so, there is also a history of successful military reform upon which the Army might draw for historical support. The Prussian Army reforms of 1815,[2] the British military reforms in the late nineteenth century, the work of Elihu Root, Secretary of War from 1899 to 1904, who reorganized the American Army under general staff principles, are all good examples. Military systems can be changed for the better, although the exact calculus must in each case be worked out. To be sure, where governments tend to centralization and minimize pluralism, reforms can be made more quickly and with less concern for democratic sensitivities. Where a system is irreversibly pluralistic, as in the United States, then military reform is far more problematic, as opponents of change can invoke the support of multiple allies against what to them may be radical shifts in values and authority. Since a substantial reason for the difficulties faced by the Army in Vietnam is traceable to the officer corps, it seems therefore sensible to root suggested change at the threshold in which the officer corps comes to be the primary focus of internal reform. To the extent that this analysis has placed much of the blame for the general institutional malaise of the Army at the feet of the officer corps, reforms in the behavior, attitudes, and ethics of the corps itself will have a beneficial impact upon the Army as a whole. Any attempt at reform which leaves the officer corps unchanged is doomed to failure.

A much-heralded value in the U.S. Army is the concept of command responsibility and its attendant prerogatives. Although the prerogatives are guarded dearly, command responsibility is often avoided or transferred to subordinates when operations go poorly. The concept of command responsibility is, it seems to us, overdrawn insofar as it localizes responsibility in one commander. A somewhat more admirable model can be found in the successful Prussian institution of joint command responsibility placed upon the commanding general and his chief of staff. While this institution is peculiar to Prussia, it does possess that American political quality of checking and balancing while enjoining a moral constraint upon chiefs of staff to restrain any tendencies to irrationality by commanding generals. We suspect that some of the American command failures cited earlier and evidenced in indicators of disintegration might have been avoided or at least minimized had a series of constraining devices been built into the system. One device might have been the concept of joint responsibility operationalized within the context of the American military structure. Another might have been an investigative, prosecutorial element located within the Army and parallel with but not subordinate to the field chain of command. Such an element may have been in the form of an Inspector General divorced from command control except at the secretarial level. Such an institution would be clearly consistent with our larger cultural value of checking and balancing organizational power.

Currently the Inspector General occupies a staff slot, beginning usually at the division echelon. In theory the IG may and is enjoined in a very general sense to investigate command, administrative, and legal irregularities. In practice, however, the IG investigates at command behest or at the behest of ordinary soldiers who feel some grievance deserves redress. Normally grievances are resolved by command action. For common and often trivial abuses the IG, as constituted, appears reasonably adequate. In the matter of serious offenses, especially those involving senior officers, the IG system is quite inadequate for two reasons. First, if the matter is serious enough it may be that powerful interests are at stake such as were evident in the matter of My Lai, the drug traffic, and the "Sergeants' Mafia." Because the resources of the normal IG staff are small, other agencies often take over the case but remain under immediate command control. Second, the IG-assigned officer has the same career interests as his brother officers and is just as susceptible to command pressures. So is it with other investigatory and often prosecutory instruments such as the Criminal Investigation Division (CID) of the Provost Marshal, certain intelligence elements but especially the Counter Intelligence Corps (CIC), and special officer boards for *ad hoc* inquiries. All of these instrumentalities remain, like the IG, embedded in the military command system and cannot be expected to watch critically and correct the system upon which their careers depend. They are, in short, all "on board," all "part of the team."

It is expecting too much to believe that the IG alone can enforce strict adherence to regulations, law, and custom. Neither the IG nor any of the other investigatory and control agencies are free of the career and managerial pressures which, in our judgment, affect the combat performance of the Army. The evidence marshaled from Vietnam suggests that not only were the *Rules of Land Warfare* violated without serious punishment of the offenders (My Lai), but the honored customs and traditions of military service were displaced by managerial entrepreneurialism clearly destructive of military cohesion. Little hope for system change can be placed in the IG or any other military investigatory element as presently constituted. At the same time, it is also doubtful whether direct external civilian interference can force necessary institutional pressures in the sense of a one-time intervention by, say, the Congress. What is required, clearly, is a mechanism charged with overseeing the conduct of the Army and its officers, but which is relatively free from the internally generated pressures which have already crippled the ability of existing watchdog mechanisms to function.

In principle, the concept of an Inspector General is both unexceptionable and essential. In practice, of course, the present system fails as a corrective device for major abuses of position, malfeasance by command and staff, incompetency, misleading and lying reportage, misuse of personnel, or even as a deterrent to war crimes. A casual reading of "The Peers Report"[3] reveals a lack of discipline among troops and officers, incompetent command and staff investigations, false reporting, suborning of perjury, and the art of the cover-up. While the initiatory powers of an Army IG are vague, it seems that if the My Lai investigation had been properly handled under military law and regulation, the American Division IG properly should have rapidly uncovered the circumstances of the crime and recommended immediate prosecution of the offenders. Nothing of the sort took place, and the reason is plain. An Army IG at any point in the chain of command is merely an additional command resource taking his orders from his commander. Furthermore, his career depends on his "reliability" and responsiveness to command requirements. Few if any generals would tolerate an IG who threatened their reputation or their command by speaking the truth.

We believe that the present IG structure needs to be abolished because it simply does not work. In its place we suggest a detached but parallel system of Inspectors General beginning at the division level, with appropriate rank and staff possessing the power to investigate freely; to convene investigating boards outside the command; to relieve temporarily an accused from command and staff position; and to direct prosecution. We stress that no matter of military law, regulation, custom, or accepted tradition related to order, discipline, and military performance would remain beyond the purview of these officers, be the offense criminal or a violation of honor ("conduct unbecoming an officer," resulting in mandatory dismissal). The matter could be one of either complaint by an aggrieved or IG discretionary action unconstrained by command echelon. The sole constraint would become engaged if and when the provisions of the military justice system were invoked. The autonomous IG would watch the honor, integrity, and performance of the Army on a day-to-day basis and serve as a mechanism for supporting those norms, suggested later, which are conducive to unit cohesion.

Since all men appear to be corruptible if only in small ways, existing formal and legal procedures specifying military/judicial due process naturally would remain in effect. Although the object of investigation would not in all cases be permitted knowledge of IG scrutiny—security cases in particular—the usual IG investigation would be as it is now, relatively open within military channels. However, it should be emphasized that the new IG system should be under direct civilian control since the final authority would be the civilian secretary alone, whether Secretary of the Army or Secretary of Defense, depending on the command involved. It is true that the perennial problem of *cuis custodiet ipsos custodiet?* is in perfect terms impossible of solution. But since this is not a counsel of perfection, and the objective is a better, not a perfect, military system, we suggest the potential for abuses in an autonomous IG system can be minimized.

The principal problem is how and from where to recruit Inspectors General. Career officers are not acceptable for obvious reasons. We suggest instead military personnel with a continuing interest in cohesive, effective, and disciplined military forces, but with no personal career investment. Two possibilities come to mind. The first is the pool of retired military officers and former senior non-commissioned officers with extraordinary military and post-retirement records. The second might be a very select group of veterans and reserve officers of singular military and civilian achievements. In all cases the officers and NCO's would be selected for voluntary six-month to two-year tours to be placed into the IG structure at points appropriate to their experience and skills, retaining their retired or former active rank and pay, but no higher. Ideally, no such person would act in organizational parallel with former peers and friends, and preferably would work in a branch different from his original one. None would ever be eligible for promotion, decoration, public citation, or *any* singular honor; they would serve in the anonymity traditional to the German general staff officer.[4]

The selection of these men would be difficult. Possibly a detailed examination of records might reveal men who never lied, who demonstrated genuine creativity during their service, and who stood up for their men. Even persons who might have been a bit eccentric, often getting "poor" efficiency ratings because of their integrity, might be selected. In this regard, one desirable sign might be a bad rating or two for "tact." Above all, one criterion would be the individual's battle experience and performance. Conduct and achievement in post-retirement could also provide indicators. Nomination of potential IG's might also be solicited from peers and subordinates both active and retired but only rarely from former superiors. Of course *no* volunteers would be selected. Within the system itself, any "commanding" IG could be removed by his coresponsible deputy for cause, and both would remain subject to investigation thereafter. Finally, all such IG's would be subject to the Universal Code of Military Justice.

Here then is a group of custodians none of whom is permanent; their assignments could not be self-perpetuating; all final selections after screening would be at random; the men chosen could not be promoted, decorated, or honored; they could not have a career. Such men would have little likely interest in corrupting the system and every likely interest in improving it.

Creating an independent military Inspector General will entail the requirement of widespread military reeducation and training of officers and the troops. Added to this must be the formal injunction to all that in the event of a breach of military law, custom, or tradition for which an inappropriate command action has been taken, or no action has been taken at all, by the responsible commander, then the *failure* to report such a breach to the new IG by persons directly involved might itself be actionable. This same constraint would, of course, apply to the IG group. In a sense they will build upon the honor code of West Point, which, as we know, does not appear to be transmitted to the Army, despite the intense socialization of cadets over a four-year period.

Obviously an autonomous IG is an institutional reform designed to restore traditional propriety in the behavior of officers and NCO's and which could be effected by Army initiative. But since the new IG will doubtless be perceived for some time as an external alternative and possibly even as a threat until cultural adjustments have been made, there is need for another institutional change which is *internal* to the system but which would apply solely to officer conduct. This institutional reform is that of an Army-wide system of honor boards to be employed on an *ad hoc* basis. These boards would not exist except as needed and would have no permanent institutional existence. We do not intend, of course, that in every instance of a violation of a military norm that the IG be called upon to intervene or that an honor board be convened. Indeed, first recourse should always be the immediate superior, but failing that, other internal recourses and resources are essential. Here the honor board appears particularly appropriate. Honor boards have been used for centuries in European military services as watchdogs of officer conduct and, as we know, at the Military Academy itself. At West Point these cadet boards function under the guise of honor boards and as investigating mechanisms. Unfortunately, the tradition of the honor board *as such* appears to stop upon graduation from West Point, with the newly commissioned officer adapting rapidly to the prevailing entrepreneurial norms of the Army structure. We do not visualize a system of Army-wide honor boards as detached from the command network. Rather, the convening of any board for whatever matter would be with the concurrence of the senior commander at the level immediately above that echelon directly concerned with the problem, together with the commander directly concerned. Naturally either of the commanders could deny permission to convene the honor board but would have to consider and risk the alternative of an appeal to the autonomous IG. The honor board rests on the notion of peer judgment and is congruent with older military norms, that is, of officers within a grade or so of the "plaintiff" or the "accused," or both, considering the merits of the issue. An additional safeguard might provide that members of the board could be drawn from units or commands different from those of the immediate parties.

It is doubtful that any request to convene a board of honor would be for trivial reasons, and it is accepted that a great deal of intermediate prudential action would intervene before calling such a board into action. Still, in matters where an officer's integrity or the integrity of a unit is at stake—an unjust efficiency report, orders to falsify reports, mistreatment of enlisted men, clear incompetency so as to endanger a command—honor boards might become a very useful institution.

The honor board might assume semi-judicial functions in that it might find a matter so serious as to request IG intervention; or the findings of the board, say, in the case of a seriously false efficiency rating verging on slander, might recommend court-martial, admonition, or official reprimand of the offender. Also, another aspect suggests itself. In cases where the board finds that the conduct under examination was serious enough to be characterized as "conduct unbecoming an officer," the person found against might well be asked to resign from the service. In this instance, the boards assume the role of an Army reform mechanism appropriately and specifically elaborated to aid the enforcement of an ethical code. Is it too much to suggest that if the honor board system had been in effect during My Lai, together with the autonomous IG, even if the cover-up and false reporting had taken place, *some* officer of integrity and courage might well have demanded a board to inquire into the conduct of Major General Koster? Moreover, it would have been very risky for the higher command to subvert such an effort since this automatically would activate a full-scale IG inquiry. The Army could quickly have cleaned its own house rather than face the years of serious criticism and embarrassment that followed and in fact continue.

Naturally there is more to be said about what code of conduct is to be enforced. The Army, however, lacks a specific code; the brief code of officer conduct cited earlier is far too general. More specific norms are required. But since this chapter deals essentially with the structure of institutional reforms, a later one will suggest a detailed code of ethical behavior.

We have dealt with the destructiveness of the managerial ambience in the officer corps. Historically we know that cohesion is also strongly related to officer stability and that no army to our knowledge has used an "up or out" policy as a permanent feature.of its operational processes. Germany used a variation of such a policy during the Weimar Republic, but only under the duress of Versailles and for reasons not related to careerism. Further, unit cohesion appears directly related to the relative permanence of officers serving in particular combat units. The American Army has created other causes of instability; short overseas tours, excessive military schooling, separations, and extreme rotation policies. Turbulence produced directly by these policies exacerbates a situation which is already disastrous to small-unit cohesion. Worse, the "up or out" pressures place a premium on self-interest translated into careerism. In fact, a long-term stabilized assignment is usually regarded as bad for a career. Much of this has been discussed already, but what has not been observed is the connection between the sheer numbers of officers as they affect cohesion *and* "up or out" as the basis for personnel policies. It seems probable that if the "up or out" policy were set aside, the numbers of officers could conceivably be reduced.[5] Naturally, many officers being retained in grade but not promoted would remain in skilled positions for a protracted period. A variety of fields come to mind, such as intelligence, electronics, vehicular maintenance, helicopter flying, general and special combat elements such as Special Forces and Ranger units, parachute formations, and personnel management. If elimination of "up or out" were coupled with a sizable reduction of about 20 to 30 percent in the officer corps, there might well be substantial financial savings (smaller payrolls and reduced retirement costs), greater stability, slower promotion.

The most important savings rest, however, in the probable increases in military cohesion to the extent that stable long-term leadership directly affects cohesion. As promotion rates must inevitably slow down, so must the passage of officers in and out of key combat formations. Obviously the numbers of officers at various schools at all levels and in the replacement pipeline will decline, with additional savings in school staff and pipeline administrators. An objection that can be raised here is the danger of a static, immobile army with a tendency to a permanent cadre frozen in rank. But surely a balance can be achieved between manic turbulence and immobility of personnel. Performance will be closely watched as a basis of both promotion and the elimination of the unfit. It is difficult to see how the Army benefits by the present extensive turbulence because the costs of unit fragmentation are so high. By lessening turbulence through long-term unit tours, stabilized grades with assured tenure but not promotion, a variety of benefits potentially accrue. Unit replacement of overseas combat elements becomes much more feasible: reduction of the large numbers of dependents in Europe since *unit* tours might be but one year; relative ease in fixing responsibility for unit performance since the excuse of rapid command turnover would be gone. The longest tenure in a combat branch probably should not exceed twenty years. Where forty-year-old captains might not be uncommon, there would be no fifty-year-old company commanders. Similar standards would be easy enough to apply to all ranks.

Another and more serious objection is that the ready replacement pool of officers for war might be so small that battle losses could rapidly outstrip replacement capability. The answer is to raise the quality of the National Guard and the reserves as combat-ready units. Still, even if a major war in Europe developed into a protracted battle of attrition, the chances are that the necessary number of combat leaders could be found, assuming that the Army had adjusted to austere officer manning levels as did the Germans, and if the National Guard and reserves were qualitatively upgraded. We know that a future war as large as the Vietnam War would best be fought with long-term volunteers and professionals operating a Spartan-like field army, which is what the army we have in mind would be in any case. It is important to remember that of almost 600,000 men in Vietnam, only 80,000 were combat troops. In any spartan professional force it should not be impossible to field 100,000 troops—50,000 of which in the theater would be combat elements.

Quite aside from the problem of force manning levels, grade structure, and the inflated number of officers, the principal benefits from eliminating the "up or out" policy are social and psychological. The tendency to be disloyal to peers and subordinates because of competition would certainly be reduced. The pressures of near-frenzied career competition and for advantageous assignments could be minimized; many of the pathologies cited in the Army War College study would be eliminated or would be less severe. Finally, the concept of permanent but nonpromotable status is compatible with both an autonomous IG and with the notion of the honor board in that career aspirations are not preeminent while personal stability, reliability, capability, integrity, and honor are. If we honor the position of professional company commander, we do exactly what the Roman legions did to ensure their own long-term stability. In effect, we create a guild of truly professional small-unit leaders.

The necessity to stabilize the officer corps and to provide an atmosphere supportive of integrity, honor, and professional performance united by a community sense of shared values is self-evident. But the creation of an autonomous Inspector General, elimination of "up or out" policies, and honor boards, however linked in support of unit cohesion, are alone insufficient to restore and maintain a cohesive military system. We know that in World War II the American Army achieved an acceptable level of cohesion traceable to the impact of squad- and platoon-level primary groups but, in our judgment, did not reach levels of cohesion achieved and maintained by the German Army. During the Korean War, U.S. Army unit-cohesion levels contracted to the buddy system, and during Vietnam the level of disintegration was dangerously advanced to the point that the Field Army was possibly without functioning military primary groups. As a factor in disintegration, officer behavior is of course an important element in the process. However, officer behavior is not the sole variable in the disintegration process; and other factors were perhaps of equal importance and must be addressed. This is to say that given the most effective and professional leadership imaginable, if the material of war, the ordinary soldier, must operate within an atmosphere of social uncertainty, turbulence, and unit discontinuity, a high level of cohesiveness remains unachievable. The contemporary system of military training and replacement appears linked to the absence of primary military groups in the Army.

Soldiers in successful armies have historically identified with a single unit during their military lives. Be that unit the XX Valeria Victrix Legion, in Britain for centuries, or the XXI Rapax Legion, or the *Limes* in Germany, or the Irish Guards, all had long-term leadership and long enlisted service. Obviously the U.S. Army will not and cannot repeat the experience of the legions, spending decades and centuries in the same territory with soldiers serving twenty-five-year enlistments; nor will it duplicate the experience of the British, in which regiments served a century or more on the North-West Frontier of India. One important fact from which we can learn, however, is that many of the very cohesive formations in history trained their own men and thus unit identification began at the outset of military service which lasted a lifetime. So, of course, did most of the great British regiments in training and retraining their own recruits, and in many cases the strong German divisions on the Eastern Front in World War II did likewise.

The lesson here is that the prevailing method of recruit training in the American Army, the use of enormous identity-less replacement training centers judged "cost effective" by military managers, does not contribute to combat-unit cohesion to the extent that a unit training system might. The consolidated replacement training center (RTC) is attractive largely to the managerial officer, not to the leader concerned with an integrated unit. In our judgment, the

RTC is destructive of cohesion because it isolates individuals and produces soldiers with no sense of belonging. All successful professional military units are in the end strong social units and it is necessary to create them with care and to treat them with sophistication. To be avoided above all is the mass producing of troops as if they were utensils. Consider the recruit coming into the training pipelines and the problems of identity he faces. Most RTC's are ephemeral and devoid of tradition. Can anyone identify with the Fort Leonard Wood 1st Replacement Training Brigade, Second Battalion, A Company, when the recruit's experience there lasts but eight to twelve weeks and is followed by advanced training somewhere else? These appalling training machines spring up during each mobilizing crisis, usually in inactive, run-down, and remote training camps of World War II vintage. Military lash-ups of this form produce troops like sausages; troops characterized by poor training, doubtful combat skills, and an even more doubtful reliability, if the Vietnam experience tells us anything at all.

To gain some notion of the personnel turbulence to which the forces are subject, some of the data in Table 13 are illuminating. The table notes that in the total defense establishment, circa 1976, of 2.1 million persons, 85 percent experienced a "permanent change of station" (PCS) in one year. This figure does not, of course, include assignments for school or temporary duty at one place or another. For the Army alone, fiscal year 1976 planning accepted a level of 193,000 overseas moves.[6] With a budgeted strength for fiscal 1976 of 785,000, then 24.6 percent of the Army would rotate overseas in one year alone. The cumulative turbulence from this same factor within the Army within the United States would equal at least twice the foregoing percentage, or 49.2 percent. Further indicators of turbulence, specifically in the officer corps, are revealed by the data in Table 14. Approximately 50 percent of the officer corps, the junior officer, is not retained, a situation clearly contributing to turbulence. With the decline in the retention rate of West Point graduates and the higher retention rates of OCS graduates, quantity tends to dilute quality; the same effect is evident in enlisted ranks. The percentage of high-school graduates in the Army in 1966 was 77 percent, but had declined to 54 percent by 1975.[7] Since roughly 20 percent of the Army is separated each year, resulting in a separation-recruitment turbulence of 40 percent, we can sense the extent of the cumulative turbulence from permanent changes of station within the country and overseas, officer separations, and the yearly discharge rate without even having to attempt to estimate the flow of personnel to and from schools and temporary-duty assignments and their effect on stability. That the Army has any stability at all may be illusory as well might be its capacity to fight a protracted land war in Europe or anywhere else. When no one, leaders in particular, is ever anywhere long enough to be effective in the small, then the effectiveness of the entire Army in the large is very much in doubt.

Something better can surely be devised. One alternative is suggested by both British and German experience. In Britain the old formal regimental is a thing of the past. What remains is regimental sentiment. The sentiment is continued because the British regiment is now essentially a training instrumentality. The Black Watch in World War II consisted at one time of over eighty field battalions, almost all trained in the regimental center in Scotland. But at that center, all the regimental panoply, symbols, and customs remained enshrined—centuries of history, battles, and heroism against a staggering variety of enemies. In all fairness the U.S. Army has little hope of replicating this quintessential British style since the old American Army regiments are too long gone and the discontinuity in tradition too great. But extrapolating from the German practice of divisional training centers, we see a possibility appropriate to the American experience. The relatively permanent combat divisions are readily available and some of them have great histories and records of performance. These include the 82nd and 101st airborne divisions, and the famous 3rd Armored Division; some of them with evident stability and continuity. Except for what the managerials will pose as objectionable costs, there is no reason against and every reason for basing all combat training in the division, whether at the actual division site in the United States or at a division training command in-country when the parent division is overseas or in battle. Assuming that the necessary personnel arrangements can be made, which include the rigorous prohibition against trivial personnel transfers, guaranteed assignments for enlistment duration in the same unit, longer-term enlistment, and stability in the leadership elements, a training structure of this nature creates at the outset a core of identity for the newest soldier. Also, with the stabilization of the officer corps, the recruit after training would spend the majority of his time with the same unit *and* leaders. When an officer or soldier was transferred, in most cases temporarily, say to support maneuvers, training exercises, and other activities, he would retain his divisional identification and expect to return to his unit, as the British do. Severe restrictions would control and, in most cases, prevent the assignment to temporary duty of staggering numbers of officers and men; repeated short tours and excessive schooling would be eliminated. The prevalent practice of general officers selecting their own staffs at each assignment or the stripping of combat units for military advisory functions would be prohibited.

We suggest further that uniform standardization in the Army be abolished and division and brigade uniform variations be permitted. Such items as berets, special unit insignia, and perhaps even dress uniforms signifying unit history and experience might be encouraged. While battle dress is of course standard, parade dress and semi-dress admit of many possible variations. There is no reason why armored troops should not wear black berets or that armored cavalry regiments should not be permitted to wear the older cavalry broad-brimmed hat. Unquestionably, many of these symbolic trappings appear childish—and of course they may well be. But we are not concerned with maturity versus adolescence. It may be that war is both primitive and childish, but if one must fight it is best to do so with cohesive and disciplined units, and there is no doubt that a feeling of belonging, pride in one's unit, is historically vital to high cohesion. From the latter stems the building block of cohesion, namely, primary-group identification. This identification takes not only time but protracted professional leadership coupled with appropriate symbolic expressions.

Reduction in both officer and enlisted turbulence tied to a change in training procedures, basing the combat training component in the division, leads logically to a *unit* overseas replacement and rotation policy. It would probably be unnecessary to rotate entire divisions yearly. In case of divisions based in Europe, the division training element, a brigade, together with combat battalions not due for overseas duty, would remain in the United States. For strategic reserve divisions in the United States there is no special problem in the division training its own recruits. It is not suggested that there be permanent overseas divisions, for the good reason that some parts of the Army would never serve overseas. A reasonable policy, it seems to us, would be to set the division tour at three years, at the end of which a division stationed at home would replace it. Still, no battalion would serve more than two years abroad. In any case, there are a variety of rotation options to avoid excessive time out of the country and, concurrently, to remove gradually the mass of dependents in Europe who would create a serious problem in the event of war. Exceptions can and should be made for key staffs, in particular intelligence staffs at Field Army and army group level. But the great bulk of officers and men are not in this category, or at least should not be if staffs can be cut, units and transfers stabilized, and the replacement and training system reformed and first priorities placed on long service with the same unit.

Policies which direct or encourage the frequent rotation of officers through a series of varied assignments must be radically altered. The notion that every lieutenant is a potential chief of staff and, therefore, must have a very wide variety of successive jobs is patent nonsense. Because of the individual rotation of officers, units of assignment become a place from which to get a good efficiency report. Obviously the current rotation policy is considered as the only way to higher rank and the rank of general, to which far too many officers are induced to aspire. In interviews with senior officers, including several general officers, a common observation which emerged was that the frequency of job rotation, coupled with a wide array of assignments, mostly staff and school posts, too often resulted in the promotion of people, to include brigadier and beyond, who were not really prepared for their new jobs. Often efficiency reports, frequently prepared by officers not much better qualified in the first place, had a disproportionate impact upon the selection process. Very little of the Army's performance in Vietnam counters the suggestion here that the "Peter Principle" has run wild. Thousands appear to have been promoted beyond their levels of competence. Surely the indicators of disintegration cited earlier are a fair test of whether the Army had been well led in Vietnam, and the judgment, it seems to us, is not a favorable one. Even more strangely, this high level of turbulence is accompanied by a huge flow of awards and decorations.

Accompanying rapid job shifts has been an inflation of the Army awards system. As it stands, officers rotating out of staffs expect and receive an inordinate number of commendations. The gross swelling of awards and decorations in Vietnam has been noted earlier. We noted that as casualties decreased, awards for *valor* increased, and almost as many Medals of Honor were awarded in Vietnam as in World War II. But even in peacetime, certain awards have increased to the point that men who have never seen battle, nor can probably be expected to, are festooned with varieties of badges, ribbons, and medals often given for the most ordinary of performances. In some cases, service with the Joint Chiefs of Staff or the Department of the Army rates an ornate badge more appropriate to an elderly archduke. Indeed, even the recipients find it difficult to take such awards seriously, referring to at least one such staff award as "The Liver Patch." Why not simply cease giving staff awards and various commendation ribbons and award *no* medals not connected with combat? Another alternative is to require all staff awards to be worn on the right side of the chest, reserving the place of honor over the heart for combat-associated awards. As it stands, most officers connected with higher staff appear to receive an award of one sort or another. By restricting all awards to combat or to rare acts of peacetime bravery, the special importance of battle decorations can be restored. The Israeli Army gives virtually *no* decorations on the grounds that each soldier is expected to perform bravely; special bravery is not to be publicly recognized. Israeli performance, to say the least, does not appear to have suffered.

The problems of the Army are not a seamless web, and it is clear that multiple factors must be applied to the solutions. Parallel to turbulence and an excessive number of officers is the proliferation of staff agencies and the acceleration of promotion rates. An enormous number of officers moving rapidly in and out of an increasing number of staff activities tends to accelerate promotion rates and create a "rank-heavy" military organization. There is an inexorable tendency in any special part of the military bureaucracy that as it waxes in size it operates to obtain "its own general" so that its special interests become represented at the highest level. For example, Military Intelligence in the Army once had no general at all. Then it had one, and now has a major general at Department of the Army level and others at lower levels. Generals by their existence proliferate staffs. It seems plainly foolish that an Army of roughly 785,000 men requires 457 general officers. All these general officer slots generate aides, drivers, often enlisted servants and additional supportive staff. Clearly a reduction in general officers to possibly 200–250 would be a bearable burden for the Army with a consequent change in general-to-enlisted ratios from 1:1,717, as it is now, to 1:3,140, a ratio still far higher than during World War II (see Table 6). Similar reductions should be imposed on the entire officer corps. We have suggested an overall reduction of 20 to 30 percent. At this time (1977) officer strength of total Army strength is 12.5 percent. To reduce this percentage to 6 or 8 percent seems sensible and desirable in the interest of cohesion and discipline. Coupled with stabilization of tours, stress on service in combat units, and lower promotion rates, these reforms should combine to

produce a better professional officer corps if only because lengthened experience in their jobs will better train them for battle. The
psychosis of "ticket punching" might markedly be reduced, since
any officer would have the chance to "fail" briefly and recover,
while a single "failure" today, however trivial, frequently is considered a career disaster. Further, much of the needed reform could
be achieved if anticipated service were lengthened. In other words,
eliminate the twenty-year career as a norm, require thirty years,
possibly combined with contributory retirement. Taken together,
our recommendations will tend to increase professionalism and stability.

With emphasis on the readiness of the Army for battle, no soldier or officer should be exempt from at least two years in a combat
unit: exceptions should be rare indeed. The first duty of any soldier is to master combat skills. More important, the soldier must be
exposed to the atmosphere of the combat unit, not only to build an
awareness of its social context, but to inculcate the ethos of the
legion. Vietnam produced the worst of all military worlds. Far too
many regarded the "grunt," the combat soldier, with contempt or
even ridicule because he was not smart enough to get himself an assignment away from the guns. Even the officers regarded their
combat tours as merely ticket punching, a fact attested to by the
unfair combat rotation policy for officers. One way to restore respect for the combat soldier is to require that the combat unit be
the major environment attending a military career and to allow the
combat soldier the opportunity to *see* his officers in the difficult and
dangerous environment that field service represents.

Without an intensive study of present-day Army schooling for
officers, we can only suggest that it is far too staff-oriented at far
too high a level and only remotely connected with the details of
small-unit combat. Few officers, in our judgment, genuinely comprehend the details and complexities of squad-, platoon-, or company-sized battle. With the stress on staff training, there has been a
deemphasis of the true skills of the soldier. It is a sad commentary
that after officer basic branch school, there are few places where a

young officer can learn the art of war. Indeed, this peculiarity of technical and staff training detached from the realities of battle has been a long tradition in the American Army, where only since 1924 have terrain models been used for tactical instruction, even though the Romans used them commonly centuries ago. Existing command and staff schools do not so much teach battle tactics or even command so much as they focus on the art of bureaucratic staff control and manipulation, namely, "management." To be specific, any officer at any level should be well versed in the detailed technique of conducting a squad, platoon, or company combined-arms assault or defense with thorough knowledge of weapons, new techniques, and communications and to do so on any terrain anywhere in the world, to include desert, mountain, tundra, steppe, city, or jungle. We suspect that very few officers, in fact, could meet such a demand and, moreover, that this incapacity increases with rank.

The schooling system should be changed to include the "tactical walk" first practiced by the Prussian officer corps. Officers would be posted in some area for a year and required to solve a series of posed tactical problems. At the end of the "tactical walk" and after the submission of a written report, a detailed written and oral examination would be given. Some of the tactical walks would serve as ongoing analyses and critiques of existing forward deployments and war plans. Complementing the tactical walk would be frequent but brief attendance at combat schools stressing small-unit combat, new and old techniques, and new weaponry. We realize, of course, that staff officers are essential to modern operations, but certainly not in their present numbers. Obviously a number of staff specialty schools are needed, but emphasis should be placed on schools with priority given to combat at battalion and lower echelons. Further, these schools should stress refresher courses in small-unit battle for *all* ranks. Additionally, there is good reason to institute a series of examinations, either at the time of promotion or every two years or so, to determine if the officer is keeping pace with modern battle techniques. (How many generals today really understand the capabilities and limits of the modern tank, American or Soviet?) Requalification testing would apply to *all* ranks, generals not exempted, and specialties, even those officers who elect to pursue a career as a "professional" staff officer, say, in intelligence or logistics. The intent of all this is not, of course, merely to ensure the largest number of leaders possible with high combat skills, but to reinforce the fact that the basic task of the Army is combat. One proposition already put forth is that the Army has far too many officers and certainly far too many senior ones. If it is essential that the officer corps be reduced by 20 to 30 percent, much greater emphasis must be placed on combat skills if the Army is to function as a cohesive organization when placed under combat stress.

With emphasis on combat-unit assignment, competitive pressures will rise; but all officers cannot command combat units because such commands will be long-term. The problem is one of selection. We can find no research that provides a psychological profile of the good combat leader. Behavioral research is needed and we suspect that the state of the art does indeed permit the construction of such a profile. Still, lacking the profile, to reduce pressures for ticket punching in a reformed system, certain institutional changes can be initiated. Since all combat command assignments should be for relatively protracted periods, and since command at company or battalion level will in no way assure promotion (the Army War College study suggests an additional officer grade be created to be called senior captain—a permanent company commander), competition for these slots might not be all that intense. In fact, successful company command might last five years or more, thus reducing upward mobility across the board. In any event, promotion would be based on multiple factors, not merely command time, but combat potential, together with initiative, creativity, and integrity. Another way to reduce instability would be to prohibit the "nominating" of officers for assignment or the request for specific individuals by generals for their staffs or combat units in their divisions.

Promotion selection itself might well be broadened by rank peer ratings directed from the Department of the Army, particularly for colonels selected for brigadier general. All colonels on a promotion list would be rated by their grade peers. Other procedures would simplify separation of officers; retired officers would be selected for promotion and separation boards by the same standards we have suggested for selecting the autonomous Inspector General; this practice would reduce the amount of quantification on readiness reporting and efficiency reports, and move to a "pass/fail standard" of judgment; each decision would be fully justified by detailed written assessment and, of course, strict enforcement of an "Officer's Code." [8]

A clear case seems to exist for a thoroughgoing military reform in the United States Army. Without this reform, we believe the pathologies exhibited during the last years of the Vietnam War may, in all likelihood will, continue to characterize any future period of combat stress. In fact, disciplinary problems continue to persist in Europe, not the least of which is drug use and indiscipline. To attempt to reform the Army by exhortation, to pay lip service to military ideals will not suffice. The very conditions which led to the Army War College study have not, in our judgment, been corrected. Universal managerialism, obsessive careerism, "up or out," high levels of personal turbulence, tremendous overburdens of administrative staffs, excessive numbers of poor officers and far too many senior officers, competent or not, still persist. Unless these conditions are changed, the ability of the Army to fight successfully will be in grave doubt.

Pathological signs of inability to make far-reaching changes persist in the Army as late as summer 1977. The idea of "up or out" was defended before the Congress earlier in the year, and was this spring justified on the grounds that this policy encourages the "hard charger," the careerist. In effect, collectors of "max" efficiency reports. Certainly the "hardest" of chargers would be the generals. In a recent survey of general officers, Douglas Kinnard, Brigadier General, U.S.A. Retired, interviewed 173 generals who served in Vietnam during the war (a parenthetical note in the *Wash-*

ington Post observes that General Kinnard "planned the Cambodian invasion"). Of the general-officer sample, 61 percent stated that the body counts were grossly exaggerated (how the exaggeration was achieved is not clear—was the body count correct in absolute numbers but not in terms of combatants?); 25 percent of the respondents said too much close air and fire support was employed; and 28 percent of the generals said that "the results of the war 'were not worth the effort.' " Over half of the generals faulted the search-and-destroy missions, and 70 percent stated that "Washington ran the war badly." Asked why the generals had not spoken out on this issue during the war, Kinnard, now a professor of political science at the University of Vermont, said: "The only thing I can think of is careerism. And I think there was a great deal of that at every level." General Kinnard, a military-academy graduate, began his survey in late 1974 and received replies from 64 percent of the generals, or some 110 generals. This represents over 20 percent of the approximately 500 general officers on active duty at the time. Since only three years have passed since Kinnard's survey, it must be assumed that careerist attitudes persist in the Army and that they remain essentially unchanged since Vietnam.[9]

One important indication of the Army's ability to resist change can be found in a statement by the Army Chief of Staff, General Bernard Rogers, directing that all regulations which suggest the lack of officer integrity (excessive certification of truthfulness in reports, countersigning of readiness statements) should be expunged. General Rogers was quoted in July 1977 as saying that there was no need for special officer codes and creeds. We must presume that the Army (and Rogers is Chief of Staff) still clings to the belief that honor and traditional behavior will automatically lead to an intuitive sense of right military conduct.[10]

Concern about the Army's battle readiness has also been expressed. In June 1977 the General Accounting office expressed strong doubts that the stateside divisions were fully ready for deployment overseas. The General Accounting office believed that the basic reporting system, the Readiness Report, did not provide an accurate assessment of the combat potential of the Army.[11] Truth-in-readiness reporting can be quickly career destructive.

If careerism is still pervasive, particularly in the higher ranks, nothing in the available data shows an effort to reduce careerists in the officer corps. At the end of fiscal year 1977 (30 June 1977), officers constituted 12.4 percent of the 784,600 men and women in the U.S. Army. The number of programming permanent changes of station of this force in fiscal year 1977 is 693,000; 88 percent of the Army will move in a twelve-month period.[12] This level of turbulence must be destructive of cohesion. Such fluid units cannot be expected to perform well even under the relatively mild stresses of peacetime training and maneuver. In one case during 1977, a NATO tank crew competition was held. Tank crews from most NATO nations competed at the British training center in Sennelager, West Germany. The American crew placed last and, prior to the NATO competition, apparently had not qualified on their *own* tank-crew proficiency course.

One important dimension must be added—the racial one. The following is from the Army's own paper: "The racial composition of the Army, and in particular its combat forces, is greatly unbalanced by heavy black soldier reenlistment. While this was probably brought about by an open volunteer force, depressed economic circumstances among black youth, and greater opportunities in the Army for blacks compared to the 'outside,' the result is a disproportionate number of blacks in the line units. Blacks, who constitute some 12 percent of the total population, have gone from 18.4 percent of enlisted strength in fiscal year 1973 to 25.5 percent in fiscal year 1977. However, '. . . four of the Army's 16 divisions and two separate brigades have black strengths exceeding 30 percent. The remaining 12 active Army divisions have black strengths totaling about 25 percent. The 197th Inf Bde [sic] at Fort Benning, Ga., continues to have the Army's highest percentage of blacks, 41.6 percent . . .'* Any future war will at the outset engage the

---

*The Army Times, September 5, 1977, p. 12.

Army as it stands. Casualties will be heavy and the burden borne by black soldiers will be massively disproportionate to their numbers in the society at large. The question arises as to how the black soldier will perceive his share of death and wounds when far more blacks in the immediate fighting units die than white soldiers. We can only speculate here, but the effect cannot be favorable to military cohesion over any length of time."

Stability, effectiveness, discipline, training, dedication, and overall efficiency are the announced doctrine and goals of the Army. The 1976 Army Budget Hearings before the House Subcommittee of the Committee on Appropriations provides verbatim testimony by the Secretary of the Army, Howard H. Callaway, and the Chief of Staff, General Frederick C. Weyand, that the Army has changed and improved in most respects, and certainly with respect to training and discipline.[13] The tragic fact is that little is provided by this testimony to substantiate the claims of improvement. Under ordinary circumstances, claims concerning military order, discipline, and esprit would be accepted. But since Vietnam, claims by Army leaders must be suspect, and more so given the present analysis. But what is more suspect is that virtually no institutional changes have been undertaken to reverse those internal organizational conditions which, as they did in Vietnam, lead to military disintegration. Any Army claim to "change for the better" must be treated with strong doubt, especially since *any* land war in Europe will be intense by many orders of magnitude beyond Vietnam. Ultimately, the intent of reform is to improve military professionalism. The object is a military community structured with and dominated by traditional military values and behavior. Measured by these goals, the search for honor goes on.

VI

Effecting Change
in Military Values

The loss of traditional military cohesion seems closely connected to
the transformation of the American military from a *corporative* bureaucratic structure into a largely *entrepreneurial* one. If the officer
corps is to return to its traditional role of contributing to cohesion,
there must be a change of values away from those rooted in the entrepreneurial ethos to those typical of corporative, quasi-monastic
institutions. How, then, do military institutions change their values? How do they adopt new ones; how do these variables affect
behavior? What are the variables involved in the process? Can a
model be developed that may, perhaps, be used as a guide to policy? Obviously crucial to an understanding of how military bureaucracies adopt and inculcate new values is an understanding of the
differences between entrepreneurial and corporative bureaucratic
structures. The argument swings on the proposition that the military must model itself on the corporative structure if cohesion is to
be achieved and that the officer corps in particular must return to
the values inherent in this model if it is to play the positive role
that it has traditionally played in contributing to the overall cohesion of the military institution. How, then, do entrepreneurial and
corporative bureaucracies differ; and what is it about military institutions that makes them markedly different from the business cor-

poration which has served so often as a model for American organizational development since World War II?

One of the clearest differences between the two models of bureaucracy is the doctrine of rationality.[1] The doctrine of economic rationality requires that entrepreneurial bureaucracies be "rational" in that norms and values are perceived to have worth only in terms of the "products" produced by the organization. Corporative bureaucracies, on the other hand, often develop operating procedures and norms that are "arational" in that they come to be valued for themselves far more than for the contribution they make to the product. Thus, honor codes, medals, and parades in the military or the ritual and ceremony of the monastery are valued in themselves. To the extent that traditions operate in entrepreneurial bureaucracies, they must be continually and demonstrably functional in the rational sense;[2] in corporative bureaucracies, such traditions come to have an independent value.[3]

Entrepreneurial bureaucracies classically stress the ethics of self-interest both in an organizational and individual sense,[4] the latter being relied upon to motivate the individual to desired modes of behavior. Corporative bureaucracies, by contrast, stress an ethic of community interest. Accordingly, individuals work in an entrepreneurial bureaucracy because it is in their perceived self-interest (usually material) to do so, that is, to earn money, rewards, prestige, larger offices, etc. To the extent that corporative bureaucracies stress "self-interest" at all, they suggest that it can only be attained through serving the community. An ethic of community obligation or community service supplants rapacious individual laissez-faire or uncontrolled free enterprise.

The entrepreneurial bureaucracy denigrates nonmaterial rewards as being destructive of individual initiative, which, it is feared, may become submerged in a sense of community identification. Accordingly, the "logic of profit" is extended to include organizational norms intended to stimulate individual advancement and initiative. Here the contrast with the corporative bureaucracy is most marked. Corporative bureaucracies have a tendency to define rewards in psychic and ritualistic terms most specifically expressed as a recognition of contributions made by the individual to the community of which he is a member. For example, the presentation of a Medal of Honor is usually made with much ceremony and pomp. It is a recognition of a contribution to one's comrades. The recognition is itself the reward. The material aspects are either absent or insignificant. Accordingly, the role of psychological and ritualistic rewards tends to be much larger in corporative bureaucracies than in entrepreneurial ones, the latter tending to stress rewards which are largely material and highly transferable.[5]

There is another important difference. Corporative bureaucracies rely much more heavily upon "higher code" justifications for developing organizational norms and compelling individual behavior. The stress on higher code justifications within corporative bureaucracies leads them to place greater emphasis upon "values" as opposed to "interests" to motivate individual behavior.[6] It is expected, of course, that such values—defined mostly in nonmaterial terms—will become internalized to a great extent and thus compel acceptable behavior. Clearly, in corporative bureaucracies such as the officer corps, one is expected to behave in a manner which is consistent with given accepted values but which would be regarded by the entrepreneur as highly counterproductive in that material self-interest is not served.

A final point of comparison between the two bureaucracies has to do with the means of compelling acceptable behavior. In entrepreneurial structures, the means of compelling conformity are immediately available and quickly operative; in corporative structures the means are usually remote and slow to operate. Thus, in an entrepreneurial bureaucracy a superior can usually dismiss a subordinate on the spot, deny a promotion, or hold up a raise. In corporative structures, these powers are diffused, sometimes even throughout the entire community. Accordingly, when it comes to compelling acceptable behavior, corporative structures tend to rely on indirect means such as peer pressure, internalized norms, values, etc. Indeed, because the motivational incentives are internalized, the need for formal, rapid means of enforcing conformity are considerably less in corporative bureaucracies.

The preceding distinctions represent two bureaucratic models, the corporative and the entrepreneurial. If one were to imagine a continuum with the entrepreneurial model at one pole and the corporative model at the other, a successful military institution would be placed at a point on the continuum to the right of the center line approaching the corporative model. A "successful" military institution is defined here as one displaying a high degree of cohesion under conditions of high combat stress. The Israeli Army comes immediately to mind as an excellent example of extraordinary cohesion. To be sure, the American military structure, like all military bureaucracies, is a mixture of both models. Nonetheless, we believe that successful military organizations more closely approximate corporative structures. Military organizations are simply not analogous to the modern business corporation. It strikes us that the argument that the development of modern technology requires the adoption of modern entrepreneurial mechanisms of management is an empty one. For their time, both the Roman and German Armies were marvels of technology and yet maintained high levels of corporative cohesion. Technology per se compels nothing—certainly not an impetus to ape the modern bureaucratic entrepreneur.

In general, the modern business bureaucracy (an entrepreneurial bureaucracy) develops administrative ideologies which are basically *secular* in nature and rooted in economic values. Corporative values are subordinated to concepts of "self-interest" and "profit." Corporative bureaucracies, on the other hand, develop administrative ideologies which are patently *communal*. The stress is placed upon community obligations, norms of service, higher code justifications, and internalized values subjectively defined in terms of psychic and ritualistic rewards as the primary means of defining and motivating organizational and individual behavior. These two models develop very different standards of acceptable behavior. The difficulty arises, of course, when an organization whose effectiveness depends upon its remaining corporative begins to imitate the practices of an entrepreneurial bureaucracy.[7] This process is well under way in the American Army, and the Vietnam experience may simply have exacerbated a tendency which really began during World War II. If a military system modeled on corporative lines is a precondition for rebuilding and maintaining unit cohesion, the question is: "*How* does one get an institution to accept new values or adjust old ones in order to achieve what is seen as a desirable form of behavior?"

Very little in the way of theory has been developed which addresses the problem. Indeed, what "change models" we do have are heavily rooted in the ethos of the entrepreneurial bureaucracy, which we have already argued to be inappropriate.[8] Thus, the need for a new theoretical approach is clear. We hope that the model put forth here will aid in constructing a theory and also provide some insights which heretofore may have been obscured by the marked tendency to adopt entrepreneurial solutions to corporative problems.

The difficulty may be stated simply. How do we get an existing organization to adopt new values and to make these values take root? How is this to be accomplished in military bureaucracies in general and in the officer corps in particular? The terms of the problem require further clarification. The military bureaucracy is more a corporative than an entrepreneurial entity, with all that implies in terms of the characteristics and limits upon individual behavior. Military bureaucracies are institutions which are "value-infused"[9] as opposed to organizations which are only instrumentalities for marshaling human energy to accomplish a given task. As institutions, they have a "history," which has established a heavy investment in existing practices, norms, and values. To the extent that any proposed change in values runs counter to the history and values of the institution, the more difficult will it be for the new value or policy to take root and gain internal support and compliance. Finally, there is a distinction between the adoption of totally new values and the adoption of latent and cognate values. Latent values are those which enjoy the support of the bureaucracy but which do not compel individual behavior;[10] cognate values are those which can be directly deduced from existing values. The point is that institutional resistance to new values is likely to be greater than to latent and cognate values. With the latter, it may only be a matter of making already acceptable and publicly supported values operative. Given these few preliminary distinctions, what factors play a role in the process of adopting new values in military bureaucracies?

Among the most important variables in the value-change process is the extent of open, formal, and forceful support which must be forthcoming from the elites positioned at the highest levels within the corporative structure.[11] In a military bureaucracy, the highest levels of command and staff must marshal the full force of their authority and prestige behind the adoption of a new value. Failure to do so will result in the lower ranks being unclear as to what behavior their superiors expect.[12] Additionally, open support of high-ranking officers within a corporative bureaucracy serves the important purpose of formally clarifying changes in policy, thus removing as much ambiguity as possible as to what behavior is expected among subordinate levels of the bureaucracy.

While active elite support of new values is clearly important, it is probably more important that military elites charged with initiating and overseeing the transmission of new values share such values. Above all, they must publicly support the new value. Since the lower ranks of the bureaucracy, especially the officer corps, observe elite behavior, the effect of elite conformity to these values cannot be overestimated.[13]

The problem is how to "convert" the elite to the new values when, at the outset, the very success of their careers has been predicated on their ability to internalize and behave in accordance with the very values which are being supplanted. Clearly this presents a major difficulty. Two solutions come to mind. In the first instance, pressure can be brought to bear from outside authorities upon which the initial bureaucracy is dependent and with which it must interact.[14] While more will be said of this later, suffice it to say that legal and political directives may be issued by congressional or presidential authority requiring support for new values. However, the most direct way of ensuring elite support is simply to remove those elites who do not support the new values and replace them with new elites whose position is predicated upon such support. This practice of "circulation of elites" is hardly a new one to the American Army, especially when promotion to general officer often requires that one be "on the right side" of some policy debate. Further, this process of "accelerated circulation" of elites is very common to the military structures of under-developed countries and even some highly developed ones.[15] It might be added that such a practice would have the additional effect of reinforcing the perceptions of lower-ranking officers that the institution means to enforce new values.

We also suggest the use of strong ethical indoctrination programs at all ranks. Such programs must be particularly strong at the entrance level, for it is the young officers who can be expected to carry the new values throughout their careers and to eventually internalize them, so that they become part of their personal and organizational codes. Middle- and upper-tier officers could be "reeducated" with series of seminars, although how much real change can be expected through this process is unclear. The key point, however, is that the indoctrination of junior officers at the entrance level will place limits upon the behavior of senior officers. Faced with a junior officer corps indoctrinated in a clear "code of honor" (read: new values), existing military elites are less likely to violate this code because of the serious risks of exposure.[16] To be sure, this requires that the military be prepared to develop and observe such codes of behavior, which entails a return to the corporative ethos and a move away from the ethos of the modern business corporation.

Change won't take place unless there is strong support for new values evident within the informal groups in the bureaucracy.[17] In practical terms, this suggests that there is a strong necessity for peer support at all ranks for the new values. Such support will, of course, take time to materialize but it should be rooted in a common indoctrination experience and, as the organization develops, in the realization that observing the new values is essential to a successful career. Without peer-group support, especially in the lower ranks of the officer corps, few individuals can be expected to stand alone in support of new values.[18]

Important to the success of new values is the officer's perception that he is a member of a community. The individual officer must perceive a link between supporting the new value and the behavior it compels: to advance both his "self-interest" and the military community as a whole.[19] It is important to stress that the "self-interest" of the individual officer is not limited to personal advancement. The assumption is that there is a whole range of goals relevant to and supported by the military community that transcend the crass careerism of the military entrepreneur. Here the concept of "self-interest" really translates as "communal values" in that the individual officer perceives that the observance of new values will be congruent with the sense of communal identification basic to all corporative structures.[20] Enforcement of new values must also consistently demonstrate to the members of the officer corps that such values and their concomitant behavior strengthen communal and integrative links with one's peers and superiors.

Also relevant to the extent to which new values will take hold is the fact that the experience of the individual officer, both personal and anecdotal, must demonstrate that new values and their implied behavior are functional to career advancement and survival within the institution.[21] Official support in terms of public rewards and sanctions must be consistent with new values. If official rewards and punishments are not constantly and consistently marshaled in support of the desired behavior, then newly adopted values will be gradually weakened. While lip service will be paid to such values, their effect on behavior will be minimal or sporadic. In either case, deep behavioral change will not result.

It seems clear that, in a democracy at least, bureaucracies respond most rapidly when pressured from the outside.[22] This is especially the case when pressure is brought to bear by bureaucracies that are legally superior to it and which have the means of enforcing compliance. Both the Presidency and the Congress are good examples of such institutions. New values are more likely to take root *within* the military if strong *external* support for them can be brought to bear. Perhaps it is unfair to expect total "in-house" reforms. What may be required are externally generated norms (laws?) which clearly require some types of behavior and forbid others. Such external pressure would go a long way in supporting those within the military who wish to adopt new values.[23]

The final and in some ways the most important factor in the process is time. The transformation of an organization into an institution is a slow process. This transformation is, among other things, a function of the adjustments that the organization makes to its own experiences. The organization's experiences have created a "history," which in turn affects the way in which its members perceive their world. It is this history which must be overcome if the introduction of new values is to be successful. Further, this history can only be less influential when the experiences which result from the adoption and application of new values are sufficient to provide the experimental base for the development of a "new history." The critical element is time. Thus, it is unrealistic to expect new values to "take hold" immediately. Rather, one must look for the gradual transmission and inculcation of new values against the background of the passage of time; time constitutes a major influence in any proposed change.

What we have attempted to do is to identify those factors or variables which we suspect are important to developing a model of value change in a military bureaucracy. There are eight of these: (1) overt elite support, (2) elite conversion, (3) indoctrination, (4) peer support, (5) perceptions of communal interest, (6) functional linking of behavior to career survival, (7) external support, and (8) time. The list, however, does not show how the variables are connected in terms of a sequence of interactions. We must fit the variables into a model and develop a preliminary paradigm which specifies the rules of interaction among the variables within the model.

Our model must suggest how a military bureaucracy will come to adopt new values. Models are often confused with theories and both with explanations.[24] A model is a simplification of reality; it attempts to provide insights into a problem by removing much of the complexity attendant on the empirical situation. Accordingly, a model is an approximation of reality and does not represent empirical reality.[25]

Our model proceeds from the following basic proposition:[26] any stimulus will produce a response only after that stimulus has been "interpreted" by the organism or actor which is expected to behave. The behaviorist approach is rejected in favor of the more general and accurate behavioralist orientation.[27] As a result, it becomes necessary to identify the variables responsible to understand how the actor interprets the stimuli to which he is exposed and is expected to respond.

Once this basic orientation is understood, the terms of the model are comprehensible. The "stimulus" is really the new value which the bureaucracy seeks to adopt and transmit. The value itself takes on the character of a stimulus only to the extent that it is formulated as a policy to which the system may react. The "actor" is the individual officer confronted with the problem of modifying his behavior in light of new policy formulated by the bureaucracy. The response variable is self-explanatory in that it represents the overt behavior which we expect the actor to adopt if the system works successfully. A further dimension of response is accomplished over time, that is, reinforcing behavior leads formally to a systems change insofar as new values now become productive of the kind of behavior that was desired to begin with. The model appears in graphic form in Figure 1 (in the Appendix). Clearly the model describes a process, and what remains is to detail the interactions which are expected to occur among the variables.

The model assumes that the value change will be expressed in terms of a formal policy promulgated by top bureaucratic elites. Critical, of course, is the strength of the stimulus. It seems clear that stimulus strength depends on three sub-variables: elite conversion, external support, and authority support. Elite conversion to new values can be accomplished either through indoctrination or by replacing some of the old elites with new ones.[28] No policy of either elite conversion or replacement can occur without external support. Thus, another factor entering into the strength of the stimulus is the extent to which outside legal and political pressure is brought to bear upon the bureaucracy to adopt and transmit new values. Together, external support and elite conversion produce the third variable, authority support. An elite convinced of new values and supported by external centers of influence is likely to produce formal and open support for them; and this support, all other things equal, will extend throughout the bureaucratic structure.[29]

It seems clear that the extent to which top levels of the bureaucratic hierarchy can be relied upon to continue support for new values over time depends upon the degree to which they perceive the new values to be producing the kinds of effects that they define as useful. In line with the premises of the model, as time passes accumulated experience transforms itself into a "history" supportive of new values.[30] As a supportive experience grows, the process of internalizing new values and their concomitant behavior begin to emerge. This results in the absorption of these values into the administrative ideology, so that modification of the institution's value structure begins to occur.

The model assumes that no official policy will truly produce lasting behavioral results unless the individual military officer "interprets" such policies correctly. Correct interpretation implies that the officer perceives new values as "right" and worthy of his support. In time, he will internalize the values. As specified in Figure 1, the actor in the model will begin to correctly interpret new values largely as a result of four sub-variables: indoctrination, career functionalism, peer support, and communal identification.

Within an existing institution, the actor must first be exposed to the new values that he is expected to observe. In this regard, indoctrination becomes the first active variable in the system in that it is through this process that the individual officer is made aware of the desire of the hierarchy to introduce new values.[31] Indoctrination communicates to the individual and his peers just what kind of behavior is expected by the institution. Accordingly, it allows the officer to begin to restructure his reward-punishment calculus as a guide for future action.[32] It cannot be stressed too strongly that institutions which seek to introduce new codes of behavior must make certain that such codes are unambiguously clear at all levels of the bureaucracy, if any chance of success is to be expected. This includes an unambiguous officer's code.

Once the actor has been made aware of new values and the behavior expected, it is highly probable that he will begin to assess the new code in terms of how helpful it is likely to be for his career. Since he will have no pertinent history upon which to draw in formulating his estimates, he will initially be forced to rely heavily on demonstrated elite support and their public actions to provide him with cues as to how he himself must behave. The individual officer will remain cautious until his own experiences provide him with sufficient evidence to begin making his own judgments as to the career value of one course of action over another. Much of the success or failure of adopting new values will depend upon the ability of the military hierarchy through word and deed to convince the individual officer that it is sincere about rewarding behavior consistent with expressed values. Elite hypocrisy or any evidence of a double standard will quickly be perceived as such by the individual officer, who will adjust his behavior accordingly, in which case the process of value change will likely fail.

Once aware of a new code and once reasonably convinced that the military hierarchy is sincere in its efforts to transmit new values throughout the bureaucracy, the individual officer must now make such cues operative on a day-to-day basis. It is here that observance or noncompliance will be encountered. Critical to the individual officer's willingness and ability to comply with new values is the degree of peer support that he receives. As the individual officer perceives that his peers share his values and are willing to support him, he will likely comply with the new code. The value of peer support cannot be overstated. As a member of a corporative bureaucracy, heavy reliance is necessarily placed upon identification with and recognition by one's peers virtually as a means of identifying what one's "self" truly is. Isolated from peer support, few individual officers can be expected to comply with a value promulgated by the military hierarchy but which goes unsupported by one's brother officers in the day-to-day business of living and working together.[33]

Once the individual officer is convinced that the values he is expected to maintain are supported by the military hierarchy and are shared and observed by his peers, the internalization of that value and its concomitant behavior are required as a means of establishing a psychic sense of communal identification with the institution to which he belongs. In short, the individual officer begins to identify with the values and codes that he and his brother officers, but especially his superiors, share. Such values and codes of behavior make him, in effect, what he is, just as the codes and values of a monastic order define what a monk is. Clearly, this sense of communal identification is the mark of an officer who is the very antithesis of the military entrepreneur, and the institution which requires and supports such identification is most certainly not an entrepreneurial bureaucracy but a corporative one.

The response element of the model can be expected to occur with reasonable certainty once the specified conditions are met; to wit, it is reasonable to expect that some value change is occurring. However, it must be stressed that the variables identified here will be assessed by the actor insofar as the effects which they produce over time reasonably support new values. As both personal and organizational experiences are perceived as reinforcing new values, the variables which produce it will in time sustain the new code. To the extent that the elements of the model perform correctly, a qualitative systems change may be anticipated to incorporate the new codes of behavior into the official administrative ideology of the bureaucratic institution. Obviously the speed and depth of change will be largely a function of the extent to which historical reaction to the effects of observing the code produces a reinforcing experience for the individual officer and, collectively, for the institution as a whole.[34]

The model is offered because there appears to be a significant lack of attention to the problem insofar as it relates to the military. This is not to suggest that the literature is totally devoid of "change models." Rather, change models that have been developed to aid in our understanding of value change are by and large not very relevant to military bureaucracies. Indeed, as we have asserted, existing models draw far too heavily upon the entrepreneurial ethos and experience. Such models are not applicable to the military bureaucracy.

The reliance upon entrepreneurial models has led scholars and policy makers to overlook a basic fact: successful military bureaucracies are basically corporative in nature and, indeed, whenever a military institution begins to show signs of adopting entrepreneurial ethics or practices such signs are to be taken as indications of an undesirable change. Again it is stressed that the elements which make for cohesion and success in a corporative military bureaucracy are virtually the antithesis of those elements which bind the individual to the business-entrepreneurial organization. The variables which are important in stimulating behavior required of officers in a military institution are categorically different from those which motivate the business executive. Current terminology notwithstanding, military officers are not "middle-tier managers"; nor can they ever be if the military institution is to be truly successful.

It would be naïve to maintain that the American military bureaucracy in general and the officer corps in particular have not manifested, in at least some instances over the last decade, the values and ethics of the entrepreneurial bureaucracy. Indeed, even much of the terminology has been adopted *in toto*. The Vietnam experience did not cause such a shift away from the corporative model; it merely accelerated it and brought to public attention a change that had been under way for many years. Whatever the cause or causes, it seems clear that the American military and its officer corps must begin to undertake a serious self-reevaluation in order to search for ways to return to the communal ethics characteristic of corporative institutions. The "officer as entrepreneur" must be replaced and the emphasis on careerism abandoned. To this end, our model offers some suggestions as to how this may be accomplished.

VII
Reform and the Search for Honor

The problem of the quality of the officer corps did not begin with, nor has it ended with, the Vietnam conflict. Vietnam merely exacerbated and accelerated tendencies that were already clearly evident within the military structure. The key question is: "Has the military undergone the kind of self-examination and criticism that would lead it to make the kinds of reforms that are needed to correct those pathologies that surfaced during Vietnam?" We think not.

The evidence we have at our disposal suggests that not much in the way of substantive, penetrating, and genuine reform has taken place within the military structure in general. Even less seems to have taken place within the officer corps; to some extent reform in the latter can only come about as a reflection of larger institutional change. The most damning piece of evidence in support of this contention was the fact that General William Westmoreland, when Chief of Staff of the Army, ordered the Army War College to produce a study on the officer corps to determine what was wrong with it.[1] When confronted with the findings that the corps was in terrible shape and in need of much reform, he immediately ordered the study suppressed and made available only to general officers. The study has since been made available to interested scholars.

Additionally, the RIF policies adopted after Vietnam forced the

Army to choose those officers that it wanted to keep and those it would terminate. To the best of our knowledge, personal connections, educational background (the West Point Protective Association), and the ticket-punching calculus of career advancement were the criteria for the RIF. As a result, many of the Army's better officers, especially at the rank of captain, were terminated without mercy. A breach developed within the officer corps between "regulars"—those who had tenure—and the reserve officer, the most likely candidate for a RIF. At some levels, although mostly within staffs, this breach frequently paralyzed action since reserve officers were afraid to make decisions, take the initiative, or otherwise act in a responsible manner for fear that one mistake would lead to their removal from service as a result of a bad efficiency report. In the end, while a large number of reserve officers survived, a bitter taste was left in the mouths of all, especially those junior reserve officers who must now look forward to the anticipated trauma of possibly failing to make their reserve majority. Such a failure, which can occur prior to eighteen years of service, results in dismissal from the service and loss of retirement benefits. This threat can only breed further caution and a tendency to "get on board" and not "rock the boat." According to Robert Presthus, a tendency toward an "upward looking posture"[2] has developed, a condition which can only stifle further criticism and comment within the Army. Of some importance in noting the problems associated with the RIF, it is interesting to mention that while the Army removed well over 10,000 junior officers—mostly combat-experienced captains—it removed only 600 field-grade officers and most of them were at the very bottom of the barrel of the major rank and had spent most of their careers in staff positions.

General Maxwell Taylor once suggested that the Army "is more like a church." While the suggestion may be too strong insofar as organized religious creeds often call for the abandonment of the self and, at times, even the family in total devotion to one's beliefs, it is not incorrect to suggest that the analogy of the military life to that of a monastery may be more accurate. What religious orders and successful military organizations—by which we mean those that can establish functional combat units which cohere under combat stress—have in common is that both have established what might be called the "price of belonging" and have evolved a set of behavioral guidelines for demonstrating how that "price" is to be paid. To speak of the "price of belonging" is to suggest that there is a common code of ethics agreed on and observed to such an extent that one's definition of what one truly is, is defined in terms of one's ability and willingness to observe the code. Accordingly, a monk is said to be a good monk when he observes and practices the values which the monastic order holds dear. Analogously, a "good" officer is one who recognizes a set of values and obligations which are common to his brother officers and observes them, demanding a high degree of selflessness. Entrance into the community is predicated upon recognition and observance of commonly held values. One is sustained within the community by strict fidelity to such values. With a breach of values, summary expulsion from the community may occur, perhaps because of "conduct unbecoming." In a very real sense, a bad officer and a bad monk are not expelled from the community by the rejection of their peers, although this would seem to be the effect of a violation of the code. More importantly, when the price of belonging is a mechanism for holding an officer faithful to his duty, the fact that an officer may violate the code really means, in true tribal fashion, that he has by his own action placed himself outside the community. It is his action which rejects the community and its values; it is he who has failed to pay the price of belonging or has signaled that he is no longer prepared to pay the price. The formal dismissal or rejection by his peers merely formalizes what has already occurred, namely, a breakdown in the communal relationship; that symbiotic relationshhip that binds the individual officer to the loyalty and expectations of his peers.

In this sense, it is clear that the Army is indeed not for everybody in the same way that a monastery is not for everybody. The commitment is special. Such is not the case in the everyday business of earning a living. Working for IBM is truly much the same as working for GM or ITT. Careerism and entrepreneurialism are accepted and considered to be desirable. Military life, on the other hand, is unique in that it clearly levels upon the officer, or any other member for that matter, responsibilities which transcend his career or material self-interest. The problem has been, however, a failure to realize this and to regard the military life as the same as working at any other occupation. This equation is false, misleading, and ultimately dangerous, for it does not recognize that at some point an officer may be called upon to do his duty and "be faithful unto death." That alone, the burden of expectation, is sufficient in itself to distinguish the military way from the business way. Clearly, as long as attempts at reform within the military are aimed at changing operating procedures without addressing this critical fact which actually fuels the organizational engine, such attempts cannot succeed.

If the quality of the American officer has suffered somewhat because of the system, it seems equally relevant to note that the major thrust of this system, at least as it affects officers seeking to choose a pattern leading to a "successful" career, is for the officer to seek staff work and staff assignments over command assignments. It is as if the military has developed an informal norm which suggests the perversion of the old Germanic axiom that "*Stabs Officieren habt keinen Namen*" ("Staff officers have no names"). In short, one can go from one staff assignment to another and still make one's promotion schedules on time. With a touch of luck and some political skill this route can lead to the rank of colonel with little effort. The point is that the adoption of the ethos of the entrepreneurial bureaucracy has led the military to become enamored with the "scientific management of its personnel assets." As a result, not only have we a substantially high number of people involved in the business of "career management" but, more to the point, the American military has become permeated with a background ambience that is more supportive of the staff officer than the combat officer. To be sure, this tendency emerged most blatantly in Vietnam, when a formal effort was made to ensure that staff and combat tours were shared and, at the least, combat officers were sometimes viewed by their peers as misguided for not avoiding dangerous assignments—an end, by the way, which was quite easy to achieve.

The reforms which have been suggested earlier in this work cannot be expected to come about, operate, or sustain themselves in a vacuum of values. There is a clear need for the development of what we have called a "background ambience" which supports such reforms. To be sure, the manner in which institutional and ambience variables interact is obscure, but the reciprocal pattern seems to suggest at least one model of operation. Having discussed the kinds of institutional reforms at issue, it seems fair to inquire how the directions of these changes may be formalized. What we need, of course, is to establish the "price of belonging" (which has been identified as characteristic of the corporative institution) needed to sustain cohesion within military units. We must try to provide a code of behavior and values which offer a set of *prescriptive ethics* for the Army officer if he is to keep faith with himself, his peers, his men, and his profession.

The American officer corps has given precious little attention to evolving a code of behavior or a statement of ethics according to which its officers would be expected to perform. Indeed, it is no misstatement to say that no such formal, official code exists within the American military. The reasons why no such code has been developed are, no doubt, complex, but at least one reason stands out. In America, nothing is prized so highly as individual freedom. It is this freedom, and the right to pursue it, which is deeply ingrained in our political, economic, and social life. Three major philosophical strains have strongly shaped the nature of America's institutions: Madisonian politics, laissez-faire economics, and Darwinist social doctrines have strongly influenced the shape of the American sociopolitical order. The three philosophical perspectives share the belief that if individuals are left alone to pursue what they believe is "right," the result of the clash of individual interests will be the evolution of the common good. As a consequence, there is little need to regulate individual values since, in the long run, "functional" ones survive and "dysfunctional" ones wither. A kind of Gresham's Law begins to operate in which all individuals are allowed the free pursuit of ethical values, and it is the process of interplay itself which is expected to produce a semi-solid code to which most members more or less subscribe. Given such a historio-social perspective, it is hardly surprising that the military has failed to evolve a code. Such an effort would, in the strict philosophical sense, be superfluous since a sense of ethics is held to emerge automatically from the interplay of individual ethical perspectives. Nations which have developed codes of behavior for its officers are nations which lack the strong individualistic philosophical strains which have characterized American development, and tend to be nations with more communal orientations toward the process of social development.

The fact remains that the American officer corps has not stressed the need to develop a code of behavior which would formally establish the "price of belonging" for its members. By analogy, such a situation is akin to trying to run a monastery or, in General Taylor's analogy, a church, without a strict code of rules governing ethical behavior. Cohesion and ethical codes go hand in hand and are mutually reinforcing. While the problem of which variable came first remains unanswered, it is clear that the failure to develop a code of behavior for the American officer corps is at once a reflection and a cause of its failure to develop a strong sense of community around which cohesion could be built. Moreover, it is among the strongest indicators that the American military in general and the officer corps in particular are thoroughly penetrated by the ethos of the modern entrepreneurial bureaucracy.

Yet, in at least one instance, an attempt was made to develop such a code. This resulted from the study conducted by the Army War College in 1970 at the request of then Chief of Staff William C. Westmoreland.[3] As we have already indicated, the findings of this study were such as to convince Westmoreland that the study should be suppressed and its circulation limited to the general officer corps. However, General Westmoreland's directives to the authors of the study that pertain to the existence of an "officer's creed" are instructive. Referring to "several unfavorable events" which had occurred within the Army during the past few years (a rather oblique reference to My Lai and other Vietnam horrors), Westmoreland charged the authors of the professionalism study "to ensure that an analysis of the moral and professional climate is conducted with the utmost thoroughness and mature perspective."[4] The General then adds his own view by saying "by no means do I believe that the Army as an institution is in a moral crisis."[5] If there is no serious moral crisis within the Army, then why the need to investigate "the moral and professional climate" of the Army at all?

Whatever his motives, and in retrospect it seems that the initiation of the study was never intended by the Chief of Staff to serve more than a propaganda function (otherwise he would not have suppressed it when the results turned out unfavorably), Westmoreland does raise the question of a code of behavior for officers: "In making your study, I should like particularly to have developed an Officer's Code." He then goes on to negate the very purpose of such a code by saying that "its only purpose would be to guide officers in exercising their authority and performing their duties."[6] In short, there is a singular lack of awareness that the purpose of a code of ethics as it relates to a corporative institution like the military is to create a sense of communal identification and to establish a sense of belonging among one's "brothers." In Westmoreland's view, there is no need to develop such a broad code. Failures within the organization are individual failures. The possibility that the institution is lacking in a primary element which cements its parts to the whole was never considered and it is precisely this perspective which has been traditionally associated with attempts at establishing codes of behavior for the American military. A brief illustration can be obtained from an examination of the "Code of Conduct" developed in 1954 at the order of President Eisenhower because of the failure of American prisoners of war during Korea to withstand interrogation. Nowhere in this code can one find the concept that certain things should be done because they are "right." Rather, in typical American entrepreneurial fashion, the code stresses function. Accordingly, one does certain things because they work or serve the mission. To be sure, it may be a question of stress rather than a truly qualitative difference. Nonetheless, it remains true that no serious attempts have been made by the military to establish an "officer's creed" that would serve to establish the "price of belonging" to the officer corps.

The "Officer's Creed" quoted earlier clearly reflects many of those tensions which we find in the American officer corps. A large segment of it is, characteristically, devoted to the premise that the American officer is not becoming "a legionnaire." Accordingly, the civilian's traditional fear of the professional military is expressed in the sections dealing with the source of military authority, namely, the civilian political establishment. The sections, also substantial in length, dealing with private morality and conducting oneself in a manner "free from the appearance of impropriety" reflects once again the typical American concern with public action associated with trivialities. The "Officer's Creed" reflects the morality of the fraternity house, equally devoted to the trivial, as well as the ineffectual and sophomoric West Point "honor code." Other nations have not felt it necessary to rail against trivia. In the British experience, indeed, one suspects that personal eccentricity—to be extremely kind to men such as Haig, Kitchener, and Gordon—not only had little to do with their military professionalism but was indeed cultivated as a way of attracting attention. In any case, it is our argument that the present code—officially nonexistent—is inadequate in any case, and that what is required is a true code of military ethics which would define the nature of membership in the officer corps.

The code offered below is but one of several institutional mechanisms necessary if the American military is to change in such a manner as to increase cohesion in its combat units. Accordingly, it cannot stand alone. As a single variable in a highly complex equation of institutional change, the most that can be said for it is that it aims directly at altering that "background ambience" so vital to the support of larger institutional reforms. Furthermore, the purpose of an alternative code is not merely to quibble about words, but to do battle over concepts central to the organizational life of the officer corps. The code offered here has a singular advantage over that in the Army War College study: it seeks to spell out an officer's specific obligations against the background of a more general ambience dedicated to values associated with *combat, command,* and the *responsibilities* derived from them. Here the ethics of the staff officer, the organization man, the ticket puncher, the military manager—ethics associated with the notion of entrepreneurial bureaucracies—are subordinated or rejected in favor of those values which are perceived to emerge from the crucible of risk associated with combat. Collectively, these ethics constitute that ambience associated, not with the business executive, but with those of the warrior monk. Such a creed might contain elements of the precepts offered below:

Officer's Code of Honor

- The nature of any command is a moral charge which places each officer at the center of ethical responsibility.
- An officer's sense of moral integrity is at the center of his leadership effectiveness. The advancement of one's career is never justified at the expense of violating one's sense of honor.
- Every officer holds a special position of moral trust and responsibility. No officer will ever violate that trust or avoid his responsibility for any of his actions regardless of the personal cost.
- An officer's first loyalty is to the welfare of his command. He will never allow his men to be misused or abused in any way.
- An officer will never require his men to endure hardships or suffer dangers to which he is unwilling to expose himself.

Every officer must openly share the burden of risk and sacrifice to which his men are exposed.

- An officer is first and foremost a leader of men. He must lead his men by example and personal actions. He cannot manage his command to effectiveness . . . they must be led; an officer must therefore set the standard for personal bravery and leadership.

- An officer will *never* execute an order which he regards to be ethically wrong and he will report all such orders, policies, or actions to appropriate authorities.

- No officer will willfully conceal any act of his superiors, subordinates, or peers that violates his sense of ethics.

- No officer will punish, allow the punishment of, or in any way discriminate against a subordinate or peer for telling the truth about any matter.

- All officers are responsible for the actions of all their brother officers. The dishonorable acts of one officer diminish the corps; the actions of the officer corps are only determined by the acts of its members and these actions must always be above reproach.

The code has a built-in distinct philosophical and ethical bias. It is the purpose of this bias, as argued previously, to develop and sustain the background ambience which has traditionally been associated with the "way of the legion." The bias is almost religious in that it seeks to define the officer in a manner that is far more extensive and far more intensive than what we have come to associate with definitions of the officer as manager or as military entrepreneur. Clearly, the purpose of any code goes beyond the engendering of a "feeling of belonging," beyond an attempt to establish a sense of community. More specifically, it seeks to engender the feeling of belonging by prescribing and proscribing certain actions which, in themselves, come to define membership in the larger value group. The group can become "value-infused"[7] only when its members recognize and follow the code.

The precepts aim at stimulating specific types of behavior. They are types of behavior which are congruent with reinforcing the specific kinds of larger institutional reforms which we believe are essential. Each of the code's precepts should offer support for the reforms which have already been suggested.

In the first instance, the code affirms that command is a "moral charge" which places the officer at the center of reciprocal ethical responsibility. Accordingly, command is never just one more ticket to be punched to achieve the next higher rank. Indeed, command is the very essence of military life; and it is its prerogatives, but mostly its responsibilities, which come to define what the "way of the legion" is all about. It will avail a military organization nothing if its staff work and staff support are all in order if the organization finds itself incapable of producing commanders. War is the art of conflict, and command is an expression of that art which assumes an almost mystical place in the litany of military values and most certainly occupies a central place on the altar of military ethics. The failure to recognize command as the center of military moral responsibility and to recognize that the officer must bear this responsibility is to deny that there is any difference between the military and any other occupation, a proposition which has already been laid to rest.

The notion that moral integrity is at the center of a leader's effectiveness suggests that the compromise of one's moral standards can never be truly hidden from one's brother officers or, indeed, in most instances, from the men in his command. The notion is simple enough: there are just some things that are not done. There is a line beyond which a truly ethical man will not go. Accordingly, the notion that one "has to go along to get along" is rejected as the first step to greater compromises of one's integrity. In addition, the code maintains that to be an officer is to occupy a "special position of moral trust" and that this trust—which clearly goes hand in glove with personal integrity—must never be violated. Certainly, if there are circumstances in which it must be violated, career advancement is never to be among them. There comes a moment in the career of every officer when the choice has to be made between pleasing one's superiors and staying loyal to oneself and one's values. At times, the rewards for betraying one's values are great, indeed being too often reflected in promotion or other gains. The code sets up the simple standard that personal integrity and one's position as an officer are inseparable and to violate one is to violate the other. An officer must never betray his position, for to do so is to betray his inner ethical self.

The proposition that an officer's first loyalty is to the welfare of his men does not mean that he should be fearful of putting them in harm's way. Indeed not, for it is the fundamental purpose of a military organization to engage in combat. The point is that an officer must never allow his men to be squandered or used in a manner that is not directly related to the true purpose of a command. In this regard, the idiot who ordered the same company back up Hamburger Hill in Vietnam after it had been virtually decimated, or the fool who sent a platoon down a well-ambushed road to retrieve a burnt-out armored personnel carrier are prime examples of officers who allowed their men to be misused. Danger is central to combat; the object is to expose one's command to that danger only in pursuit of "legitimate" military goals. Clearly, what constitutes a legitimate objective and what constitutes an illegitimate one is a determination that each officer will have to make when he finds himself in a situation that makes him doubt the wisdom of his superiors in ordering a given action. He must be prepared in defense of his oath as an officer to question his superiors on a specific order and, if he deems it necessary, to refuse to expose his men to risks to achieve goals which are of doubtful value. To be sure, he must never allow his command to become the tool of the advancement of his superiors, as happened upon occasion in Vietnam when some commanders ordered their men into dubious actions to increase the "body count," or to inflate the degree of combat activity as a way of padding their own efficiency reports.

Perhaps most central to this book is the proposition that a good officer must share the risks and dangers of combat to which his men are exposed and, if necessary, be willing to accept the ultimate sacrifice himself. This, above all, is what differentiates the military profession from others. Among the major findings which emerged from the research on the performance of the military during Vietnam was the fact that officers often avoided the risks of combat by various means. The dictum of "good management is good leadership," itself erroneous, became perverted even more into the belief that an officer could literally manage his men to their deaths in support of a mission. What evidence we have suggests clearly that this belief was wrong and that it did not work. The American Army seems to have forgotten the basic lesson which commanders since the time of Thermopylae have always known: to be effective, a commander must be seen on the field of battle by his men. No less a man than George Patton realized the importance of being seen— indeed, he had a reputation for exposing himself to combat risks— ·and even suggested the somewhat bizarre step of wearing a red cloak in combat (a habit affected by Julius Caesar) in order to increase his visibility on the battlefield. Erwin Rommel knew the value of being seen in combat. Indeed, the Germans developed a term of derision for those officers who paraded bedecked in shined boots and ribbons but never exposed themselves to the enemy. They called them "golden pheasants." In a word, a good officer realizes that his men will follow his judgment if they are convinced that he too is prepared to risk his life in their defense. In Vietnam, too often the troops perceived their officers as unwilling to assume the burdens of combat that they themselves carried and reacted in a most violent manner—they tried to kill them. If the Army is to change, every officer must come to accept the responsibility of exposing himself to the dangers to which his men are exposed and, if necessary, to follow the dictum of the British NCO who, when asked where his officers were, replied, "When it comes time to die, they'll be with us."

One of the pressing strains of reform which resulted from the American experience in Vietnam was associated with the concept that a military officer could not escape responsibility before the law or before his own conscience for certain acts. Among the most notorious of these actions was, of course, My Lai. Yet the problem of "following orders" actually is faced day in and day out by numerous officers outside the combat zone. For example, the system of checking readiness status in use today virtually forces hundreds of officers to report equipment ready for action when, in fact, it is not. In other instances, officers are witness to actions which they know to be wrong and which they conveniently ignore on the grounds that to report violations will "rock the boat" or result in a poor efficiency report. Accordingly, the injunction that an officer will never execute any order which he regards to be ethically wrong goes far beyond the bounds of actions which one is likely to encounter in a combat zone. It also addresses activities which often permeate a highly bureaucratic military establishment such as ours. Cost overruns, falsified intelligence reports, falsified readiness reports, all are examples of the kinds of "orders, policies, and actions" which occur almost daily within the military establishment. The directed moral change is that an officer is in violation of his honor—in betrayal of his ethical trust—if he has knowledge of such occurrences and either acquiesces in them or fails to report them.

It has always struck us that the quality of loyalty, once part of the official efficiency report, has been a misplaced value. What, in reality, does it mean to be loyal to a superior? Surely, whatever loyalty is owed to a superior cannot logically or ethically be construed to extend to a willingness to cover up his failings or conceal his shortcomings, especially when they bear on the ability of a unit to perform its mission. There must certainly be a higher loyalty and that is to the officer corps, the men in the command, and one's sense of ethics. In this sense, loyalty should never be interpreted to mean that policies, orders, or actions which are thought to be detrimental to the cohesion and effectiveness of the unit are to be tolerated by subordinate officers. Such toleration violates their higher obligation to the corps and to the men they command. Loyalty to one's superior is never anything but a conditional relationship predicated upon the continuing perception of his subordinates that he is acting honorably in his position of command. The Romans called this quality *fides* and distinguished it clearly from *obsequium*. Once superiors begin to act otherwise, even that relationship is dissolved and the obligation to make appropriate authority aware of existing circumstances must take precedence.

It is a truism that "the truth will make one free." It is, however, naïve to believe that such a statement is an accurate description of reality. Nonetheless, regardless of what one thinks of the inherent value of truth, no organization can respond to pathologies which may develop within itself unless it has adequate information on which to base corrective measures. There is, then, an *organizational imperative* for telling the truth to one's superiors or to others in authority. In the end, there is only one way in which members of any organization will "tell it like it is" and that is if they can be reasonably certain that telling the truth will not be regarded by superiors or peers as "fighting the problem," not being a "team player," or, as in some cases, showing disloyalty bordering upon treason. For this reason, the officer corps must never strike at any brother officer for exposing even the most heinous of crimes or shortcomings within the corps or the military establishment itself. The far greater crime would be to hide the truth. Falsehoods and cover-ups can never contribute to freedom or reform. If we hold an officer responsible for a higher ethical code in the same way that we hold a member of a religious community responsible, the truth will not be punished. To punish the truth sayer automatically negates the value of the other ethical norms to which allegiance is pledged. There can be no question of destroying truth in order to save it.

Finally, to come to grips with ethical guidelines for the military officer, we must never lose sight of the fact that the officer corps is akin to a religious brotherhood, or at least ought to be if military units are to be cohesive. Thus, all officers are brothers in the same sense that monks are brothers and, in specific terms, this means that the dishonorable action of one necessarily reflects upon and diminishes one's brothers. Responsibility becomes, in a real sense, collective in that the community of brothers is unwilling to permit or tolerate in their midst one who fails to observe the code of honor at the center of the community itself. Every officer is thus responsible for his brothers and this imposes the awesome responsibility of ensuring that one's brothers remain loyal to communal values. The officer corps must, therefore, be ready to dismiss summarily those officers whose actions testify to their inability or unwillingness to pay the price of belonging. Moreover, this responsibility bears most heavily upon those senior-grade officers who occupy strategic positions within the organization, for they, above all others, truly have the power to enforce the code. Indeed, as was suggested earlier, a basic precondition for the acceptance of any new value within an institution is the readiness of institutional elites to give full and overt support to the new value. So it is with a code of honor for the officer corps. Unwillingness to remove the "deadwood," or any hint that a "West Point Protective Association" is operating, or further evidence of hypocrisy at the top, will do much to erode the compelling power of the code. With rank goes power and with that power goes the responsibility of ensuring that the code of honor used by the officer corps is enforced at all levels of command.

It is, of course, painfully clear to even the most naïve student of bureaucracies that the mere promulgation of a code of honor for the military will not ensure its effectiveness. Yet we cannot resist pointing out that it is unrealistic to expect the officer corps to act honorably when no such code has yet been promulgated. It is possible that our suggestions are unworkable, but surely it is an acceptable proposition that it is possible to develop a workable code. The time is long past when we can continue to rely on the ethics of the marketplace to set the standards of behavior for the officer corps. Something more is needed, as the American experience in Vietnam has demonstrated all too clearly. What is suggested here is open to debate. What is beyond debate is that it is past time for the military to turn its attention to developing such a code of honor for its officer corps.

It would be unfair if we did not acknowledge that many of our perspectives and arguments are shared by our "brother officers" who remain within the officer corps, or if we did not admit that some debate concerning the question of reform is going on within the military and even, on some issues at least, growing in intensity and scope. Yet, despite the sincere efforts by those who stayed behind to "change the system," it strikes us that the case for reform will never be truly articulated by the Army itself or, indeed, by its officer corps, for the simple reason that institutions do not reform themselves without a great amount of external pressure being brought to bear first. Too many sunk costs, too many careers, too many status roles, are invested in the status quo. By definition, those who have risen to positions of highest rank, authority, and influence have done so by successfully mastering and manipulating the very system that some now seek to change. *Ab initio* they would have the most to lose by reform. It is they who have the greatest psychic investments in the present state of things and it is they who would have to admit that many of the things they have given their lives to were empty and who would have to witness "the truths [they've] spoken twisted by knaves to make a trap for fools." [8] Men do not easily repudiate their personal histories.

Consequently, the case for reform cannot reasonably be expected to emerge from within. For essentially the same reasons, change in the direction of restoring corporative values and rituals can hardly be expected to emerge. In the end, it seems inescapable that both the policies of reform and the momentum for their implementation must come from agencies outside the military itself. To be sure, the military will have to cooperate in their implementation, but the stimulus for reform must come initially from other centers of influence. To assert this is simply to recognize that the Army as an organization operates within the context of a larger democratic and pluralistic political system and must interact with other centers of influence, some of which are legally superior to it. It is here, at the points where the military establishment meshes with the wider decision-making systems, that the initiative for reform must be aroused.

Reform must be a cooperative effort between the civilian authorities and the military. Let there be no mistake, the dogs of war are to be harnessed by their civilian keepers and the decision to loose them can only legitimately be made by the political leadership. Yet this control carries with it severe responsibilities; chief among them is the responsibility to assure that the military is capable of carrying out its mission and, when that capability is in doubt, to take the necessary steps to correct the situation. There should be no wish to grasp control of these reins or, indeed, even to resist serious civilian initiatives at reform. Accordingly, every consideration must be given to the fact that policies of reform within the military must remain consistent with the values of civilian preeminence over military affairs. The creation of an effective combat killing force through reform that resulted in the creation of a "state within a state" is unacceptable from any perspective. Equally unacceptable is the continuation of a military structure that can no longer perform its mission, or an officer corps which has lost both its ethical bearings and the ability to develop and lead cohesive combat units. There *is* a middle ground; balance is the keystone. It is likely that the question of reform will remain a problem for many years. Certainly, major changes will not be brought about overnight, and the task will be difficult. But no matter how difficult the task, it behooves us to attempt a solution. As A. E. Housman has suggested:

> If it chance your eye offend you,
> Pluck it out, lad, and be sound . . .
> But play the man, stand up and end you,
> When your sickness is your soul.[9]

There is a sickness in the soul of the Army and reform is the only alternative. If the experiences in Vietnam are any indication, the risks of doing nothing are simply too great to tolerate.

Postscript

The critiques of the officer corps which underlie our argument cry out for some definition of just what the "good officer" is. More important, how are we to locate him within the vast military bureaucracy? This search assumes major importance since it is clear that rapid and deep reform is simply not going to come about. What chance does exist for changing the military rests with men who share corporative values which are seen to be fundamental to establishing a corporative sense of the military way and who will eventually find themselves in positions where they are able to effectuate change. Accordingly, it is helpful if we can identify some of those officers in the hope that they will be selected for promotion. What criteria can be developed so that the military, as presently structured, can select its "best men for the right job"?

To be able to identify good officers within the confines of the available data within the Army's present promotion system works against an attempt to develop some sort of pristine model against which selection would take place. Far more realistic is the hope that one can develop some unobtrusive indicators associated with the corporative notion of a good officer. Several of these unobtrusive indicators seem relevant:

- Distrust any officer with a perfect or near perfect record of efficiency reports. He is conforming to the existing value system and will have no interest in changing it.

- Look carefully at a man who gets low marks on "tact" and who "deviates from accepted doctrine." He may be creative.
- An officer who gets low marks on loyalty is especially valuable, for he is unwilling to acquiesce in his superior's policies without debate. He is likely to have an independent mind.
- Be suspicious of any officer who has accumulated awards for valor without having sustained any physical injury. Trust a Purple Heart wearer.
- Distrust any officer who has had "all his tickets punched" and who sports an array of staff awards on his chest. He is likely to be a manager playing the system.
- Distrust all officers who use "buzz words" and have a poor vocabulary. They tend to be managers of the most obsequious type. True leadership is likely to be foreign to them.
- Trust a man who heads for sounds of the guns and has repeated tours of combat and command duty at all unit levels; it is preferable that he have only minimal exposure to staff work.
- Trust an officer who was seen by his men in combat and whose command performed well and showed low rates of drug use, fragging, body counting, etc.
- Search for the officer whose readiness reports indicate a high percentage of equipment which is deficient. He is a man addicted to the truth.

To be sure, the foregoing unobtrusive indicators of the "good officer" beg the question in many ways. On the other hand, those characteristics which are denigrated in the above list are often the very qualities considered to be important in the present military establishment. Further, only we Americans are so addicted to the penchant for legalistic definition and writing things down. This is a shortcoming which leads us to fail to realize that some things are not so easily graspable but are, in a very real sense, felt by the individual involved. Thus it is that the British sense of "the military way" and the French sense of "élan" are qualities that escape definition but quite clearly exist and affect the behavior of their respective armies. That a similar "sense of the legion" is lacking in the American military in general and the officer corps in particular has been the major thrust of this book. In the end, we are forced to admit that we may be unable to define it in an exact sense. What we are sure of, however, is that such an entity exists and that when it is in evidence, its impact is felt upon the cohesion and unit integrity of a military force. What we are equally certain of, however, is that the American officer corps, in the main, does not now reflect it. It is this quality, the discovering of a sense of community, a sense of honor, a sense of the "way of the legion," which we must attain.

Tables and Figure

TABLE 1   *Desertion Rates for U.S. Army Forces in World War II, Korea, Vietnam in Rate Per Thousand*

World War II			Korea			Vietnam		
Fiscal year	*Rate*	*% change ea. yr.*	*Fiscal year*	*Rate*	*% change ea. yr.*	*Fiscal year*	*Rate*	*% change ca. yr.*
1945	45.2	−28.3	1954	15.7	−30.0	1972	53.2	−27.6
1944	63.0		1953	22.3	+ 0.0	1971	73.4	+40.5
1943	Not avail.		1952	22.0	+54.0	1970	52.3	+23.3
1942	Not avail.		1951	14.3		1969	42.4	+45.7
						1968	29.1	+35.9
						1967	21.4	+45.5
						1966	14.7	− 6.7
						1965	15.7	

Source: Department of Defense

TABLE 2 Data Relating Overall Army Strength to Overall Vietnam Forces Level to Desertion Rates and Deaths Due to Hostile Action by Year of Engagement

Data and Strength Cross Section

Year	Strength of the Army* Officer	Strength of the Army* Enlisted	Total ground forces strength Vietnam†	Deaths due to hostile action‡	U.S. Army desertion rate per 1,000	U.S. Army deserters in percent
1965	111,541	1,079,750	184,300		15.7	1.10 (n=13,177)
1966	117,205	1,296,600	385,300		14.7	3.12 (n=44,244)
1967	142,964	1,401,750	485,600	8,581**	21.4	1.73 (n=26,782)
1968	165,569	1,357,000	543,400	9,387	29.1	2.58 (n=39,321)
1969	171,182	1,153,000	475,200	7,043	42.4	4.27 (n=56,608)
1970	160,814	1,161,444	343,600	3,911	52.3	6.07 (n=76,643)
1971	144,595	962,605	139,000	1,449	73.4	7.13 (n=79,027)
1972	120,982	686,692	25,200	195	53.2	5.52 (n=44,643)
1973	117,860	703,031	—	—	37.3	3.95 (n=32,500)

(Total n=380,445)

* Strength of the Army figures extracted from Fiscal Year 1974, Authorizations for Military Procurement, Research and Development, Construction Authorization for the Safeguard ABM, and Active Duty and Selected Reserve Strengths: Hearings Before the Committee on Armed Services; United States Senate. (Previous Fiscal year hearings for additional data.) Also, Department of Defense Appropriations for 1974; Hearings Before a Subcommittee on Appropriations, House of Representatives. (Previous year hearings for additional data.)

† These figures extracted from The New York Times over several years and from the Index to the Times.

‡ "Killed in Action" was not used in Vietnam in official reports. "Death Due to Hostile Action" was substituted.

** Cumulative deaths from 1961.

TABLE 3   Assaults with Explosive Devices—Vietnam (As of 31 December 1972)

	Total incidents	Category AA*	PA†	Deaths	Injuries	OFF/NCO	Intended Victim EM	VN	Unk.
CY 1969	126 (239)	96	30	37	191	70	17	7	32
CY 1970	271 (386)	209	62	34	306	154	40	20	57
CY 1971	333	222	111	12	198	158	43	28	104
CY 1972	58	27	31	3	19	31	7	4	20
Totals	788 (1016)	554	234	86	714	413	107	59	213

* Actual Assaults: Motive determined as intent to kill, do bodily harm, or to intimidate.

† Possible Assaults: Possible motive determined as intent to kill, do bodily harm, or to intimidate.

Source: Reproduced verbatim from Department of Defense source. Figures in parentheses obtained from congressional hearings; see note 24, chapter II.

TABLE 4 *Percentage of U.S. Army Using Drugs in the Last Twelve Months (1971) by Place of Service*

Service location	Marijuana %	Type of Drug Other psychedelic drugs %	Stimulants %	Depressants %	Narcotic drugs %
Continental U.S.	41.3	28.4	28.9	21.5	20.1
Europe	40.2	33.0	23.0	14.0	13.1
Vietnam	50.9	30.8	31.9	25.1	28.5
Other S.E. Asia	42.0	23.2	24.7	18.1	17.6
Total Army	42.7	29.4	28.0	20.4	20.1

Source: *Drug Abuse in the Military: Hearing Before the Subcommittee on Drug Abuse in the Military of the Committee on Armed Services, United States Senate, Ninety-second Congress*, 1972, p. 127

TABLE 5   Strength of the Army, 1867–1974: Officer-Enlisted Comparison

Year	Officer strength	Enlisted strength	Total strength of the Army	Officer-enlisted ratio	Officer percent of total strength
1867*	3,056	54,138	57,194	1:17.7	5.34
1898	10,516	199,198	209,714	1:18.94	5.01
1900	4,227	97,486	101,713	1:23.06	4.15
1918	130,485	2,265,257	2,395,742	1:17.36	5.44
1945	891,663	7,376,295	8,267,958	1:8.27	10.78
	(481,466)†	(5,741,729)	(6,223,195)	(1:11.92)	(7.73)
1953	145,683	1,388,182	1,533,815	1:9.53	9.49
1955	121,947	987,349	1,109,296	1:8.1	11.0
1956	118,364	907,414	1,025,778	1:7.7	11.5
1957	111,187	886,807	997,994	1:8.0	11.1
1958	104,716	794,209	898,925	1:7.6	11.6
1959	101,690	760,274	861,964	1:7.5	11.8
1960	101,236	771,842	873,078	1:7.6	11.6
1961	100,335	776,327	876,662	1:7.7	11.4
1962	115,578	950,826	1,066,404	1:8.2	10.83
1963	108,299	867,617	975,916	1:8.01	11.09
1964	110,276	854,950	965,226	1:7.42	11.42
1965‡	111,541	1,079,700	1,191,241	1:9.68	9.36
1966	117,205	1,296,600	1,413,805	1:11.06	8.29
(Buildup)					
1967	142,964	1,401,700	1,544,664	1:9.8	9.25
(Tet)					
1968	165,569	1,357,000	1,522,569	1:8.07	11.01
(Fragging begins)					
1969	171,882	1,153,000	1,324,882	1:6.7	13.08
1970	160,814	1,161,444	1,262,258	1:7.2	12.6
1971	148,623	971,871	1,120,494	1:6.5	13.26
(End of U.S. ground war)					
1972	120,982	686,692	807,674	1:5.7	14.97
1973	117,860	703,031	820,891	1:5.96	14.35
1974	110,260	689,646	799,906	1:6.25	13.78

* 1867–1964 figures from Russell F. Weigley, *History of the United States Army* (New York: Macmillan, 1967), pp. 566–69.

† Data in parentheses reflect strengths of the Army *minus* the Army Air Force. Data from *Strength of the Army, 1 June 1945* (Copy No. 40, RSC, GC-P3-31).

‡ For all officer data after 1965 warrant officers are included. Strength figures gathered from multiple congressional sources but primarily from *Senate Armed Services Committee and House of Representatives Committee on Appropriations*, fiscal years 1966–75.

TABLE 6   Officer-Enlisted Ratios: World War II, Korea, Vietnam

Rank	World War II (1945)* No.	Enl. ratio	Korea (1953) No.	Enl. ratio	Vietnam (1971)† No.	Enl. ratio
General	1,168	1:4,916	479	1:2,953	498	1:1,952
Colonel	8,547	1:672	5,155	1:274	5,947	1:163
Lt. Colonel	22,184	1:258	13,100	1:108	14,577	1:67
Major	48,794	1:118	18,271	1:77	22,266	1:44
Captain	135,348	1:42	33,410	1:42	49,073	1:20
1/Lt.	166,238	1:35	31,920	1:44	23,907	1:41
2/Lt.	75,368	1:76	31,467	1:45	13,666	1:71
W.O. 1–4	23,819	1:242	13,483	1:105	18,689	1:52
Total officers	481,466 = 1:11.9		147,285 = 1:9.6		148,623 = 1:6.5	
Total enlisted	5,741,729		1,414,711		971,871	

Source: Figures for 1945 and 1953 from *Strength of the Army, 1 June 1945* (Copy No. 40, RCS, GC-P 3–31), *Strength of the Army, 30 June 1953* (Copy No. 122, RCS, CSGPA-332). Data on Vietnam peak strength from *Hearings Before the Committee on Armed Services, United States Senate, Ninety-third Congress, on S-1263, Part 8, Manpower*, p. 5443. *Strength of the Army* reports from 1961 on remain classified according to a Senate source.

* U.S. Army Air Force strength in World War II subtracted.

† This date is used since fragging, desertion, and drug indicators were at their highest.

TABLE 7 *Officer-Enlisted Ratios: Deaths among Battle Casualties*

Rank	World War II (1941–45)*		Korea (1950–53)†		Vietnam (1961–72)‡	
	No.	Enl. ratio	No.	Enl. ratio	No.	Enl. ratio
General	25	1:6,796	2	1:13,084	3	1:9,074
Colonel	77	1:2,206	5	1:5,234	8	1:3,407
Lt. Colonel	338	1:503	21	1:1,246	55	1:495
Major	466	1:365	71	1:369	135	1:201
Captain	2,115	1:80	252	1:104	720	1:38
1/Lt.	5,168	1:33	716	1:37	1,206	1:23
2/Lt.	4,499	1:38	445	1:58	463	1:59
W.O. 1–4	122	1:1,393	23	1:1,138	679	1:40
Total officer losses	12,810 = 1:13.26		1,512 = 1:17.31		3,269 = 1:8.33	
Total enlisted losses	169,891		26,169		27,222	

* *Army Battle Casualties—Final Report* (RCS, CSAP [OT] 87,1953, Adjutant General U.S.A.). U.S. Army Air Force losses excluded.

† *Battle Casualties of the Army* (RCS, CSGPA-363,1954, OACSG1, U.S.A.).

‡ Department of Defense *Computer Study of Casualties in Vietnam.*

TABLE 8 Comparative Trends in Relative Strengths by Grade and Losses: World War II, Korea, Vietnam

	World War II %	Korea %	Vietnam % (1972)
Officer strength of the Army	7.29	10.5	14.97*
Officer deaths of all deaths due to hostile action	7.01	5.45	10.7 (8.4)†
Senior officer strength (general to major) of officer corps	16.74	25.12	29.12‡
Senior officer deaths of all officer deaths due to hostile action	7.07	4.47	6.1

* See Table 5. By 1972 officer strength had reached 14.97 percent of total strength.

† Percentage in parentheses shows officer losses with warrant officer deaths in action removed.

‡ See Table 6. General officers alone increased their numbers by 152.0 percent. In bureaucratic terms the presence of generals creates the Byzantine effect. The higher the rank, the greater pressures for numbers needed to affirm the importance of the personage with the rank: a type of military Parkinsonism.

TABLE 9 *Distribution of Casualties between RA Volunteer and Draftee in Vietnam*

	1968	1969	1970	Percentage rate of increase or decrease 1968–70
Draftee				
% of Army in Vietnam	42.0	39.0	39.0	−3.0
% of casualties	58.0	62.0	65.0	+7.0
Volunteer				
% of Army in Vietnam	58.0	61.0	61.0	+3.0
% of casualties	42.0	38.0	35.0	−7.0

Source: *Congressional Record,* August 21, 1970, pp. 29700–29704, citing "National Journal Studies Role of Draftees in Vietnam"

TABLE 10   *Reserve Officers' Training Corps Enrollment,*
1960–72* (In thousands, for May, end of school year)

Branch of Service	1960	1965	1967	1968	1969	1970	1971	1972
Senior ROTC, total	230	231	216	196	175	123	92	73
Army	133	142	152	141	125	87	63	45
Navy	10	7	9	9	9	8	7	7
Air Force	87	82	56	45	41	28	23	21
Junior ROTC, total†	87	88	95	111	122	126	124	121

*From *Statistical Abstract of the United States, 1973,* Bureau of the Census, p. 270.

† Consists of high schools, academies, junior colleges, and National Defense Cadet Corps Schools; beginning 1967, includes enrollment in Army, Navy, Marine Corps, and Air Force Junior ROTC, and in National Defense Cadet Corps. Source: U.S. Department of Defense, Office of the Secretary, unpublished data.

TABLE 11 Statistical Analysis of Question 9, "Individual Questionnaire," by Grade

S = 410*

Question 9: "Do you feel that, within the officer corps as a whole, there is a discernible difference between the ideal standards and those that actually exist?"

Officer Rank	Number	None (1)	Slight (2)	Moderate (3)	Consider-able (4)	Great (5)	Mean
0-1							
0-2							
0-3	67	0	7	33	24	3	3.24
		0%	10.0%	49.0%	36.0%	4.0%	
0-4	76	0	9	45	19	3	3.21
		0%	11.8%	59.2%	25.0%	3.9%	
0-5	150	3	42	78	23	4	2.89
		2.0%	28.0%	52.0%	15.3%	2.7%	
06+	117	1	35	61	17	3	2.88
		0.9%	30.2%	51.7%	14.7%	2.6%	
Total		4	93	217	83	13	
		1%	23%	53%	20%	3%	

The intensity columns (None, Slight, Moderate, Considerable, Great) fall under the spanning header *Intensity*.

Source: Reproduced verbatim from *Study on Military Professionalism*, United States Army War College, 30 June 1970, p. B-2-2

* Total sample computed in table.

TABLE 12 Statistical Analysis of Answers to Question 9 on the Basis of Various Biographic Factors

$S = 415$

Question 9: "Do you feel that, within the officer corps as a whole, there is a discernible difference between the ideal standards and those that actually exist?"

1. A detailed breakdown of this attitude by various biographic factors is as follows:

Total months of command	S	X*	Total months of command	S	X
6 or less	54	3.19	36	35	2.79
12	68	3.27	42	18	2.67
18	48	2.83	48	28	2.96
24	36	3.06	54	50	2.90
30	40	3.05	60 or more	38	3.05

Source	S	X	Branch	S	X	Educational Level	S	X
USMA	105	3.03	Arms	322	2.99	12 or less	5	3.00
ROTC	151	2.97	Services	93	3.10	13–14	25	3.29
OCS	97	3.05				15–16	178	3.05
Direct	47	3.09				17 or more	207	2.97
Other	15	3.00						

2. Correlation of Question 9 vs. the variables indicated in Part I.

Variable	r=	Variable	r=
Grade	−.21	Educational level	−.09
Total months of command	−.11	Military education	−.29
Source	.01	Level of staff	−.22
Branch	.06	Level of command	−.13

Source: Same as Table 11

* X represents the mean arithmetic response, expressing degree of difference between ideal and existing standards, based on a scale from 1 ("no difference") to 5 ("great difference").

TABLE 13   *Department of Defense: Overseas and PCS* Moves by All Ranks in One Year*

Type of Move	Number of DOD Moves
Rotational (tour over or beginning)	467,635
Accessional (change of strength)	100,245
Separation (discharge)	107,916
Total PCS overseas moves	675,796
Total PCS moves	1,805,741†
Overseas moves as percentage of total moves	37%
Cost of all moves	$1,647,635,000

Source: *Department of Defense Appropriations for 1976; Hearing Before a Subcommittee of the Committee on Appropriations, House of Representatives, Ninety-fourth Congress, First Session,* Part 3, p. 364

* "Permanent change of station."

† All services.

TABLE 14   *Army Officer Retention Rates in Percentage,
Fiscal Years 1966–74 by Commission Source, Service One Year
Beyond Initial Obligation*

	Commission Source		
Year	U.S. Military Academy %	ROTC %	OCS %
1966	Unk.	20	56
1967	97	15	56
1968	96	14	48
1969	98	25	34
1970	77	11	22
1971	72	22	26
1972	72	19	30
1973	Unk.	47	62
1974	76	41	50

Source: Same as Table 13

FIGURE 1
Model of the Dynamics of Value Change
in a Military Bureaucracy

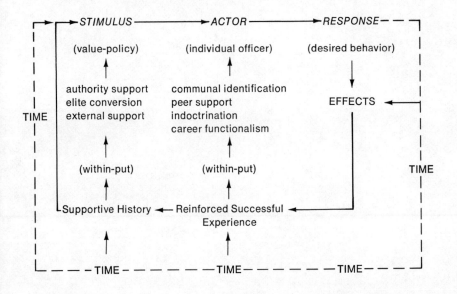

Notes

CHAPTER I

1. The difficulties involved in forcing a bureaucracy to initiate change are addressed by Anthony Downs's classic work, *Inside Bureaucracy* (Boston: Little, Brown, 1967), chapter 16.

2. The study eventually produced by the War College was entitled *Study on Military Professionalism* (Carlisle Barracks, Pa.: U.S. Army War College, 30 June 1970).

3. For an excellent examination of the role played by General Haig in the Nixon resignation, see the account contained in Woodward and Bernstein's *The Final Days*. The critical aspect of Secretary Schlesinger's role involved his decision to require that all orders to all military units originating in the White House first pass through the office of the Secretary of Defense.

4. The importance of the French defeat at Dien Bien Phu has been greatly exaggerated. Even after the battle, the French military establishment was largely intact throughout Indochina and was in control of most of the country, including all its major population centers. From a purely military perspective, the French were quite capable of continuing the war. Indeed, it was the Viet Minh who had largely reached the limit of their military capacity and this fact was one of the primary considerations in Ho's decision to go to Geneva. For more on this point see Richard A. Gabriel, *The Tactical and Strategic Failures of Dien Bien Phu* (Fort Huachuca, Ariz.: U.S. Army Intelligence School Archives, 1976).

5. There is no question in our minds that the United States could have imposed a purely military solution upon North Vietnam, but the price to

be paid in Vietnamese civilian casualties would have been morally repugnant even to Tacitus, who said of Rome's military policies that "they make a desert and call it peace."

6. Some of the arguments in support of this particular case can be found in Paul L. Savage and Richard A. Gabriel, "Cohesion and Disintegration in the American Army: An Alternative Perspective," *Armed Forces and Society*, Vol. 2, No. 3 (May 1976), pp. 340–76.

7. Edward A. Shils and Morris Janowitz, "Cohesion and Disintegration in the German Wehrmacht in World War II," *Public Opinion Quarterly*, Vol. 12 (1948), pp. 280–315.

8. "The impact of individually assigned DEROS dates as opposed to a tour of duty lasting for 'the duration' or having units assigned DEROS dates upon the cohesion of American units in Vietnam," can be found in Charles C. Moskos, Jr., "The American Combat Soldier in Vietnam," in *Journal of Social Issues*, Vol. 31 (1975), pp. 25–37.

9. By comparison, despite staggering losses, the German officer corps during World War II did not see fit to lower its qualifications for men awarded commissions.

10. Or, as put by Rudyard Kipling in his poem "The Vampire": "And it isn't the shame and it isn't the blame / That stings like a white-hot brand— / It's coming to know that she never knew why / (Seeing at last she could never know why) / And never could understand."

11. Moskos, *op. cit.*

12. Some data are provided by William L. Hauser, *America's Army in Crisis* (Baltimore: Johns Hopkins University Press, 1973), p. 175.

13. Such a statistical system was developed and employed by General Julian Ewell and was regarded by many officers, including the MACV commander General Abrams, with derision.

14. Our investigations have been unable to uncover any *official* directives authorizing the use of award "packages." However, interviews with a substantial number of officers, including Adjutant General officers whose task it was to award such packages, confirm beyond any doubt in our minds that such practices were widespread in Vietnam.

15. Comparative figures can be found in Savage and Gabriel, *op. cit.*

16. The use of the term "gladiatorial" in relation to the American military establishment is taken from *The Professional Soldier* by Morris Janowitz (New York: Free Press, 1971), who virtually pioneered the field of military sociology.

17. Among those who suggest the military is categorically different from civilian forms of social organization is Charles C. Moskos, Jr.,

"Trends in Military Social Organization," paper presented at the Center for Continuing Education, University of Chicago (June 1976). Along the same lines, General Maxwell Taylor's comment that "the Army is not for everyone . . . it is like a church," is instructive as well.

18. The burden of exposure to risk, especially within the enlisted ranks, was divided further. Career soldiers, the "lifers," were often able to manipulate the system to avoid combat exposure, especially during second tours of duty. Draftees were usually not so "lucky."

19. The notion that the officer corps is largely a reflection of its society and, indeed, is becoming more of a reflection is found in Franklin D. Margiotta, "A Military Elite in Transition: Air Force Leaders in the 1980's," *Armed Forces and Society*, Winter 1976, pp. 155–84. Margiotta's comments are of course directed at Air Force officers.

20. The Armies of Rome, for instance, were marvels of technology for their time and yet their fighting units retained high levels of cohesion. Technology per se compels nothing, and certainly no necessary alterations in basic military values. See Jacques Ellul, *The Technological Society* (New York: Alfred A. Knopf, 1964), pp. 29–32.

21. This point is supported by Bernard Crick, *In Defense of Politics* (London: Penguin Books, 1972), chapter 2.

22. The notion that the expansion of a group's social values to the larger society is related to its perceptions of external threats to its own core values finds support in R. L. Neiburg, *Political Violence: The Behavioral Process* (New York: St. Martin's Press, 1969), chapter 5.

Chapter II

1. See "Trends in Military Social Organization," paper presented at the Center for Continuing Education, University of Chicago (June 1976).

2. Morris Janowitz, *The Professional Soldier* (New York: Free Press, 1971), p. 425. It may be that disintegration of the U.S. Army is associated with the rise of managerials and their (extreme) displacement of Janowitz's "heroic" images—i.e., men seeking privilege and displacing men of honor.

3. See Theodore Ropp, *War in the Modern World* (New York: Collier, 1965), p. 250; and Leon Wolff, *In Flanders Fields* (New York: Ballantine, 1958), p. 73.

4. The general staff organization of the American Army, as in many other Western armies, is a variation of the Prussian system of command and staff. American field regulations governing the conduct of armies in

the field are derived, also, from Prussian influence. For example, see Leon Friedman, ed., *The Law of War* (New York: Random House, 1972), Vol. 1, pp. xv–xviii.

5. See Edward A. Shils and Morris Janowitz, "Cohesion and Disintegration in the German Wehrmacht in World War II," *Public Opinion Quarterly*, Vol. 12 (1948), pp. 280–315.

6. *Ibid.*, p. 281.

7. *Ibid.*, pp. 284, 287, 295–97. In addition to the usual esteem held by German soldiers for their immediate superiors, primary-group cohesion was further strengthened by a "hard core" which had a "gratifying adolescence under National Socialism" (p. 286). Even this small hard core was militarily oriented, not political.

8. *Ibid.*, p. 299.

9. *Ibid.*, p. 295.

10. Data obtained from Burkhardt Mueller-Hillebrand, *Das Heer, 1933–1945*, Vol. 3 of *Der Zweifrontenkrieg* (Frankfurt am Main: Verlag E. S. Mittler & Sohn, 1969), pp. 248–66.

11. Mueller-Hillebrand (*ibid.*) does not provide running data. Officer data here are interpolated. However, by 1945 German officer strength in front-line units had fallen to 50 percent of authorization. See Shils and Janowitz, *op. cit.*, p. 295. None of the figures includes missing in action.

12. See Paul Carell, *Scorched Earth* (New York: Ballantine, 1971), pp. 596–97.

13. See Josef Folttmann and Hans Moeller-Witten, *Opfergang der Generale* (Berlin: Verlag Bernard und Graefe, 1959), p. 85.

14. Dr. Matthias Graf von Schmettow, *Gedenkbuch des Deutschen Adels* (Limburg a.d. Lahn: C. A. Starke Verlag, 1967), p. x. No similar study exists on American "elites." In any case, the Brahmins of Boston do not seem to appear too often in the casualty lists, and almost never in the Vietnam War casualty lists.

15. Other data support the sense of duty and cohesion in the German Army. One example was the very low desertion rate. Cf. Shils and Janowitz, *op. cit.*, p. 285. Mueller-Hillebrand, *supra*, notes that only 2,600 men were listed as actual deserters in the total Wehrmacht: Army, Waffen SS, Luftwaffe, and Navy, *op. cit.*, p. 262.

16. A sharply illustrative and autobiographical account of small-unit warfare and the cohesion of German combat units is Guy Sajer, *The Forgotten Soldier* (New York: Harper & Row, 1971). This account stresses the regard German soldiers had for their officers, especially at the company level. Cf. Shils and Janowitz, *op. cit.*, p. 298.

17. Shils and Janowitz, *op. cit.*, pp. 287–88.

18. See Morris Janowitz and Roger Little, *Sociology and the Military Establishment* (New York: Russell Sage Foundation, 1965), pp. 82–83.

19. By minimal stress we mean: a situation in which an army experiences discontinuous combat, low levels of combat intensity, plus low casualties, all of which takes place over a protracted period of time. As we have emphasized, history is replete with examples of armies fighting under maximum stress and experiencing high casualties with no loss of cohesion.

20. Data from unpublished Veterans Administration Reports: *Data on Vietnam Era Veterans, June 1971* (Reports and Statistics Service, Office of the Controller, Veterans Administration, Washington, D.C.), p. 7. The VA data reveal the educational levels for veterans between the ages of 20 and 24 years in three conflicts. More college *dropouts* served in Vietnam than in World War II, but *fewer* college graduates served in Vietnam by some 69.41 percent.

21. There is some evidence that college-educated middle-class enlisted men decrease cohesion in primary groups. See Charles C. Moskos, Jr., *The American Enlisted Man* (New York: Russell Sage Foundation, 1970), pp. 74–76.

22. Studies of the American soldier in World War II reduced the conventional image of an ideologically committed soldier to shards. See Samuel Stouffer et al., *The American Soldier* (Princeton: Princeton University Press, 1949), Vol. 1, pp. 484–89; "The general picture of this volume, of men preoccupied with minimizing their discomforts, acquiring higher rank or pay, securing safe jobs which would offer training useful in civilian life, displaying aggressions against the Army in many different ways, and in getting out of the Army as fast as possible does not suggest a particularly inspired work performance in the American Army." The sense of commitment and generalized system dedication was found to be equally irrelevant in the Korean War by Roger Little. (See Janowitz and Little, *supra.*, pp. 77–79.) See Roger Little, "Deterioration of Military Work Groups Under Stress," in Morris Janowitz, ed., *The New Military* (New York: W. W. Norton, 1969), pp. 195–223. From a Marxist perspective, John Helmer, in *Bringing the War Home* (New York: Free Press, 1974), argues that the working-class soldiers in Vietnam became "alienated" and did so for "ideological" reasons. Moreover, they actively "resisted" for reasons of class-based ideology. Helmer surveyed Vietnam veterans in the Boston area. His sample totaled 90 respondents. See Helmer, pp. 43–105, *passim*, for "design study."

23. See Eugene Linden, "Fragging and Other Withdrawal Symptoms," *Saturday Review*, January 8, 1972, p. 12. Data on assassination of officers or

NCO's are, understandably, difficult to acquire. What data we present above are figures obtained from the Department of Defense and must be considered with suspicion if only because they tend to be overly conservative.

24. Inserted figures in Table 3 are from testimony by Major General Walter Kerwin, *Subcommittee on Appropriations, House of Representatives, Ninety-second Congress: Department of Defense Appropriations, 1972*, Part III, pp. 473–74. General Kerwin's figures do not agree with those in Table 3. We are inclined to accept the higher figures. Since the Pentagon is understandably sensitive about "fragging," they will not inflate such figures as they did other data—for example, "body counts." In the same hearing the General was asked if there were figures on the number brought to trial for such actions. He did not know, but said he would find out. Inserted later in the record was the following: "inquiry to U.S. Army Vietnam revealed that this information was not available." The probabilities are that the number of "fraggings" was much higher. Testimony of General Davis at the same hearing stated: "Fragging is not particularly new in warfare." He cited an incident of threats of violence by men against their officers at the Battle of Cedar Mountain in the Civil War. He denied as well that "fraggings" in Vietnam were beyond similar violence against officers in other American wars. It may be superfluous to add that General Davis was not in command of military history.

25. See Charles C. Moskos, Jr., "The American Combat Soldier in Vietnam," *Journal of Social Issues*, Vol. 31, No. 4 (1975), pp. 25–37.

26. Personal letter, Department of the Army, dated 26 July 1972, signed by Clayton N. Gompf, Acting Deputy for Military Personnel Policy and Programs. Such a gap in Pentagon data banks seems equivalent to the British Admiralty denying that any record was made of the Bounty Mutiny or, indeed, of the Napoleonic Wars mutinies, not to mention the French neglecting the mutinies of 1917.

27. *Nomination of Robert R. Froehlke: Hearing Before the Committee on Armed Services, United States Senate, June 1971*, pp. 9–11.

28. Although much remains secret about the French Army mutinies even today, some facts are known. The mutinies followed the disastrous Nivelle offensive beginning on April 16, 1917. By May 3, the French Army had lost 120,000 men for a gain of two miles. The mutiny began in the 21st Division of Colonial Infantry (Sinhalese). Outright deserters totaled 21,174 French. (See Wolff, cited *supra*, pp. 68–69.) Another source observes that "nearly 25,000 men were court-martialed . . . only 55 were shot and a few hundred sent to penal colonies . . . and a few officers had been attacked." (See Ropp, cited *supra*, p. 263.) French soldiers were

quoted as describing the (Nivelle) offensives as senseless. Many of the French mutinous outbreaks consisted of units which, saying they would fight defensively, refused, however, to attack.

29. Lee N. Robbins, *The Vietnam Drug User Returns* (Washington, D.C.: U.S. Government Printing Office, 1974).

30. Humrro Study, p. 423. Other findings reveal an inverse relation between drugs and the level of education (p. 428); blacks with a slightly higher use than whites (p. 480); daily usage higher among technicians than infantry (p. 432); users reported drugs easily available on base, ship, or town (p. 439). Data source is Senate hearing cited in Table 4, which reproduced the Humrro Study quoted.

31. Alfred W. McCoy et al., *The Politics of Heroin in Southeast Asia* (New York: Harper & Row, 1972), pp. 171–72, 218.

32. *Ibid.*, pp. 247, 262–64.

33. *Ibid.*, pp. 350–51.

34. Those so inclined are invited to read in the reports of congressional hearings the weak replies given by generals to questions by senators and representatives about fraggings, mutinies, desertion, and drugs. More remarkable is the prolonged unwillingness of the Congress to conduct detailed inquiries as to why such expensive armed systems were allowed to disintegrate. As an example, see hearings cited in note 24, *supra.*, pp. 220–51.

Chapter III

1. "Continuity was provided by the centurions, of whom there were six in each cohort. These formidable men combined the functions and prestige of a modern company commander and sergeant major or top sergeant." The historian Livy writes of such an officer of the early second century B.C., Spurius Ligustinus. By the time he was in his fifties and had undertaken twenty-two years of service, he had served four times as the senior centurion of his legion, and had won thirty-four decorations, including six civic crowns. A legion had ten cohorts of three maniples each, in turn containing two centuries of 80 men; each century was divided into ten mess units or *contabernia*. Thus, the legion's strength was some 4,800. See Michael Grant, *The Army of the Caesars* (New York: Charles Scribner's Sons, 1974), p. xxxiii.

2. Robert Ardrey, *The Territorial Imperative* (New York: Atheneum, 1966); Konrad Lorenz, *On Aggression* (London: Methuen, 1966); Lionel Tiger and Robin Fox, *The Imperial Animal* (New York: Holt, Rinehart and

Winston, 1971); and by the same authors, *Men in Groups* (New York: Random House, 1969).

3. *Study on Military Professionalism* (Carlisle Barracks, Pa.: U.S. Army War College, June 1970). Copy No. 250. Cited hereafter as AWC study. While not generally circulated, copies were provided to us on request to the War College.

4. AWC study, p. 55.

5. See *The Washington Post*, June 24, 1971, p. F6.

6. The differences were even greater for Korea than for the other two conflicts (see Table 8). However, when we discuss "linear" as contrasted to "confined" or "circular" warfare, it will be made clear why the conspicuous relatively low rate of officer losses in Korea did not impinge on enlisted perception horizons, as it did in Vietnam. Briefly, troops in both World War II and Korea rarely saw many officers in their transition to the lines, much less high-ranking ones. The situation was quite the reverse in Vietnam.

7. *Britannica Book of the Year*, 1954, p. 61. See Orville D. Menard, *The Army and the Fifth Republic* (Lincoln: University of Nebraska Press, 1967), p. 69.

8. See Menard, *op. cit.*, p. 58. In the entire Indochina war, Joseph Buttinger reports, 29,605 French and 11,620 Foreign Legionnaires for a total of 41,225 were lost. The remaining 41,995 were "colonials." See Joseph Buttinger, *A Dragon Embattled*, Vol. 2 (New York: Praeger, 1967), p. 1071, n. 2. One reason the OAS during the Algerian affair was able to persist for so long was the deep loyalty French enlisted men felt for their officers. There was clear recognition that French officers never sent their men to die alone.

9. Data from *Secrétariat d'Etat aux Anciens Combattants, République Française*, personal letter, 26 September 1974.

10. The one-year tour was also military policy in Korea during the combat phase. Yet disintegration indicators were not evident among the American units in Korea.

11. See Charles C. Moskos, Jr., *The American Enlisted Man* (New York: Russell Sage Foundation, 1970), pp. 7, 24, 30; and Roger Little, *op. cit.*, *supra*.

12. In Moskos, "The American Combat Soldier in Vietnam," *Journal of Social Issues*, Vol. 31, No. 4 (1975), pp. 33–34.

13. This argument was made in a letter received from a senior officer of the U.S. Army. In the same letter, the discriminatory distribution of losses among RA and draftee was justified on the grounds of economy: the volunteer had a longer-term value.

14. See William L. Hauser, *America's Army in Crisis* (Baltimore: Johns Hopkins University Press, 1973). See as well William R. Corson, *The Betrayal* (New York: Ace Books, 1968); Edward L. King, *The Death of the Army* (New York: Saturday Review Press, 1972); Ward Just, *Military Men* (New York: Alfred A. Knopf, 1970). One writer observed that over one half of the general officers serving in Vietnam received decorations for bravery. (King, *op. cit.*, pp. 103, 210–11.) Observing the same curious inflation of awards for general officers, Hauser provides further data on decorations given in Vietnam. In 1968, 416,693 awards of all types were passed out while total Americans killed in all services amounted to 14,592; in 1970, with total killed amounting to 3,946, some 522,905 medals were awarded. Incidents are given of fraudulent awards for senior officers who were given Silver Stars for acts not involving bravery of any special quality or for acts that were imaginary. (Hauser, *op. cit.*, p. 175.) *It should be added that as casualties lessened, together with sizable force reductions, awards for bravery accelerated!* No student of this subject appears to have noted the anomaly concerning large numbers of awards for bravery being issued to generals, namely, that medals for valor are often accompanied by the Purple Heart or given posthumously. With respect to generals in Vietnam, we have already shown that they do not die very often. Hauser's book recognizes that the Army is in peril, but fails to come to grips with root causes. He tends to attribute blame to forces outside of the Army—a proposition which we maintain is not credible. In the end, he has written a military apologia. His solution for the regeneration of the Army is to divide the institution into two strata. One level would be an elite, even Spartan fighting force; the other a semi-civilianized support system. (Hauser, *op. cit.*, pp. 201–28 *passim*.) For all the interest in leadership, little attention has been given to the relation of losses to performance in the Israeli Army. In the 1973 war, Israel lost 2,500 KIA of which 25 percent were officers. However, of the 2,500 killed, only 85 individuals were "private" soldiers. Thus, more than 95 percent of the dead were officers and NCO's. See Ward Just, "Israel," *Atlantic*, June 1975, p. 11. Just attributes his information to "private" sources. His data are, however, most credible.

15. Stuart H. Loory, *Defeated* (New York: Random House, 1973).

16. AWC study. In both the survey and the "Q" sort, the same themes emerged: careerism, self-seeking, and hypocrisy. It should be added that "Q" sorting properly applied permits the respondents to evolve as self-selected models. The report gave no details as to the exact "Q Sort Technique," although the method was attributed to Victor H. Vroom, *Work and Motivation* (New York: John Wiley and Sons, 1964); see p. B-30, AWC study. The study, conducted under Army War College control, also in-

cluded officers at a variety of higher army schools, among them the Command and General Staff College, and included junior officers.

17. AWC study; pp. 30–32 contain all quotations from the conclusions in the AWC study.

18. AWC study, pp. 28–29.

19. The number of cadets formally accused of cheating was 184, all apparently from the junior class. Allegations have been made that possibly 600 may have been involved. See *The New York Times*, July 24, 1976, p. 26; *ibid.*, July 25, 1976, p. 24. See Joseph Ellis and Robert Moore, *School for Soldiers* (New York: Oxford University Press, 1974), pp. 160–222, *passim.* The curious ethical and practical isolation of the Academy from the Army is well illustrated.

20. AWC study, pp. 28–29.

21. *Comprehensive Report: Leadership for the 1970's, USWAC Study of Leadership for the Professional Soldier* (Carlisle Barracks, Pa.: U.S. Army War College, 20 October, 1971), p. 27. This document is not classified; neither has it to our knowledge been widely circulated in nonmilitary circles.

22. Samuel Rolbant, *The Israeli Soldier: Profile of an Army* (South Brunswick: Thomas Yoseloff, 1970).

23. *Ibid.*, pp. 167–68.

24. *Ibid.*, p. 168.

25. *Ibid.*, pp. 169–72. The heavy losses among Israeli leaders rested on the tradition that the commander is always at the head of his troops. But "deeply imbedded in this custom was the conviction that all fighting men's lives were equally valuable. . . . There is no doubt that the fact that so many commanders, proportionately, fell in battle had a salutary effect on the morale of the troops." (*Ibid.*, p. 176.)

26. *Ibid.*, pp. 169–72.

Chapter IV

1. The exaggeration of careerism as a value to the neglect of other traditional military values is one of the major conclusions found in the study conducted for General Westmoreland by the Army War College on the subject of military professionalism. See AWC study, *op. cit.*

2. Some of the practical operational difficulties which confronted the American Army in Vietnam as they resulted from endemic structural problems are examined by Paul L. Savage and Richard A. Gabriel, "Cohesion and Disintegration in the American Army: An Alternative Perspective," *Armed Forces and Society*, Vol. 2, No. 3 (May 1976).

3. For more on the distinction between organizations as "occupations" versus "institutions," see Charles C. Moskos, Jr., "Trends in Military Social Organization," paper presented at the Center for Continuing Education, University of Chicago (June 1976).

4. A relatively good account of these scandals can be found in *Time*, June 7, 1976.

5. An excellent analysis of the results that can be expected when an individual is caught between the press of a course of action which he regards as morally wrong and the imperatives of organizational pressure can be found in Stanley Milgram, *Obedience to Authority* (London: Tavistock, 1974).

6. The American Army does subscribe to the Geneva Convention. Further, every young officer is told at some point in his career that he may refuse an order, but it is quickly added that every order is presumed to be legal until proven otherwise. Anyone who has had the experience of sitting through these basic indoctrination lectures is quite aware that they are not regarded as serious guides to action. Indeed, the notion of abiding by the rules of "civilized combat" as specified in the Geneva Convention are often treated as impractical and with contempt. In any event, a doctrine of moral resistance for the military officer has never been developed by the American Army, nor has it received the kind of informal support which would be required if such a doctrine were to function successfully. Even so, the United States government has refused to publish "The Rules of Engagement" written for Vietnam, those rules implementing the Geneva Convention. The New York Bar Association in 1972 asked President Nixon to reveal these rules. The reply from the President was dated February 15, 1972. The letter declined to reveal the "Rules of Engagement" on the grounds that "knowledge of the limitations imposed by the rules on United States . . . operations could be of substantial value to hostile forces in Indochina." The letter was signed by Nixon's counsel, John W. Dean III.

7. While clearly the impact upon policy that the resignation of any general officer will make remains an open question, in the main it seems obvious that had several generals resigned in the face of the Vietnam conflict, public support for the war would have faded rapidly. Further, civilian policy makers would have had to formulate policy with a view toward how the military would react to it in the public forum and this may well have led to an abandonment of some of the harsher policies of the war.

8. Principally, *respondeat superior* has been used as a defense against charges of war crimes during World War II, and rejected by international military tribunals. This concept has, of course, broader dimensions. Two further dimensions come to mind. The first is that Western military codes

enjoin obedience to *legal* orders. (Article 47 of *The German Military Penal Code of 1847:* ". . . the superior is alone responsible for illegal orders [but] . . . the obeying subordinate shall be punished as an accomplice . . .") Further, criminal responsibility for illegal acts increases as the chain of command rises so far as the crime comes unambiguously under international (criminal) law of war. Indeed, where war crimes occur, failure to exercise control associated with crime among subordinates, even in the absence of knowledge thereof, is no defense. See *In Re Yamashita* 327 U.S. 1 (1946) and dissents by Justices Murphy and Rutledge; also Leon Friedman, ed., *The Laws of War* (New York: Random House, 1972), Vol. 2, pp. 1430–70. Essentially, he who commands is responsible, though more so than his subordinates who are culpable mostly in terms mitigated by the actual situation. An even older legal norm of *respondeat superior* applies, of course, to the superior society as well, holding in common and code law in most Western nations that the "master" is responsible for the actions of his servants. See L. Oppenheim, *International Law: A Treatise* (8th ed.; New York: David McKay, 1965), pp. 339, 389, 493, 560, 574; *Register of International Law*, Vol. 10 (Washington, D.C.: Department of State Publication 8354, 1968), pp. 883, 941–42. Far deeper in the history of Western civilization is the concept of the just war. While no space may be taken for an examination in depth, the heritage of such an ethical construct is that violence in pursuit of national goals is governed by clear ethical constraints. The imperative, rested on individual participants, is to be responsible that these constraints not be violated. See Friedman, *op. cit.*, Vol. 1, pp. 3–15. From our position we affirm a direct linkage between the military ethic and law of the past, and forms of moral protest legitimately available to military professionals today.

9. We are not suggesting that the failure of junior officers to resign in deference to perpetuating their careers is an admirable act, but only that it is more understandable in practical terms. This is precisely why alternatives to resignation consistent with moral protest must be developed. Otherwise, the junior officer has little chance of being able to effectuate moral protest in the face of policies he considers immoral.

10. Such obligations spring from many sources, not the least of which are the values of the society that an officer has sworn to uphold as well as the military organization of which he is a part. In any event, such obligations are personally imposed and the obligation would exist *qua* obligation whether the means to effectuate it are functional to career advancement or not. In short, the case for circumstantial ethics is rejected.

11. In deference to the traditional Russian practice, we may call this assumption the "little father imperative."

12. By definition, moral imperatives are "ought" propositions and can never be demonstrated to be "true" in any empirical sense. Accordingly, the assumption of a moral obligation is to take an absolute position which, in and of itself, can brook no compromise. In short, the argument is not for a set of circumstantial ethics—often confused with prudential judgment—but for moral obligations, once assumed, as absolute constraints setting definite limits on human action.

13. The important point here is that the refusal to execute an order per se is not the end of the judgmental process. Whether in military or civilian society, that act is judged at a later time as to its acceptability or unacceptability. Thus, the willingness to "accept the consequences" of one's act of refusal is really a statement of readiness to justify one's actions at some appropriate time. It is *not* an assumption of *a priori* guilt or of one's preparedness to accept summary justice.

14. Ironically, such a tradition may be rooted in the fact that the military in both countries has drawn heavily upon the aristocracy for its members. This suggests that military officers who chose resignation still had alternative social and career roles to play outside the military. Additionally, it is probable that since both Britain and France have long traditions of parliamentary government where resignations of heads of state and cabinet ministers are commonplace, much of the trauma which we Americans tend to associate with resignation from public positions is reduced.

15. In this regard one recalls the suicide of the commanding officer of the *Graf Spee*. Further, it is also likely that the German officer corps, being drawn heavily from the Junker aristocracy, was able to employ the option of resignation for reasons similar to those in Britain and France, namely the existence of alternative social roles.

16. One may clearly have some doubts about the validity of such a doctrine. Yet it seemed to apply most often to officers of high rank, suggesting, if nothing else, that it was no empty code used to retain the loyalty and control of the junior officer corps.

17. It is axiomatic in the study of bureaucracies that formal rules of operation are heavily conditioned by the informal norms, values, and practices which constitute the milieu in which formal rules must operate. For more on this point see Anthony Downs, *Inside Bureaucracy* (Boston: Little, Brown, 1967), chapter 6.

18. Many policies in Vietnam were executed for over a decade and long after they had been shown to be not contributing to the aims of the war, largely because of the number of careers and interests involved in these policies. Such policies included "search and destroy," massive bombing in "free-fire zones," bombing of North Vietnam, and possibly "Operation

Phoenix" as well. Surely, one of the tests of the policies in the end was whether enemy strength was deeply affected by all of this. The catastrophic collapse of the South Vietnamese Army, an Army trained for almost twenty years by the United States, in a matter of days, if not hours, appears to us valid evidence of years of failing policies. Given the vast wealth of sophisticated equipment available to the South Vietnamese, their collapse can only have been caused by a total lack of cohesion, itself attributable to a failure to absorb even the most rudimentary of military ethics. See Frances FitzGerald, *Fire in the Lake* (Boston: Little, Brown, 1972), pp. 403–42 *passim*.

19. Which, by the way, is the contention that rests at the very base of the argument against an all-volunteer military force.

CHAPTER V

1. See Theodore H. Lowi, *The End of Liberalism* (New York: W. W. Norton, 1969). For all its humanistic intentions to equalize the distribution of income and pursue social justice, however defined, the benefits of politically institutionalized liberalism flow somewhat less to the more unfortunate strata of our society than to the bureaucrats who create the apparatuses. This is to say that the salaries and perquisites of office in the Department of Health, Education and Welfare far exceed the relative benefits which trickle to the lower-income groups. Alternatively, complex welfare systems create a class of civil servants with, first, a vested interest in their careers, and second, preserving to some degree the deprived clientele and associated social conditions that justify the continuance of the welfare system.

2. One of the more "rational" administrative and military systems created by a conscious reform effort was that of Prussia in the early nineteenth century. The entire Prussian system of government—military and civil—was reorganized with the intention of achieving maximum rationality and efficiency, an objective largely achieved, even over the opposition of the Prussian and East Elbian Junkerdom. The latter were simply coopted into the system. Given the basic Junker ethic of hard work, frugality, integrity, dedication, and military heritage, the cooptation was not difficult. See Herbert Jacob, *German Administration Since Bismarck* (New Haven: Yale University Press, 1963); Hans Rosenberg, *Bureaucracy, Aristocracy and Autocracy—The Prussian Experience, 1660–1815* (Boston: Beacon Press, 1966).

3. See "The Peers Report," *Report of the Department of the Army Review of*

the Preliminary Investigations into the My Lai Incident, 14 March 1970, Dept. of the Army (Washington, D.C.).

4. An autonomous IG is properly anonymous. Awards and decorations are superfluous in this setting. We will have more to say on awards and decorations later.

5. For analyses of the general effects of "grade creep" and rank inflation, see *Pyramids and Squishy Spheres: The Dynamic Context of Military Grade Creep*, Vols. 1 and 2, Executive Summary, Military Issues Research Memorandum (MIRM 74–76) dated 20 November 1974 (Carlisle Barracks, Pa.: U.S. Army War College, Strategic Studies Institute, 1974). These studies are ambivalent on both the cause of and future trends with respect to rank distributions in large organizations, civil and military. The studies do demonstrate that rank inflation is characteristic of technocratic societies. The studies do not deal with the consequences of rank inflation, which do not contribute to good performance.

6. *Department of Defense Appropriations for 1976; Hearing Before a Subcommittee on Appropriations, House of Representatives, Ninety-fourth Congress, First Session*, Part II, p. 366.

7. *Ibid.*, Part III, p. 577.

8. *Study on Military Professionalism* (Carlisle Barracks, Pa.: U.S. Army War College, June 1970), pp. vi–ix. As pointed out, some follow-up on the original AWC study was done in 1971. We are informed that a final data base of over 30,000 is planned.

9. *The Washington Post*, Sunday, August 27, 1977, p. A14. This commentary by Bill Peterson states that Kinnard will publish an article on his findings in the September 1977 issue of *Human Behavior*. Two other findings of importance by Kinnard are "a striking lack of communication between the generals and political leaders" and "the lack of consensus among the generals and their sharp division over war tactics."

10. *The Army Times*, 16 July 1977, p. 2.

11. *Ibid.*, 27 June 1977, p. 12.

12. *Department of Defense Appropriations for 1978, Hearings Before a Subcommittee on Appropriations, House of Representatives, Ninety-fifth Congress, First Session*, Part I, Budget Overview, pp. 183 and 220–21. In some fairness, it must be pointed out that officer strength had been reduced by 22,000 since 1972 in a period when the Army has added three new divisions. "Officers to man these divisions were obtained by eliminating seven major headquarters, reorganizing the Army staff, and pursuing officer reductions in the remaining headquarters. A stable officer strength at the 98,000 level is necessary *through FY 1982* [our emphasis] to procure the officers required as leaders and managers [sic.]." It is superfluous to point out that officer infla-

tion will continue into the 1980's. From a view of another service, the opinion of Admiral Hyman Rickover seems apt; namely, that in his judgment the quality of flag officers is very low and their numbers could be cut by 50 percent. See *The Army Times*, 18 April 1977.

13. House of Representatives Hearings cited above. See pp. 177–87, 208–13, 226–30—a recounting of a semi-mutiny by twenty-two men in Battery C of the 94th Artillery, Berlin Brigade. The event was called a "sit-in" with the soldiers demanding, among other things, "the right to approve all asignments of leadership positions" and that the Army remove leaders whom they did not approve. Some courts-martial resulted from all this, together with other disciplinary actions. The event took place on 25 November 1974.

CHAPTER VI

1. The doctrine of rationality is heavily embedded in entrepreneurial notions of bureaucracy, probably, as Dwight Waldo suggests, because the first schools of public administration were financed by business corporations in an effort to apply the "rational" calculations of the Smithian marketplace to public administration. In any event, a reading of Anthony Downs, *An Economic Theory of Democracy* (New York: Harper & Row, 1957), clearly reflects the rationalist bias of many bureaucratic theorists.

2. The application of cost-benefit analysis as a means of functionally measuring rationality is the most widely used method of deciding which practices to maintain and which to abandon.

3. Indeed, one of the major difficulties of attempting to assess the "value" of a given procedure in a corporative bureaucracy is precisely the fact that such procedures often have no "economic" facets by which they can be measured. A similar problem is encountered in attempting to employ cost-benefit analysis in public administration programs. For more on this difficulty, see Anthony Downs, *Inside Bureaucracy* (Boston: Little Brown, 1967), chapter 4.

4. The proposition legitimizing the pursuit of one's own self-interest is so heavily ingrained in American social, economic, and political thought as to border on the self-evident. Its roots run to the free enterprise of Adam Smith, the social Darwinism of Herbert Spencer, and the political laissez-faire of James Madison. For an examination of the literature as it relates specifically to the area of bureaucracy, see William Scott and Terence Mitchell, *Organization Theory: A Structural and Behavioral Analysis* (Homewood, Ill.: Dorsey Press, 1972).

5. The role of psychological factors in motivation has been explored by Chris Argyris, *Personality and Organization* (New York: Harper Torch Books, 1957); Herbert Simon, *Administrative Behavior* (Chicago: Free Press, 1945); and Robert Presthus, *The Organizational Society* (New York: Vintage, 1962). All three analysts utilize the entrepreneurial bureaucracy as their baseline and move to the conclusion that there is more often than not an evident enmity between the individual and the organization in terms of the former's desire for psychic rewards. The point is that the ethos of the entrepreneurial bureaucracy suggests that this basic difficulty can be overcome by improving material rewards. What we are suggesting here is that these analysts may be using the wrong baseline or, more specifically, that there are different baselines for different types of organizations and that the military as an organizational type cannot be equated with the entrepreneurial.

6. Warren Bennis in his *Organizational Development* (Reading, Mass.: Addison-Wesley, 1967), agrees with Argyris and Presthus that a basic problem confronting bureaucracy in general is how to bring the values of the individual into consonance with those of the organization and still accomplish the organizational task. All suggest that the best motivator of individual action is the internalization of organizational values. Clearly this problem is much more acute in a corporative institution such as the military.

7. Of course, the reverse may occur too, in that purely entrepreneurial organizations can begin to adopt the practices of a corporative institution. Interestingly, when this does happen in the entrepreneurial world, analysts identify such a transformation as a pathology and label it "goal displacement." Strikingly, no similar analysis or terminology has been developed to address the process as it occurs in a military or corporative institution.

8. An excellent review of the models available in the literature can be found in Scott and Mitchell, *op. cit.*, chapters 15–16.

9. The term is taken directly from Anthony Downs, *Inside Bureaucracy*, whose analysis of the transition from organization to institution can be found in chapter 16 of his book.

10. Research on the American officer corps suggests that some values in military bureaucracies are frequently present only at the verbal level. Thus, such injunctions as "continue the mission," "take the initiative," and "always tell the truth" appear formally in report after report. Yet these are infrequent guides to actual behavior simply because the individual officer often perceives them as not being functional to career advancement. Such values may be termed "latent values" insofar as they are at least formally

present within the ideology of the institution; they are distinct from totally new values. For more on this point, see *Study on Military Professionalism* (Carlisle Barracks, Pa.: U.S. Army War College, June 1970); see also Paul L. Savage and Richard A. Gabriel, "Cohesion and Disintegration in the American Army: An Alternative Perspective," *Armed Forces and Society*, Vol. 2, No. 3 (May 1976).

11. Downs, *Inside Bureaucracy*.

12. Both Gordon Tullock, *The Politics of Bureaucracy* (Washington, D.C.: Public Affairs Press, 1965), and Chester I. Barnard, *The Functions of the Executive* (Cambridge: Harvard University Press, 1974), make clear that to the extent subordinate behavior depends upon executive communication, such communication must be as undistorted as possible if expected subordinate behavior is to result.

13. Tullock, drawing heavily upon Machiavelli, makes the point that elite behavior must be above reproach if it is to serve as even a general guide to subordinates seeking to adjust to a new policy. Tullock, *op. cit.*, chapters 9–12. The tendency to develop an "upward looking posture," as both Downs and Presthus suggest, seems to us to be magnified in the primary stages of initiating a new policy simply because uncertainty is increased as past behavior ceases to be a guide for future action.

14. The proposition that organizations react most swiftly to outside pressure is a major finding of Downs's work. Downs, *Inside Bureaucracy*, chapter 16.

15. Not much theoretical notice has been taken of the role of "purges" at the top as a means of converting bureaucratic elites to new policies. One of the better works on the subject is Edward Feit, *The Armed Bureaucrats* (Boston: Houghton Mifflin, 1973). In general, such purges seem confined to developing countries (Nigeria, Ghana) or to developed but highly ideological ones such as China and the Soviet Union. In any event, existing elites may well attempt to sabotage new policies because of their own career investments and because the acceleration of "new blood" to the top seems clearly to aid the conversion process.

16. In attempting to gauge elite reactions to any policy innovation, the extent to which the troops can be expected to follow elite orders is critical. Accordingly, the "law of anticipated reactions" places limits upon elite behavior simply because an officer corps convinced of its values will not lightly violate them or conceal such violations on the grounds of career advancement.

17. This proposition is virtually axiomatic in any theory of bureaucracy. A particularly good explanation of its impact can be found in Argyris, *op. cit.*

18. The ability of the individual to resist the group and group pressure ranks among the most interesting subjects in psychology. It strikes us that to the extent that the individual is able to stand alone against the organization, it is somewhat easier in an entrepreneurial bureaucracy than in a communal one if for no other reason than the psychic investment is less. By extension, then, peer support becomes more important to resisting the dictates of the organization in a corporative bureaucracy.

19. The proposition is put forth that in a truly corporative institution such as the military, there is a whole series of goals which are valued above the value of mere career advancement. If not, then the tendency toward adopting entrepreneurial ethics has gone much further than we had expected.

20. What is being addressed here is what might be called the "price of belonging" to a community. A detailed model of the process by which an individual is integrated into a community can be found in James Toscano and Karl Deutsch, *The Integration of Political Communities* (Philadelphia: J. B. Lippincott, 1964).

21. A basic proposition of this work is that the link between career survival and self-interest need not assume an entrepreneurial bureaucracy full of calculating individuals. For example, the desire of a monk to be a good monk involves calculations of career survivability yet does so within the confines of communal and peer norms expressed within a corporative bureaucratic structure. The assumption is that the officer wants to be a good officer per se and that by being a good officer he will also succeed as a career officer. In short, there is no necessity to reduce all calculations made by individuals to entrepreneurial ones. In a corporative institution, it is the logic of the monk which operates, not that of the businessman.

22. This is a basic proposition underlying Downs's work. For a fascinating study on its operation in the federal bureaucracy, see Harold Seidman, *Politics, Position and Power: The Dynamics of Federal Organization* (London: Oxford University Press, 1970).

23. To be sure, the U.S. Congress has been reluctant to issue a set of laws and the military has been even more timid. External pressure in the form of legislative statutes would have at least a communicative value and a potentially compelling value since the onus for violating such statutes would rest upon the violator even "if everyone is doing it." A more detailed treatment of this problem can be found in Richard A. Gabriel and Paul L. Savage, "Legitimate Avenues of Military Resistance in a Democratic Society," *American Sociological Association Proceedings*, Summer 1976.

24. Explanations are isomorphic "copies" of reality insofar as every theoretical element has a direct or indirect empirical referent. Models, on the

other hand, are not nearly so exact in that they are simplifications of reality, the idea being that by minimizing the complexity of reality the analyst is able to perceive relationships that were being hidden by that very complexity. For two excellent works on the nature of models and theories, see Allan C. Isaak, *Scope and Methods of Political Science* (Homewood, Ill.: Dorsey Press, 1970), and Robert Dublin, *Theory Building* (New York: Free Press, 1969).

25. This does not mean, of course, that all elements of a model lack empirical import or that because the model is not totally isomorphic that it is irrelevant to reality. Indeed, the purpose of models is to increase one's understanding of reality through simplification of it.

26. All models are driven by a calculus. Without making basic assumptions, there is no basis for a calculus and, thus, no basis for making the model work. See Isaak, *op. cit.*, chapter 8.

27. Those interested in pursuing the relative merits of the behaviorist and the behavioralist position should read David Easton, "The Current Meaning of Behavioralism in Political Science," and Heinz Eulau, "Segments of Political Science Most Susceptible to Behavioristic Treatment," both of which appear in James C. Charlesworth, ed., *The Limits of Behavioralism in Political Science* (Philadelphia: American Academy of Political and Social Science, October 1962).

28. In this regard, we suspect that while supplantation of elites leads to a more rapid adoption of new values, in the American military, indoctrination seems the more practical alternative.

29. The extent to which authority support can be expected to ramify throughout a bureaucratic hierarchy and some of the variables involved are discussed by Barnard, *op. cit.* The suggestion is clearly that existing elites are not going to cooperate in their own demise. Accordingly, it is to be expected that at least some members of the "old guard" will have to be replaced by younger aspirants who manifest new values.

30. Of course, the reverse may occur, in which case new values will either recede to the status of latent values or simply be abandoned altogether.

31. See Tullock, *op. cit.*, and Barnard, *op. cit.*, on the value of elite-subordinate communication as a stimulus to subordinate behavior.

32. Once again the reader is reminded that the term "reward-punishment calculus" should not be taken in the strict entrepreneurial sense. Rather, as it applies to the military officer, it is more accurate to describe it as the psychic "price of belonging" to a community.

33. Indeed, this is exactly what is implied by the necessity to develop

primary-group loyalty as a means of producing cohesion among the officer corps.

34. An examination of the factors involved in systems change can be found in Toscano and Deutsch, *op. cit.* The model offered here cannot predict the speed, breadth, or depth of systems change as a function of its own internal calculus. It can only suggest that such change is likely to occur given the specified interaction of the variables in the model.

CHAPTER VII

1. That study is now available under the title *Study on Military Professionalism* (Carlisle Barracks, Pa.: U.S. Army War College, June 1970).

2. Robert Presthus, *The Organizational Society* (New York: Vintage, 1962), p. 36.

3. The role of informal values as they impact upon formal instrumentalities within an organizational structure has already been explored at an earlier place in this book. Those wishing to explore the point further are referred to Anthony Downs, *Inside Bureaucracy* (Boston: Little, Brown, 1967).

4. *Study on Military Professionalism*, p. 53.

5. *Ibid.*

6. *Ibid.*

7. The term "value-infused" is taken from Downs, *op. cit.*, chapter 25.

8. Quoted from Rudyard Kipling's poem "If."

9. Quoted from "A Shropshire Lad" by A. E. Housman.

Bibliographical Essay

In the first part of this book we addressed the state of the United States Army, its leadership, and its lack of battle cohesion. The latter part suggests changes in the structure of the Army designed to increase unit cohesion. The following discussion is concerned primarily with the basic literature necessary to understand the historical and contemporary processes of military cohesion and disintegration.

The best current summary of material in military sociology is Charles C. Moskos, Jr., "The Military," in the *Annual Review of Sociology*, Vol. 2, 1976. Unavoidably some of our sources will overlap his, since our more narrow interest is that of military cohesion and disintegration. We emphasize, however, that Moskos is invaluable as a review of the field. We will not duplicate commentary found in the chapter notes except where the book or article is essential to the essay.

I
Historical Background: Men in Groups and Men in War

One category of military sociology which remains largely unexamined is that of comparative elite sacrifice and the relation elites in war may bear on the willingness of lower-status elements to assume the sacrifice of battle. By "elites in war" is meant not only the losses of officers but the visibility of leaders in battle to the primary military groups doing the fighting. John Keegan's *The Face of Battle* (New York: Viking Press, 1976) examines three engagements, Agincourt, Waterloo, and the Somme 1916. Quite aside from the vivid description of combat, one factor emerges in Keegan's study as crucial. This factor is the visibility of the leadership to the fighting formations, who perceived a willingness by their leaders to take risks equal to and usually exceeding that of the ranks. This factor applies whether the battles were medieval, nineteenth century, or in France in World War I. For whatever reasons British officers exposed themselves to risk, be it honor, promotion, or a sense of prowess, this visibility in battle directly and positively affected the cohesion of English fighting elements. Indeed, British officer losses in the First Somme approximated 75 percent of officer committed strength in the *initial* assault. An analysis of why men act as cohesive fighting groups is found in the works of Lionel Tiger and Robin Fox, *Men in Groups* (New York: Random House, 1969), and *The Imperial Animal* (New York: Holt, Rinehart and Winston, 1971). For a variety of reasons, men during their evolutionary development have tended to bond in groups. Competition for millennia over scarce resources relentlessly pressured men in hunting and war bands to wider and wider conflict. The selective process produced a survival form given to aggressive war when vital interests were at stake and, eventually as opportunity for enrichment. The implication is that the vast and complex apparatus of modern war is an evolutionary product of the basic tendency of male group bonding led by individuals distinguished in battle and with expectancies to reproduce their type. The social system of group-bonded males is biogrammatically a result of evolutionary processes predicated at least in part on the regularity of warfare. In this process the successful survive and the inept die, with the most successful individuals being the leaders. In a related context, see Stanislav Andreski, *Military Organization and Society* (London: Routledge and Kegan Paul, 1954); and Robert Ardrey, *African Genesis* (London: Collins,

1961), *The Territorial Imperative* (New York: Atheneum, 1966), and *The Social Contract* (New York: Atheneum, 1970). For an exceptional and scholarly overview of "militarism" versus the "military way," Alfred Vagts, *A History of Militarism* (New York: Free Press, 1959), is indispensable. For the classically inclined, Tacitus is recommended together with the *Anabasis* of Xenophon. From this same perspective, see as well *The Army of the Caesars*, by Michael Grant (New York: Charles Scribner's Sons, 1974). The Roman Army exceeds virtually all Western political institutions in operating with a long-term military view; this Army was, as Grant observes, the longest-lived political institution of Western civilization.

Modern war tends to kill leadership in large numbers, and while this is not demonstrably a determinant factor in cohesion, German military cohesion in World War II appears related to their high officer losses and even losses among the upper classes. The historical lesson seems to suggest that societies are hierarchical and motivated by their upper orders as exemplars. Recent research shows that some 10 percent of male English gentry were killed in action in World War II. Whatever one might say about the American establishment, there is little evidence that its youth readily face battle; they thus incurred but minimal losses in recent wars. A forthcoming article by Richard A. Gabriel and Paul L. Savage, "Comparative Elite Sacrifices in War," observes that American elites are notable by their absence in battle.

That primary groups remain essential to modern military systems is amply demonstrated in the seminal article by Edward A. Shils and Morris Janowitz, "Cohesion and Disintegration in the German Wehrmacht in World War II," *Public Opinion Quarterly*, Vol. 12, 1948. Commenting on *The American Soldier* by Samuel Stouffer et al., Hans Speier's "The American Soldier and the Sociology of Military Organization" provides great insight. See *Studies in the Scope and Method of "The American Soldier,"* in Robert K. Merton and Paul F. Lazarsfeld, eds. (New York: Free Press, 1950). An even more historic study of men in battle and the role small mutually trusting groups play in military cohesion is Ardant du Picq's *Battle Studies: Ancient and Modern,* originally published in 1880 (Harrisburg, Pa.: The Military Service Publishing Co., 1958).

Further works on the "Common Soldier" (*sic*) are outlined in Moskos's bibliographical essay (*op. cit. supra*), some of which have been considered at length in our chapter notes. More importantly we find that other less quantitative and less sociological works are invaluable for appreciating the perspective of the ranks as groups in war. Some of these are historical case studies; others are novelistic accounts. For the American experience in World War II and Korea, the books of S. L. A. Marshall—*Men Against Fire* (New York: William Morrow, 1947) and *Pork Chop Hill* (New York: William Morrow, 1956)—are vital. The French experience in the first Indochina war lives in Bernard Fall's *Street Without Joy* (Harrisburg, Pa.: Stackpole, 1964) and *Hell in a Very Small Place* (Philadelphia, J. B. Lippincott, 1967). Many novels examine the German fighting on the Eastern Front in World War II. Among the better are Willi Heinrich's *The Cross of Iron* (Indianapolis: Bobbs-Merrill, 1966), a study of a German NCO of remarkable professional detachment, capability, and ability to elicit group loyalty. *The Forgotten Soldier,* by Guy Sajer (New York: Harper & Row, 1971), is of unusual interest since it is an autobiographical account of an Alsatian volunteer in the Wehrmacht serving on the Eastern Front. The book relates the pattern of socialization of an individual into an elite division, and the system for building and maintaining small-unit cohesion detached, so far as can be gathered, from ideological pressures.

II
Contemporary Professionalism

To the extent that military professionalism relates to cohesion it would seem that the former must exhibit some regularity of behavior, notably among the leadership, and that this behavior must conform to a relatively coherent code of military ethics. The modern American military professional has been brilliantly described in *The*

Professional Soldier by Morris Janowitz (New York: Free Press, 1971). One concern of Janowitz, cited by Moskos, *supra*, was what limits there might be to the "civilianization" (convergence of values) of the military as an instrument of war and, by implication, the question of to what degree the military might or must foster a sense of isolation from civilianized (managerial?) values. Where Samuel P. Huntington, *The Soldier and the State* (Cambridge: Harvard University Press, 1967), and Janowitz diverge is that for Huntington the military needs to maintain a "corporate self identity and ultimate responsibility to the larger polity" (Moskos *supra*, p. 58). For Janowitz the problem is one of integration.

It seems that sociologists have begun to take a greater interest in the meaning of military professionalism to the extent that the *American Behavioral Scientist* devoted an entire issue to the problem of "Military Ethics and Professionalism," Vol. 19, No. 5 (May–June 1976). The first article, "Introduction: Professionalism," by Sam Sarkesian, places Professor Sarkesian solidly on the side of military-civilian convergence, arguing that no other alternative is possible in a democratic society. One excellent analysis in the issue is by Malham M. Wakin, "The Ethics of Leadership." Wakin, citing the Army War College *Study on Military Professionalism*, 1970 (cited *supra*, *passim*), writes that while officers perceive that there are higher military ideals, the military institution does not permit their achievement. Most importantly Wakin recognizes that "loyalty is best engendered in subordinates when they can reside their full trust in their leaders and that trust is readily given only to those superiors who are perceived to be persons of high moral integrity." In "Conflicting Loyalties and the American Military Ethic," Philip M. Flammer observes that genuine moral integrity among the military is rare and even rarer the higher the rank—and this applies cross-culturally and historically. This article is highly recommended. For some additional pathologies affecting the service academies, see "Professionalism and the Service Academies," by John P. Lovell. While some of the studies and articles in the *American Behavioral Scientist* are good, we are left with the belief that all remains adrift in the effort, first, clearly to define modern American military professionalism and, second, the unwillingness to formulate and enforce a code regulating the behavior associated with the military profession. Surely the credibility status of both the legal and medical professions tells us something about professions which allegedly *have* codes of ethics and what happens when the codes are transgressed or ignored.

The place in America where clear moral principles are designed to condition behavior throughout a military career would seem to be the United States Military Academy at West Point. In *School for Soldiers* (New York: Oxford University Press, 1974), Joseph Ellis and Robert Moore demonstrate that little of the West Point experience appears to prepare cadets for ethical conduct in the larger Army, nor is any *specific* ethical code taught in the curriculum. Our own examination of the West Point curriculum finds no systematic approach to ethical and moral philosophy given, say, as a series of courses throughout four years.

While the Military Academy may have neglected systematic presentation of moral philosophy or even a comprehensive and integrated course in ethics, the study of leadership has not been avoided. The Academy has an entire department created for its study. The Academy's Office of Military Leadership has produced a volume entitled *A Study of Organizational Leadership*, "Edited by the Associates in Military Leadership, United States Military Academy, West Point, New York" (1st ed., 1975). Certain curiosities about this volume are immediately obvious. The volume contains fifty-one essays and articles, including subsection introductory commentaries. Of all these efforts there appear to be but two articles centering on men in battle, and only one directly examines small groups in combat: "Why Men Fight," by Charles C. Moskos, Jr. Moskos clearly doubts the *centrality* of the primary group in Vietnam, resting such "solidarity of combat squads" as existed "as an outcome of self interest" (survival). However, Moskos recognizes that the primary cause of downgraded small-unit cohesion in Vietnam was the pernicious backdrop of the rotation system, where, as we have observed, cohesion could hardly be expected to be high. It must be noted that Moskos takes a microscopic and essential view of war, highlighting the pernicious effect that isolate *managerial* military organizations appear to have upon the building block of successful battle—highly cohesive primary military groups which do *not* operate by managerial principles. Another of the pertinent articles reviews background theory on primary groups: "Primary Groups, Organization, and Military Performance," by Alexander L. George. Summarizing the work of Ardant du Picq, Edward A. Shils, and Morris Janowitz and Roger Little on the dyadic primary group in the Korean War, George recognizes that there is "considerable variation in [the] scope and content of primary group ties [to be] expected, depending on the conditions and circumstances surrounding small military groups." In one of the very few essays that suggest starting points for an examination of the standards of military leadership and a possible detailed code that might be extracted from such standards, George lists *Factors Affecting Formation of Primary Group Ties*. These factors, summarized by us, are worth listing: (1) *Social Background of Unit Members:* National homogeneity is a "plus." (2) *Personality of Unit Members:* Members from stable social and familial background are better suited to group life. (3) *Protectiveness of Immediate Leaders:* Officers are perceived as interested and concerned; cf. the Army War College study. (4) *Performance of Immediate Leaders:* Tactical leadership is vital, and not based on threat, but on example. (5) *Military Discipline and the Role of Honor:* The need young soldiers experience for order, manliness, and "being a good soldier who gets his job done." (6) *Commitment to One's Socio-Political System, Ideology and Patriotism:* While these factors are "secondary symbols they provide the rudiments of one of the most important preconditions for the formations of primary groups which have a more positive and immediate function in strengthening the soldier's will to exert himself under dangerous conditions." This latter quote is from Edward A. Shils in his commentary on *The American Soldier* (cf. *supra*). We doubt that such feelings were even as strong as "secondary" after, say, the sixth month of Verdun in 1916, or after the Second Somme, not to mention the battles on the Eastern Front in World War II or, for that matter, among American troops in the protracted Italian campaign. Still, in our judgment, such feelings can do no harm and may do much good in the opening stages of a long war but contribute little in the lengthy periods of high attrition. (7) *War Indoctrination:* Same commentary as above and with the same limitations. (8) *Exigencies of Military Life and of the Combat Situation:* Shared hardship by all, leaders and ranks, will create elementary cohesion. (9) *Technical Aspects of Weapons Systems:* Weapons systems which maintain close personal proximity "contribute most to primary group cohesion" (Janowitz and Little, 1957). By this we mean rifle, machine gun, mortar squads, tank crews, and similar close-fighting elements. (10) *Replacement System and Rotation Policy:* Where for Moskos the individual replacement system contributed to high individual morale, it is clear that individual rotation had a very poor effect on small-unit military cohesion. The practice of *small groups in "packets"* was tried but brought "with it a different set of problems." *No* consideration is given to the possibility of large-unit replacement, i.e., battalion through division size. (11) *Social Prestige and Soldierly Profession:* Military cohesion is higher where the armed forces are held in esteem by the larger social system. An example is that of China, where though for centuries soldiers were held in low esteem, that situation now appears to have been reversed. This implies that equalization of service conditions is one factor—conspicuous consumption and luxurious privileges by leadership being radically reduced. We provide this somewhat lengthy summary for one purpose: there appear to be several cues to generate a code of leadership ethics which link readily to the sociology of men in battle but which, of course, are nowhere followed up.

Another article, by Samuel H. Hayes and William N. Thomas, "Moral Aspects of Leadership," examines in some detail what a moral code could be. They cite Kant, Plato, Aristotle, Royce, and Dewey with the intention of noting the Western tradition of creating codes of morality which in some way were systematized. In our culture most professions have long had formal and informal codes of ethics directed at the control of behavior. Among these are the legal profession, medicine, and, in different places and times, the military. The history of the military, particularly beginning in the sixteenth and seventeenth centuries and with the use of mercenary soldiery, required controlling codes and many were evolved. Hayes and Thomas then go on to discuss what duty, honor, and country entail, addressing terms derivable from this trilogy. *Duty* involves responsibility, courage, obedience, initiative, and loyalty. *Honor* demands integrity, reputation, authority, and justice. *Country* exacts loyalty to country, support of the civil-military relationship, support of policy (but with *no* suggestion that resistance by way of resignation or retirement is admissible). All these commitments also involve pathologies which break the "code."

The two foregoing articles are the closest thing we can find that suggest the need of a code and specify some basis for its elaboration. Nowhere in the text can we find a suggested and formalized code of military ethics and morality. Indeed, recognizing the fact that serious pathologies existed in the U.S. Army in Vietnam, there appears to be small serious effort directed at their correction—merely a type of persuasive continuity.

The one essay, titled "Professionalism," that is unambiguously critical of the military and points out very serious pathologies is an excerpt from *America's Army in Crisis* by William L. Hauser (Baltimore: Johns Hopkins University Press, 1973). Hauser discusses "War Crimes," "Corruption," and "Careerism" and the inflated decoration "package" policy, going on to say that a "disjuncture between the Army and society has brought about this long litany of troubles . . ." Surprisingly, Hauser notes at the same time that "the Army has been unable to *isolate* [our emphasis] itself from society sufficiently to maintain its authoritarian discipline or to prevent such social ills as racial discord and drug abuse." How can it be both ways? If the Army is to be convergent in some degree, then to that degree it must absorb the social and political values and pathologies of the civil system. To the degree that it is divergent it might fend them off and to its own benefit follow the military way instead of the managerial way. The dilemma is clear: The Army cannot have it both ways—it cannot follow the military way and be managerially civilized at the same time. Worse, it does not have a coherent code of behavior for either horn of the dilemma.

A Study of Organizational Leadership stresses overarching *organization* far too much instead of the military fighting element as a *group*—and *all* ground fighting is done in small groups. The "organization," it seems to us, can have but little meaning to fighting troops due to its inherent abstraction. A great part of the volume nonetheless is concerned with a range of abstractions dealing with the sometimes complicated dimensions of social psychology which at times assumes a perfectionist ideology such as "The Study of Man at His Best," by Abraham Maslow, where the central concern is growth and "self-actualization." How it may apply to the ferocity of ground combat escapes us.

One learned article on "Socialization," by Gertrude Jaeger Selznick, runs a lengthy hagiography of social psychologists from Pavlov and Freud through Mead and Bronfenbrenner. Central to the discussion is child and family. Such material would be unexceptionable in a course on social psychology, but in a volume on military leadership and its pragmatic demands, the article seems strangely out of place.

Leadership as such is, of course, discussed. One of the articles is "Leader Behavior—Theory and Study," by Wayne A. Wheeler and Louis S. Csoka. A point of interest is that a model called the "managerial grid," with some directions to evaluate leadership, is included. Here we find a fundamental confusion in this text as a whole and that is the fundamental confusion, a dangerous one, between managerialism and combat leadership. It is enough to say that combat leadership and management are not the same, and in fact the managerial perspective may be fatal to military cohesion at the combat-unit level.

One other section of interest in the Academy text is titled *Transactions*. It appears as a function of communications theory. One article is titled "Transactional Analysis for Managers or How to be OK with OK Organizations," by V. P. and L. L. Luchsinger. The fundamental analogous relationship used in this article is that between parent and child and manager and employee. We cannot resist quoting from the summary of this essay:

Hints for Managers

The effective manager should be able to analyze transactions with employees. . . . The manager should be able to identify the ego states from which both parties are interacting. A better understanding of himself, employees, and interactions with others will make the manager more comfortable, confident and effective. He will be aware of ego states and seek the proper ego states when interacting with employees.

It is difficult to see how this sort of thinking can be useful to soldiers.

To the greater rather than to the lesser extent this Military Academy text on organizational leadership is dominated by studies more or less similar to the foregoing. The overwhelming weight is on the side of a curious alliance between managerial theory and dubious social psychology, implying that men may be manipulated successfully, subtly if you like, to stand and fight amid the violence, confusion, noise, deprivation, sacrifice, and continuous death of high-intensity war. The actual military experience in such an environment has little time for abstractions and desperately needs clear, straightforward, and demanding guidelines that tell men what is expected of them; and more: leaders are needed who demonstrate by example the sacrifices imposed on the troops and stand readily at risk. Virtually nothing in this text suggests that. Yet it is apparently part of the incremental and fragmentary pattern in which leadership is taught at an institution which should be producing officers without peer or without reproach.

To be sure, ours is hardly the only book pointing out military deviance and the effect that such deviance might have on expected military behavior and combat reliability. *The Tarnished Shield* by George Walton, Colonel, United States Army, Retired (New York: Dodd, Mead, 1973) is forthright about military pathologies of a widespread nature. However, Colonel Walton is both an accommodationist for a "liberal" Army as well as a subscriber to the conventional wisdom that the source of the lack of discipline and military misbehavior is the "permissive" society. Even so, Walton's work is important background material.

III
Sources

Military data are necessarily more general than specific. While we have cited many governmental sources for data, none of these sources is in the ordinary sense conspicuous. For example, to use casualty data on Vietnam in the format obtained, it had first to be established that the data existed and were available. The data were not always willingly provided, especially data on "fragging," and were suspect for obvious reasons. In the case of data on mutiny we found that the existence of such information was denied—a bureaucratic response to a thoroughly uncomfortable inquiry. Still, research is possible.

First some understanding as to how the military system is organized by staff and command, along with what motivates the system, is necessary. By and large, career motivations dominate and candor suffers accordingly. Information on who and what is responsible for inquiries made to the sub-agencies responsible for, say, unit evaluations on readiness, personnel status to include drug-usage rates, desertion, personnel turbulence, and general personnel conditions, can often be obtained from the Pentagon telephone directory. The libraries of the various military academies and higher institutions are highly specialized, including the Library of the Army War College and the Command and General Staff College. The same applies to the library facilities maintained by the Department of the Army and other services in Washington. Invaluable but tedious, the appropriate congressional hearings, particularly the yearly Defense Appropriations Hearings in both Houses and their relevant subcommittees, are rich sources of information. A word of warning: We have used the word "tedious" and it is an understatement. The committee reports are badly organized, poorly indexed, if at all, and often censored for what appear to be classified reasons. Still, if important data on military performance is necessary, these reports cannot be avoided. Another usually neglected source by scholars is their congressional group, senators and representatives. These are well supported by scores of researchers who will respond to specific requests for information by constituents. Very often a reluctant bureaucrat will bury a request for data in a maze of staffing processes. If no result has been received from, say, the Department of the Army on a specific request, a similar probe through political channels will frequently get results. A caution here. Ordinarily the military are very cooperative with routine requests for information. Only when the research topic is perceived as politically sensitive will they tend to balk. Accordingly, use congressional pressure on the bureaucracy sparingly, bearing in mind that this will cause military and civil bureaucrats to be less cooperative in the future. Clearly, in research of this nature some military experience is of great use in that one can normally know where to begin to look even when material is hidden.

Selected Bibliography

Ambler, John Steward, *The French Army in Politics* (Columbus: Ohio State University, 1966).

American Behavioral Scientist, Vol. 19, No. 5 (May–June 1976): issue devoted to "Military Ethics and Professionalism," Sam C. Sarkesian and Thomas M. Gannon, eds.

Andreski, Stanislav, *Military Organization and Society* (London: Routledge and Kegan Paul, 1954).

Ardrey, Robert, *African Genesis* (London: Collins, 1961).

———, *The Territorial Imperative* (New York: Atheneum, 1966).

———, *The Social Contract* (New York: Atheneum, 1970).

Argyris, Chris, *Personality and Organization* (New York: Harper Torch Books, 1957).

Barnard, Chester L., *The Functions of the Executive* (Cambridge: Harvard University Press, 1974).

Carell, Paul, *Scorched Earth* (New York: Ballantine, 1971).

Churchill, Sir Winston, *Frontiers and Wars* (New York: Harcourt, Brace, 1962).

Crick, Bernard, *In Defense of Politics* (London: Penguin Books, 1972).

De la Gorce, Paul Marie, *The French Army: A Military-Political History* (New York: George Braziller, 1963).

Department of the Army, *Strength of the Army Reports: 1941–45, 1950–53, 1961–72.*

———, *Review of the Preliminary Investigations into the My Lai Incident*, Vol. 1, 14 March 1970.

Department of Defense, *Computer Study of Casualties in Vietnam*, 1972.

Deutsch, Karl, *Nerves of Government* (New York: Free Press, 1966).

Donovan, James A., Colonel, *Militarism U.S.A.* (New York: Charles Scribner's Sons, 1970).

Downs, Anthony, *Inside Bureaucracy* (Boston: Little, Brown, 1967).

———, *An Economic Theory of Democracy* (New York: Harper & Row, 1957).

Dublin, Robert, *Theory Building* (New York: Free Press, 1969).

Ellis, Joseph, and Moore, Robert, *School for Soldiers* (New York: Oxford University Press, 1974).

Fall, Bernard, *Street Without Joy* (Harrisburg, Pa.: Stackpole, 1964).

———, *Hell in a Very Small Place* (Philadelphia: J. B. Lippincott, 1967).

Feit, Edward, *The Armed Bureaucrats* (Boston: Houghton Mifflin, 1973).

FitzGerald, Frances, *Fire in the Lake* (Boston: Little, Brown, 1972).

Folttmann, Josef, and Moeller-Witten, Hans, *Opfergang der Generale* (Berlin: Verlag Bernard und Graefe, 1959).

Friedman, Leon, ed., *The Law of War* (2 vols.; New York: Random House, 1972).

Gabriel, Richard A., *The Tactical and Strategic Failures of Dien Bien Phu* (Fort Huachuca, Ariz.: U.S. Army Intelligence School Archives, 1976). Unclassified.

Gambrill, Eileen D., *Behavior Modification* (San Francisco: Jossey-Bass, 1977).

Glahn, Gerhard von, *Law Among Nations* (3rd ed.; New York: Macmillan, 1976).

Grant, Michael, *The Army of the Caesars* (New York: Charles Scribner's Sons, 1974).

Halberstam, David, *The Best and the Brightest* (Greenwich, Conn.: Fawcett, 1972).

Harris-Jenkins, Gwyn, and van Doorn, Jacques, eds., *The Military and the Problem of Legitimacy* (Beverly Hills: Sage Publications, 1976).

Hauser, William, *America's Army in Crisis* (Baltimore: Johns Hopkins University Press, 1973).

Heinrich, Willi, *The Cross of Iron* (Indianapolis: Bobbs-Merrill, 1966).

Helmer, John, *Bringing the War Home* (New York: Free Press, 1974).

Hermes, Walter G., *Truce Tent and Fighting Front* (Washington, D.C.: Office of the Chief of Military History, United States Army, 1966).

Huntington, Samuel P., *The Soldier and the State* (Cambridge: Harvard University Press, 1967).

Isaak, Allan C., *Scope and Methods of Political Science* (Homewood, Ill.: Dorsey Press, 1970).

Jacob, Herbert, *German Administration Since Bismarck* (New Haven: Yale University Press, 1963).

Janowitz, Morris, *The Professional Soldier* (New York: Free Press; 1971).

——, "Military Institutions and Citizenship in Western Societies," in Harris-Jenkins and van Doorn.

—— and Little, Roger, *Sociology and the Military Establishment* (New York: Russell Sage Foundation, 1965).

Just, Ward, *Military Men* (New York: Alfred A. Knopf, 1970).

Keegan, John, *The Face of Battle* (New York: Viking Press, 1976).

King, Edward L., *The Death of the Army* (New York: Saturday Review Press, 1972).

Liddell Hart, B. H., *Why Don't We Learn from History?* (New York: Hawthorn, 1944).

Linden, Eugene, "Fragging and Other Withdrawal Symptoms," *Saturday Review*, January 8, 1972.

Lowi, Theodore, *The End of Liberalism* (New York: W. W. Norton, 1969).

Luttwak, Edward N., *The Grand Strategy of the Roman Empire from the First Century A. D. to the Third* (Baltimore: Johns Hopkins University Press, 1976).

Luvaas, Jay, *The Education of an Army: British Military Thought 1815–1940* (Chicago: University of Chicago Press, 1964).

Margiotta, Franklin D., "A Military Elite in Transition: Air Force Leaders in the 1980's," *Armed Forces and Society*, Winter 1976.

Marshall, S. L. A., *Night Drop* (Boston: Little, Brown, 1962).

——, *Pork Chop Hill* (New York: William Morrow, 1956).

——, *Men Against Fire* (New York: William Morrow, 1947).

McCoy, Alfred W., et al., *The Politics of Heroin in Southeast Asia* (New York: Harper & Row, 1972).

Merton, Robert K., and Lazarsfeld, Paul F., eds., *Studies in the Scope and Method of "The American Soldier"* (New York: Free Press, 1950).

Milgram, Stanley, *Obedience to Authority* (London: Tavistock, 1974).

Millis, Walter, *Arms and the State* (New York: Twentieth Century Fund, 1958).

Moskos, Charles C., Jr., "The Military" (bibliographic essay), *Annual Review of Sociology*, Vol. 2, 1976.

——, "The American Combat Soldier in Vietnam," *Journal of Social Issues*, Vol. 31, No. 4 (1975).

——, *The American Enlisted Man* (New York: Russell Sage Foundation, 1970).

——, "Trends in Military Social Organization," paper presented at the conference on "The Consequences and Limits of Military Intervention," Center for Continuing Education, University of Chicago (June 17–19, 1976).

——, "Cohesion and Demoralization in the American Army (Vietnam),"

International Sociological Association Research Committee on Armed Forces and Society, *The End of the Mass Army*, Working Conference, Nederlandse Economische Hogeschool, Faculteit der Sociale Wetenschappen (March 1973).

———, "Studies on the American Soldier: Continuities and Discontinuities in Social Research," paper prepared for the annual meeting of the American Sociological Association, New York, 1973.

Mueller-Hillebrand, Burkhardt, *Das Heer, 1933–1945*, Vol. 3 of *Der Zweifrontenkrieg* (Frankfurt: Verlag E. S. Mittler und Sohn, 1969).

Neiburg, R. L., *Political Violence: The Behavioral Process* (New York: St. Martin's Press, 1969).

Ollard, Richard, *This War Without an Enemy: A History of the English Civil Wars* (New York: Atheneum, 1976).

Oppenheim, L., *International Law: A Treatise* (New York: David McKay, 1965).

Picq, Ardant du, *Battle Studies: Ancient and Modern* (Harrisburg, Pa.: The Military Service Publishing Company, 1950).

Presthus, Robert, *The Organizational Society* (New York: Vintage, 1962).

Robbins, Lee N., *The Vietnam Drug User Returns* (Washington, D.C.: U.S. Government Printing Office, 1974).

Rolbant, Samuel, *The Israeli Soldier: Profile of an Army* (South Brunswick: Thomas Yoseloff, 1970).

Ropp, Theodore, *War in the Modern World* (New York: Collier, 1965).

Rosenberg, Hans, *Bureaucracy, Aristocracy and Autocracy—The Prussian Experience 1660–1815* (Boston: Beacon Press, 1966).

Sajer, Guy, *The Forgotten Soldier* (New York: Harper & Row, 1971).

Sarkesian, Sam C., *The Professional Army Soldier in a Changing Society* (Chicago: Nelson-Hall, 1975).

Savage, Paul L., and Gabriel, Richard A., "Cohesion and Disintegration in the American Army: An Alternative Perspective," *Armed Forces and Society*, Vol. 2, No. 3 (May 1976).

Schmettow, Dr. Matthias Graf von, *Gedenkbuch des Deutschen Adels* (Limburg a.d. Lahn: C. A. Starke Verlag, 1967).

Scott, William, and Mitchell, Terence, *Organization Theory: A Structural and Behavioral Analysis* (Homewood, Ill.: Dorsey Press, 1972).

Seidman, Harold, *Politics, Position and Power: The Dynamics of Federal Organization* (London: Oxford University Press, 1970).

Shanahan, William C., *Prussian Military Reforms 1786–1813* (New York: AMS Press, 1966).

Shils, Edward A., "A Profile of the Military Deserter," *Armed Forces and Society*, Vol. 3, No. 3 (Spring 1977).

Shils, Edward A., and Janowitz, Morris, "Cohesion and Disintegration in the German Wehrmacht in World War II," *Public Opinion Quarterly*, Vol. 12 (1948).

Simon, Herbert, *Administrative Behavior* (Chicago: Free Press, 1945).

Smyth, Sir John, *Sandhurst* (London: Weidenfeld, 1961).

Speier, Hans, *Social Order and the Risks of War* (Cambridge: M.I.T. Press, 1952).

Stouffer, Samuel, et al., *The American Soldier* (Princeton: Princeton University Press, 1949).

Tiger, Lionel, and Fox, Robin, *The Imperial Animal* (New York: Holt, Rinehart and Winston, 1971).

———, *Men in Groups* (New York: Random House, 1969).

Tonnies, Ferdinand, *Gemeinschaft und Gesellschaft* (East Lansing: Michigan State University Press, 1957).

Toscano, James, and Deutsch, Karl, *The Integration of Political Communities* (Philadelphia: J. B. Lippincott, 1964).

Tullock, Gordon, *The Politics of Bureaucracy* (Washington, D.C.: Public Affairs Press, 1965).

United States Army War College, Carlisle Barracks, Pa., *Evaluation, Inflation and Order of Merit*, Strategic Studies Institute, March 1974.

———, *Pyramids and Squishy Spheres: The Dynamic Context of Military Grade Creep*, Strategic Studies Institute, Vols. 1 and 2, 20 November 1974.

———, *Comprehensive Report: Leadership for the 1970's*. USAWC Study for the Professional Soldier, 20 October 1971.

———, *Study on Military Professionalism*, 30 June 1970.

United States Military Academy, *A Study of Organizational Leadership* (Edited by the Associates in Military Leadership, United States Military Academy, West Point, New York, 1975).

Vagts, Alfred, *A History of Militarism* (New York: Free Press, 1959).

Walton, George, Colonel, U.S.A., Retired, *The Tarnished Shield* (New York: Dodd, Mead, 1973).

Weigley, Russell F., *History of the United States Army* (New York: Macmillan, 1967).

Wolff, Leon, *In Flanders Fields* (New York: Ballantine, 1958).

Index